A Woman's Guide
to the Temperaments

HOW UNDERSTANDING YOUR PERSONALITY
TYPE CAN ... YOUR

FOREWORD BY

Donna Partow

Zondervan Publishing House

A Woman's Guide to the Temperaments
Copyright © 1998 by Donna Partow

Requests for information should be addressed to:

📖 ZondervanPublishingHouse
Grand Rapids, Michigan 49530

Library of Congress Cataloging-in-Publication Data

Partow, Donna.
   A woman's guide to the temperaments : how understanding your personality type can enrich your relationship with your husband and your kids / Donna Partow.
      p.   cm.
   Includes bibliographical references.
   ISBN: 0–310–21204–9 (pbk. : alk. paper)
    1. Christian women—Religious life.   2. Temperament—Religious aspects—Christianity.   3. Christian women—Family relationships.   I. Title.
BV4527.P38   1998
248.8'43—dc21
                             98–10270
                                CIP

Published in association with the literary agency of Wolgemuth and Associates, Inc., 8012 Brooks Chapel Road, #243, Brentwood, Tennessee 37027

Interior design by Jody DeNeef

Printed in the United States of America

98 99 00 01 02 03 04 /❖ DC/ 10 9 8 7 6 5 4 3 2 1

THIS BOOK IS DEDICATED TO TWO OF THE
"CLASS"IEST WOMEN I KNOW:

Florence Littauer, for being a living example
of all I hope to be someday.

Thanks for daring me to dream.

AND

Marita Littauer, who has so generously shared her time
and talents to equip me to pursue that dream.

Thanks for being a mentor and a friend.

Contents

Special Thanks

To Kelly Sampson, who stood with me through "the dark night of the soul."

And to my new friends at Zondervan, in order of appearance:

Ann Spangler, who was determined to bring me into the Zondervan fold. Thanks for all the lunches out and for the special weekend getaway. When do we go back to Tanque Verde?

Stan Gundry, for traipsing through parking lots in search of Mexican food. Let's hear it for guacamole!

Scott Bolinder, for asking me questions to which I never know the answer. Thanks for challenging me to be more than I am.

Foreword

During the past thirty years, I've had the privilege of teaching the four personality types to audiences around the world. I've witnessed life-changing results in the hearts of anyone—doctors, pastors, lay people—willing to apply these truths to their daily lives. Nowhere have these results been more profound or of more eternal significance than in the home. That's why I believe this book, *A Woman's Guide to the Temperaments* by Donna Partow, is so important. Hers is the first book ever to apply the up-to-date findings of personality research to helping women maximize their roles as mothers, wives, and individuals.

In her unique, down-to-earth style, Donna has written a book that's light-and-breezy to read, while delivering a powerful message about the importance of the Bible's injunction to live with one another in an understanding way.

It's the kind of book a busy mom can pick up on the run, read a few pages, and walk away with something valuable—a new truth or fresh insight that will make an immediate difference in the way she approaches family life.

I have been acquainted with Donna's ministry for several years and have enjoyed sharing the platform with her at various Christian women's conferences. Donna is one of my Certified Personality Trainers and a graduate of CLASS, my speakers' training program. As such, I am delighted to commend to you both Donna and *A Woman's Guide to the Temperaments*.

FLORENCE LITTAUER

AUTHOR, *PERSONALITY PLUS*

Part
1

Understand
Yourself

Temperament 101

INTRODUCTION

How's this for a bold opening statement: I believe this book can dramatically change your life for the better. I believe you now hold in your hands a set of tools no less tangible than the hammers hanging in your garage. Tools you can put to use—beginning today—to improve the quality of your relationships with your husband, your children, and all those most important to you. It will even improve the quality of your interactions with neighbors, fellow church-goers, store owners, waitresses, cashiers, and total strangers. Once you learn to quickly identify the temperament of virtually anyone you meet, you'll discover just how handy this tool really is.

As I talk with women at conferences around the country, I'm continually amazed at how many of their deepest heartaches—especially in their marriage and family life—are rooted in misunderstandings and temperament conflicts. When I explain the temperaments, and especially the basic motivations and emotional needs of each, suddenly the light bulbs go on. "Wow, if only I'd realized that's how he was wired!" or "So you mean he's not really trying to drive me nuts, that's just the way he is?" I wrote this book because I was determined to provide them—and you—with some practical solutions for the homefront and beyond.

Here's how *A Woman's Guide to the Temperaments* will help you:

- You're guaranteed to gain a greater understanding of why you act the way you do. Once you understand your own motivations, you can discover positive ways to get your emotional needs met. You'll also begin to understand how others perceive you. You will develop an increased sensitivity to your weaknesses, along with some practical strategies for overcoming them. Most of all, you'll gain an appreciation of your strengths, so you can build on them.

- You'll gain an increased appreciation for your husband. Some of you may find that hard to believe, but I promise it's true! You'll rediscover God's original plan in bringing the two of you together. Even though opposites attract and then often attack, it doesn't have to be that way. Really, it doesn't! You don't have to battle with your husband for the rest of your married life. I trust you'll find freedom in the realization that just because you disagree doesn't mean one of you is wrong and the other is right. You can conserve precious time and energy once you accept that you're simply looking at life through two very different lenses. And that's not only okay, it's good.

- You'll learn the potential pitfalls in your marriage (based on you and your husband's combined temperaments) and strategies to avoid them. You'll understand why some marriages are more inclined to harmony, while others are more tempestuous by nature. You may be thinking, "Donna, it's a little too late for that information." But what about your children? This is a marvelous tool that you can use to equip them to choose a suitable life partner.

- You can set your children free to be who God created them to be. Now that's exciting, isn't it? So often, we try to force our children to fit into a particular mold, or we're baffled by their behavior. Well, kids *can* be quite baffling sometimes, but when we understand the temperaments, much of the fog clears away. Understanding the temperaments will also help you guide your children into the right profession and save them untold heartache in their own life. My six- and thirteen-year-old girls both understand the temperaments, and they can testify that it has helped them tremendously in their peer relationships.

- I think you'll have a lot of fun along the way. When folks ask me what kind of writer I am, I always say "I write for women in the bathroom."

Huh?

Yup, you read it right! I write for women in the bathroom, and if you know exactly what I'm talking about, then this book is definitely for you. I'm only able to read books about three pages at a time, in the stolen moments I manage to grab between chauffeuring my teenager from place to place, nursing my newborn, and hollering at my six-year-old. I guess that brings us to another point: I always try to be honest about my less-than-perfect life. If you like writers who've got it all figured out, we could be in trouble from the get-go.

I haven't figured it all out, but I do know one thing: understanding the temperaments has been the single most helpful tool (after the Bible, of course) I've ever found for figuring out this crazy, mixed-up world and the fruits and nuts who populate it. It has even helped me make some sense of my own zany personality, and that's saying something.

Well, if none of those benefits sound worthwhile to you and you couldn't possibly profit by understanding yourself and those around you better, by all means, put this book down immediately! But if you suspect your relationship toolbox could use some new equipment, I encourage you to read on. But don't merely read, actively seek to put to use the things you are learning. The best way to do this is to

1. Read with a highlighter in your hand. Mark anything that makes you respond with a "Wow, *now* I get it." You can even mark the stuff that makes you shout, "My husband's got to read this!" (Not too many of those, though!)
2. Take it a step further: jot down notes in the margins and at the end of each chapter, indicating how you can implement the information you've just learned.
3. Share what you're learning with someone else or several someone elses! Why not start with your husband and

kids? You can read them excerpts that strike you as particularly funny or enlightening. Better still, explain the concepts in your own words and try to think of your own stories to illustrate the temperaments in action. The best way to learn anything is to teach it to someone else.

4. Enjoy the whole book, but *focus on the emotional needs.* Although I'm certainly happy you're reading my book, there won't be much point unless this material changes the way you relate to the people you love most. It won't be worth your time, unless you invest the extra time required to apply the principles. Begin with your husband, actively trying to meet his emotional needs in fresh ways. See what a difference it makes. Next, your children. Then, your extended family. You can even have fun, as I recently did, using your tool kit (at the back of this book) as you interact with the make-up artist at the cosmetics counter. I'm telling you, this can revolutionize your life. You'll see!

5. Go back and reread the highlighted portions. Copy some of the key points onto note cards and/or sticky notes and review them on a regular basis.

6. Remove the cards included in "Your Tool Kit" at the end of this book. Carry them with you wherever you go and refer to them often.

7. Continue reviewing the material on a routine basis, until it becomes part of the fabric of your life.

If this book does make a difference for you, I hope you'll write to me and tell me all about it. Now, read on. Change your life!

SOME BACKGROUND

Chances are, you've heard the term *temperaments* before and maybe you have even attended a seminar at work or church where you charted your own. The concepts I am presenting in this book are far from new. In fact, they date back to the Greek physician-philosopher, Hippocrates (460–377 B.C.), who first developed the theory. He identified four basic temperaments: sanguine, melancholy, choleric, and phlegmatic. He attributed the differences to varying amounts of bodily substances: an abundance of blood caused a person to be Sanguine, black bile led to Choleric, yellow bile to Melancholy, and those with plenty of phlegm were the Phlegmatics. We may chuckle at the theory, but it did have a biochemical basis, and in that sense it was definitely on target.

In 1966, Dr. Tim LaHaye, a pastor and popular seminar speaker, took the Christian world by storm with his phenomenal best-seller, *The Spirit-Controlled Temperament*. Florence Littauer picked up the baton in 1983, dedicating her own international best-seller, *Personality Plus,* to Dr. LaHaye. If you are a businessperson, perhaps you've been tested using the DISC personality profile. It's exactly the same concept with different labels: **D**ominant is the Choleric, **I**nfluencing is the Sanguine, **S**teady is the Phlegmatic, and **C**onscientious is the Melancholy.

What's unique about *A Woman's Guide to the Temperaments* is that it's written especially for wives and mothers. And it's designed to help you where you live right now, in the midst of the daily juggling act: relationships with family and friends, career or ministry demands, cooking, cleaning, changing gadzillions of diapers, flagging down school buses, or homeschooling. We're not going to waste any time on theory. That paragraph about Hippocrates was it, ladies! And you won't find any of the highfalutin mumbo jumbo that some temperament books are filled with. (You need a Ph.D. just to read them!)

That's also why I won't be using the terms coined by Hippocrates. Instead, I'm going to refer to the temperaments based on the primary adjective which best describes each, as developed by the Littauers. The Sanguine's primary motivation in life is to have fun and be popular, so I'm calling her the Popular woman. Personally, I think it's just a whole lot easier to remember (not to mention *pronounce*) than the ancient Greek word. The Choleric wants power and control, so she'll be easy to remember as the Powerful woman. The Melancholy is on a mission to bring perfection to an imperfect world, so I've dubbed her the Perfect woman. Last, but certainly not least, is the Phlegmatic type, whom Hippocrates claimed suffered from an overabundance of phlegm. As you'll soon discover, these women are so easygoing they probably wouldn't put up much of a fuss, but I sure wouldn't want to be associated with phlegm. Would you? Let's call them the Peaceful women.

Okay, no Greek terminology and no psycho-babble. What's left? Just practical help for your practical, everyday life. Like how to understand yourself—why you do what you do and why you find it so doggone hard to do the things you think you *ought to* and *want to* do. And how to understand others so you can get along better with your husband, your children, and the people around you.

Before we get to the really good stuff, I want to forewarn you about a couple things. You may sense, at times, that I'm painting these temperaments in strictly primary colors. That's probably a fair assessment, first, because I'm a mom who spends lots of time around primary colors. But also because I think doing so makes these concepts easier to grasp. I do want to acknowledge, however, that even though I'm coloring with blue, red, and yellow, I know about that ninety-four-count Crayola box! We live in a world of many shades and nuances, but all come back to the primary colors. So, too, with the temperaments. Everyone you meet will be a unique blend, but the simplest way to understand them is by understanding their underlying "colors."

For the same reason, you may notice that I've incorporated some rather extreme examples of the various temperaments in action. Again, I'm not saying that everyone with this temperament will always behave thus and so. Humans are notoriously unpredictable. Nevertheless, I think a glimpse at where the temperament weaknesses—left unchecked or pushed to an extreme—can lead a person is a powerful learning tool.

And one more thing! Please don't feel hopeless when you read about the weaknesses. Just as few people have all the strengths, few people have all the weaknesses. Even if you do recognize a particular weakness, you aren't doomed. These aren't intended as death sentences for your character. We serve a mighty God and he is in the redemption business. Rather than growing discouraged, pray that God will transform you from the inside out. You should also pray for the ones you love, that God will do a great work in their lives as well. "Therefore, if anyone is in Christ, he is a new creation; the old has gone, the new has come! All this is from God, who reconciled us to himself through Christ and gave us the ministry of reconciliation" (2 Corinthians 5:17–18).

Without further ado, let's find out more about you. Any discussion of temperament must begin with understanding your own temperament. Please take your time in working through the following personality assessment tool, developed by Fred Littauer and used here with his kind permission.

PERSONALITY PROFILE[1]

Directions: In each of the following rows of four words across, place an *x* in front of the one word that most often applies to you. Continue through all forty lines. Be sure each number is marked. If you are not sure of which word "most applies," ask a spouse or a friend, and think of what your answer would have been *when you were a child*. If you have questions about these descriptions, you'll find definitions of all terms in the appendix.

1. __Adventurous	__Adaptable	__Animated	__Analytical
2. __Persistent	__Playful	__Persuasive	__Peaceful
3. __Submissive	__Self-sacrificing	__Sociable	__Strong-willed
4. __Considerate	__Controlled	__Competitive	__Convincing
5. __Refreshing	__Respectful	__Reserved	__Resourceful
6. __Satisfied	__Sensitive	__Self-reliant	__Spirited
7. __Planner	__Patient	__Positive	__Promoter
8. __Sure	__Spontaneous	__Scheduled	__Shy
9. __Orderly	__Obliging	__Outspoken	__Optimistic
10. __Friendly	__Faithful	__Funny	__Forceful
11. __Daring	__Delightful	__Diplomatic	__Detailed
12. __Cheerful	__Consistent	__Cultured	__Confident
13. __Idealistic	__Independent	__Inoffensive	__Inspiring
14. __Demonstrative	__Decisive	__Dry humor	__Deep
15. __Mediator	__Musical	__Mover	__Mixes easily
16. __Thoughtful	__Tenacious	__Talker	__Tolerant
17. __Listener	__Loyal	__Leader	__Lively

18. __Contented	__Chief	__Chartmaker	__Cute
19. __Perfectionist	__Pleasant	__Productive	__Popular
20. __Bouncy	__Bold	__Behaved	__Balanced
21. __Brassy	__Bossy	__Bashful	__Blank
22. __Undisciplined	__Unsympathetic	__Unenthusiastic	__Unforgiving
23. __Reluctant	__Resentful	__Resistant	__Repetitious
24. __Fussy	__Fearful	__Forgetful	__Frank
25. __Impatient	__Insecure	__Indecisive	__Interrupts
26. __Unpopular	__Uninvolved	__Unpredictable	__Unaffectionate
27. __Headstrong	__Haphazard	__Hard to please	__Hesitant
28. __Plain	__Pessimistic	__Proud	__Permissive
29. __Angered	__Aimless	__Argumentative	__Alienated
30. __Naive	__Negative	__Nervy	__Nonchalant
31. __Worrier	__Withdrawn	__Workaholic	__Wants credit
32. __Too sensitive	__Tactless	__Timid	__Talkative
33. __Doubtful	__Disorganized	__Domineering	__Depressed
34. __Inconsistent	__Introvert	__Intolerant	__Indifferent
35. __Messy	__Moody	__Mumbles	__Manipulative
36. __Slow	__Stubborn	__Show-off	__Skeptical
37. __Loner	__Lord over others	__Lazy	__Loud
38. __Sluggish	__Suspicious	__Short-tempered	__Scatterbrained
39. __Revengeful	__Restless	__Reluctant	__Rash
40. __Compromising	__Critical	__Crafty	__Changeable

Now you are ready to determine your temperament. The following chart features the exact same word lists as the previous page, but this time they are aligned underneath the appropriate temperament. As you transfer your answers from your answer sheet to the following score sheet, you will see your temperament revealed:

POPULAR	POWERFUL	PERFECT	PEACEFUL
1. __Animated	__Adventurous	__Analytical	__Adaptable
2. __Playful	__Persuasive	__Persistent	__Peaceful
3. __Sociable	__Strong-willed	__Self-sacrificing	__Submissive
4. __Convincing	__Competitive	__Considerate	__Controlled
5. __Refreshing	__Resourceful	__Respectful	__Reserved

6.	Spirited	Self-reliant	Sensitive	Satisfied
7.	Promoter	Positive	Planner	Patient
8.	Spontaneous	Sure	Scheduled	Shy
9.	Optimistic	Outspoken	Orderly	Obliging
10.	Funny	Forceful	Faithful	Friendly
11.	Delightful	Daring	Detailed	Diplomatic
12.	Cheerful	Confident	Cultured	Consistent
13.	Inspiring	Independent	Idealistic	Inoffensive
14.	Demonstrative	Decisive	Deep	Dry humor
15.	Mixes easily	Mover	Musical	Mediator
16.	Talker	Tenacious	Thoughtful	Tolerant
17.	Lively	Leader	Loyal	Listener
18.	Cute	Chief	Chartmaker	Contented
19.	Popular	Productive	Perfectionist	Pleasant
20.	Bouncy	Bold	Behaved	Balanced
21.	Brassy	Bossy	Bashful	Blank
22.	Undisciplined	Unsympathetic	Unforgiving	Unenthused
23.	Repetitious	Resistant	Resentful	Reluctant
24.	Forgetful	Frank	Fussy	Fearful
25.	Interrupts	Impatient	Insecure	Indecisive
26.	Unpredictable	Unaffectionate	Unpopular	Uninvolved
27.	Haphazard	Headstrong	Hard to please	Hesitant
28.	Permissive	Proud	Pessimistic	Plain
29.	Angered	Argumentative	Alienated	Aimless
30.	Naive	Nervy	Negative	Nonchalant
31.	Wants credit	Workaholic	Withdrawn	Worrier
32.	Talkative	Tactless	Too sensitive	Timid
33.	Disorganized	Domineering	Depressed	Doubtful
34.	Inconsistent	Intolerant	Introvert	Indifferent
35.	Messy	Manipulative	Moody	Mumbles
36.	Show-off	Stubborn	Skeptical	Slow
37.	Loud	Lord over others	Loner	Lazy
38.	Scatterbrained	Short-tempered	Suspicious	Sluggish
39.	Restless	Rash	Revengeful	Reluctant
40.	Changeable	Crafty	Critical	Compromising

Total 5 a 4   11 0 5   2 a 9   3 o 2

14 X 10   21 X 11   3   14*   1   X 9
     06   05   0 18   0 10

A QUICK INTRODUCTION TO TEMPERAMENTS

Now that you know which temperament you are, I'll bet you're tempted to turn to the chapters about yourself first. That's okay. In fact, it's perfectly natural. But maybe you ought to stick around for a quick overview of all four temperaments before you dash off for further self-study. I promise it'll be brief. Here's what we'll do. Let's pretend you've packed up your little cherubs in the minivan and trekked on over to the local park. While you're there, you meet each of the temperament types.

As you pull into the parking lot, you hear loud, uproarious laughter floating through the air. You notice a woman with long flowing hair, standing in the middle of a group. You also notice, even from a distance, that she's wearing a boldly colored outfit and great big dangly earrings. You couldn't *not notice* this woman if you tried. She demands attention. She is obviously talking a hundred miles a minute, and she's punctuating her delivery with wild, sweeping gestures. When you walk over to join the group, you realize this woman is not just talking, she's telling stories. If any story doesn't get the reaction she had hoped for, she immediately launches into a retelling of the *very same story*.

When she gets bored (you know, when anyone else starts talking), she dashes off and swings on the swings for a while, then strikes up a conversation with an old man on a nearby bench. For lunch, she breaks out a bag of McDonald's she picked up on the way to the park.

You've just met the *Popular* woman.

Although she's much quieter, you can't help noticing a strikingly attractive mom, stylishly dressed in a freshly ironed outfit, complete with coordinating accessories. Her neatly manicured fingernails are tinted the same color as her lips. When you comment on her clothes, her face glows as she reports (in great detail) how she found them on the clearance rack of a fashionable store for seventy-five percent off. When she speaks, she speaks quietly and uses very few gestures. In fact, she holds her arms close to her body. Her short, sleek hairstyle accentuates her facial features, which are carefully highlighted with just the right touch of makeup.

Throughout the afternoon, she keeps a careful watch over her perfectly dressed children. (Their outfits are ironed, too!) Her kids aren't allowed to play on the monkey bars, though, because she read an article last Tuesday in the *Ladies Home Journal* that said monkey bars are the leading cause of playground accidents. When lunch rolls around, she unpacks nutritious sandwiches cut into perfect triangles, wrapped in plastic, then aluminum foil for extra safety.

You've just encountered the *Perfect* woman.

There's another mom sitting at a picnic table, working on what appears to be a very important project. Although she doesn't talk much, you get the feeling she's not shy, just pre-occupied. From time to time, she gets up to organize an activity for the kids. Much to your surprise, she even disciplines *your* kids (with her hands on her hips and her pointing finger in their faces) for climbing an old apple tree. When she tells her own kids to come over for lunch, she speaks with authority and the little tykes immediately come running. During lunch, she brings up the hot debate over the local school board referendum and lets everyone know just where she stands on the issue. It's not so much what she says as it is the authoritative tone in which she says it that let's you know this woman means business. Of course, the fact that she's carrying a cellular phone will probably be your second clue!

You've witnessed the *Powerful* woman in action.

And finally, there's a very quiet woman who has laid out a picnic blanket. In fact, she has laid out two blankets, in case someone else needs a place to sit. She has brought along cold drinks and enough snacks to share with everyone. Although she doesn't talk about topics in great detail (and definitely doesn't venture an opinion during the discussion on the referendum), from time to time she'll speak up to offer food or drinks to the other women and children.

Speaking of children, you can't help noticing that her kids are almost always sitting on her lap. Even when they do venture off, she keeps them always within eyesight. She may have brought along some of her older children, whom she home-schools. Although she and her kids are very sweet, you can't help noticing that their clothes are somewhat disheveled and their grooming isn't quite up to Vidal Sassoon standards. When she sends one of her kids to retreive something from their minivan, you notice it could use a trip to the car wash.

You've had an encounter with the *Peaceful* woman.

TYPICAL COMBINATIONS

I hope those descriptions gave you an idea of what these women are generally like. Naturally, it's a bit more complicated in real life because no two human beings are exactly alike. In addition, only four percent of the population is one temperament and one temperament only. The rest of us are a combination. Chances are, you've noticed that you are a combination of two temperaments. The most frequently occurring combinations include Popular-Powerful, Perfect-Peaceful, Powerful-Perfect, and Popular-Peaceful.

The following chart should help you visualize the most common combinations, because they always occur in side-by-side or top-and-bottom boxes and are never created by crossing boxes:

POPULAR	POWERFUL
PEACEFUL	PERFECT

UNLIKELY COMBINATIONS

There are some combinations that should throw up a warning sign; combinations that do not occur naturally. Now don't panic, I'm not saying you are crazy or weird or anything like that. Just that you are letting outside forces shape who you are, rather than being the person you were originally created to be. You might think you're happy-as-a-bug-in-a-rug with your life, but maybe you'd be even happier (like a bug on a magic carpet ride), if you got back in touch with the real you.

Let me give you some examples of what I'm talking about. If your chart shows you are Popular-Perfect or Powerful-Peaceful, something may be fishy. Think about it. A person whose primary motivation in life is having fun (Popular woman) is not usually going to be concerned with doing everything perfectly (Perfect woman). And a person whose primary motivation is to take life easy (Peaceful woman) is not inclined to try to control everything around them (Powerful woman). These temperaments are polar opposites.

Just remember: Typical combinations have aligning boxes; unlikely combinations "cross the line."

What does it mean if your score reveals contrasting temperaments? There are a few possibilities. Perhaps you had over-powering parents who forced you to become something you weren't. Or perhaps your birth order played a major role. For example: You were the firstborn, you had a Popular temperament, but your parents worked day and night to make you perfect, so you ended up demonstrating many Perfect traits. Conversely, you may have been born with a Perfect temperament, but your parents pushed you to become the cheerleader and the life of the party. You began playing the part of the Popular person, although it wasn't the real you. Or your husband is a pastor and even though you are a Powerful person with lots of drive, you feel the congregation expects you to stay quietly in the background. You're afraid they won't accept the real you, so you put on a false Peaceful mask.

The key for your self-understanding is getting back in touch with who you were as a child. Or simply look at who you are when you're at your very best, your most alive. That's the ultimate you. (If you discover contrasting temperaments, I encourage you to read *Your Personality Tree* by Florence Littauer. It will help you work though these issues and get to know the real you.)

Now, what if you were a little bit of each temperament? Well, that could mean one of three things. Option #1: You are spiritually mature and well-balanced in all areas of life. You know how to kick back and have a great time, but you also know when to take life seriously. You know when it's appropriate to take charge of the situation, but you're not lacking in diplomacy. If you have walked in a close relationship with God for many years; you have simply become a reflection of your Teacher. Wonderful! The world would be a better place if there were more people like you.

Option #2: Perhaps you don't know yourself very well and you checked the wrong traits. Or you checked off what you thought you *should* be or *hope* to be, rather than what you really are. Have your spouse or a close friend take the test "for you" and see what they think. Warning: you may not like the answers you get. My husband took the test "for me" and didn't realize he could only check one trait per row. As a result, he checked off a handful of strengths and all of the weaknesses in three temperament categories. I was depressed for a week!

Option #3: You are an easygoing Peaceful type who didn't think the test was that big of a deal, so you just checked whatever came to mind. Again, invite a spouse or friend to take the test on your behalf. If you really are the Peaceful type, you don't need to worry. They'll check off all nice stuff. After all, virtually everybody likes the easygoing Peaceful types.

PRIMARY MOTIVATIONS

In terms of understanding both yourself and the people around you, one of the most powerful tools at your disposal is understanding the underlying motivation behind each temperament's behavior. Understanding your own motivations will enable you to be more realistic. In other words, is it realistic to think life will always to be fun or perfect or under control or easy? Of course not! Recognizing that will enable you to adjust your expectations and keep your frustration level to a minimum.

As you'll see in a moment, virtually everyone you meet is motivated by a desire for life to be either fun, perfect, under control, or easy. That's a bit simplistic, but as you work through this book—and evaluate whether or not the principles hold up in the real world—I think you'll discover that human motivations are often surprisingly simple. Once you understand their primary motivation, you can deal with people on their terms, which will make them far more inclined to respond favorably to you. Let's look at each temperament in turn:

- The Popular type wants to have fun and be loved. When dealing with this type, ask yourself: "How can I make this more fun?"
- The Perfect type wants to bring perfection to an imperfect world, so ask yourself, "How can I do this in an orderly fashion?"
- The Powerful type wants to control as much of their world as possible, so ask yourself, "How can I give this person (whether it's the woman in the mirror, your husband, or your children) a sense of ownership in this situation?"
- The Peaceful type wants to take life easy and live in peace. To make the most of your relationship with them, ask yourself, "How can I promote harmony in this situation?"

We'll come back to these issues again and again throughout the book, providing you with a more careful look at how these motivations play out in our own hearts, in our marriages, and in dealing with our children. For now, you've had your quick introduction to the four temperament types. You're ready to learn all you can about yourself and the people around you. Happy reading!

2

Introducing the Popular Woman

The first woman I'd like to introduce you to is the adorable, excitable Popular woman. She was a cheerleader in high school and now she's the unofficial Cheerleader of Life! The Popular woman is probably the easiest temperament to spot in a crowd. She's the one talking a hundred miles a minute, laughing loudly, and waving her arms in the air. I say "crowd" because she's always in the middle of the action, mixing and mingling with people, regaling them with grand stories that may bear little or no resemblance to the truth.

Other temperaments watch her in action and think, "Doesn't she ever get tired?" They don't realize, *this* is how she recharges her batteries. What a nice relaxing bath does for the average woman, an *audience* does for the Popular woman. That's why she's the ultimate networker. By the way, if you're new in town or at the church, just link up with a Popular woman—she knows absolutely everyone. Soon, you'll have all kinds of vicarious friends.

POPULAR STRENGTHS

I remember when Denise moved into the neighborhood. The first time we met I thought, "This is magic. All my life I've dreamed of finding a friend like this. I know we will be best friends for life." Little did I know that everyone who met Denise was thinking the very same thing. It's a tough assignment to be the whole world's best friend, but Denise does a pretty remarkable job of it.

You see, the Popular woman is everyone's very best friend, and she sincerely loves them all. However, she has an extra special place in her heart for friends who adore and idolize her—in other words, she thrives on compliments. However, if you don't make your worship obvious, she won't lose much sleep over it. In fact, even if you flat-out hurt her feelings, she won't hold a grudge. If she finds out she's done you wrong, she'll be quick to apologize. In fact, she's quick about just about everything. She's spontaneous and excitable. She's the kind of friend who calls you to say, "Let's go to the Bahamas ... this weekend." And she's so persuasive, she just might talk you into it. No wonder she's everyone's very best friend!

TALKATIVE

Generally speaking, the Popular woman is generally speaking. No doubt about it, she has what's commonly called the gift of gab. These women make great teachers and speakers because they can talk twenty-four hours a day, on any topic, with or without information. She doesn't really even need a group; an audience of one will suffice. Groups *preferred,* of course! You see, the Popular woman can talk to anyone, anywhere, anytime, about anything. Which is why her phone is permanently attached to her ear. She's a prime candidate to wear the T-shirt that says, "Help, I'm on the telephone and I can't shut up!"

If you try to call her, you'll never get through. Unless, of course, she has call waiting. In which case, you can expect your phone conversation to be interrupted every few minutes by another of her 1,001 friends.

My friend Jill recently told me the following story.

Through my business, I had been talking with a woman from California for months, but we had never met in person. When I found out she was coming to Arizona, I invited her to join me for lunch. I'd never seen a picture of her, but I figured, "How many women will be waiting at Applebees for a lunch partner? I'll find her, no problem." Well, I got to the restaurant a few minutes late and asked if there were any women waiting for someone to join them. Sure enough, she was there first. I practically ran over to the table. She stuck out her hand to shake and I said, "Oh, come on, let's hug" and gave her a huge hug. I sat down and started talking and talking. I did think some of the things she said were weird, like she thought I was in the manufacturing industry. But I found lots in common to talk about, so I didn't pay that much attention.

Then I asked her how the baby was doing. I thought she looked awfully old to have a baby, but I thought, "Hey, women are having babies later in life these days." Anyway, this time she looked at me like I was nuts and said, "I only have one child and she's twenty-seven years old." Suddenly a light went on and I said, "May I see your business card?" I took one look and realized she was the *wrong* person. I cleared my throat and said, "Um, I don't know how to say this, but . . . I'm not your lunch date, and you're not mine. I wonder if they're eating lunch together!" I jumped up and ran to the front of the restaurant. Sure enough, my real lunch date was sitting there waiting.

Only the Popular type can talk to a total stranger for twenty minutes and not even realize she's talking to a total stranger!

LIFE OF THE PARTY

Her bright cheery smile and bubbly personality make her the life of the party. And does she ever like to party! She likes to throw parties. She likes to attend parties. She loves to laugh and can have a great time doing just about anything. She's a one-woman party waiting to happen and usually arrives fashionably late singing the old Cindy Lauper tune, "Girls just wanna have fun!" Her primary goal is to enjoy life. If things get too serious, she's the first to try to lighten things up.

If your church or organization is planning a special event, put her in charge. I don't care if you're planning to sit around and watch the grass grow, she'll have everyone convinced it's the most happening event of the century. Even if she only turns out her inner circle of friends, you'll have about 250 people in attendance. She loves promoting and talking up future events. For her, the future is always full of promise. That's because she always expects the best from people and from life. She's a whirlwind of action and energy. She can go-go-go for hours, weeks, and years on end.

MOTIVATOR

The Popular woman can motivate others to action. She's fabulous at dreaming up wild schemes that someone else can do. She has an uncanny ability to inspire normally sane people to do the wackiest things. Sue's brother, John, is the most mild-mannered man you would ever meet. Unless, of course, you met Sue's husband first. Well, one St. Patrick's Day, when she was hosting another of her famous holiday festivals, she persuaded these two guys to install green toilet paper and green toilet fresheners, cover all the lamps (including the ceiling lamps, of course) with green napkins, and then practically wallpaper the neighborhood with green signs pointing to her house. These are gentlemen who would never call attention to themselves under ordinary circumstances and here they were canvassing the neighborhood in outlandish costumes complete with sparkling green headgear.

CREATIVE

She's a very creative dresser and likes to continually reinvent herself with new hairstyles and colors. She may not take the time to sew, but she sure is handy with puff-paint and a glitter glue-gun! Her creativity extends beyond her personal appearance to everything she does: decorating, baking, entertaining the kids. She's the master at inventing games, crafts, and projects for the kids. She'll throw together the most incredible Fourth of July cake and have everyone amazed. Don't ask her for the cake-making directions, though. Just as you've never seen a cake quite like that one before, you'll never see its likes again. Why? Because it never even occurred to her to write down the recipe. She'd rather come up with something brand new the next time around.

When my friend, Jill, told me her four-and-a-half-year-old daughter, Jesse, plays quietly for hours in her bedroom each morning, I couldn't believe it. Then Jill told me about the room and I *could* believe it. In fact, I wanted to rush over and play in the room myself! The headboard is a gigantic cutout cloud. The back wall is painted royal blue and has a big cutout moon and stars. That's the nighttime wall. Together, Jill and Jesse created a daytime wall by sponge-painting it light blue and white. Then her husband cut out and mounted wooden clouds. The window even has a cloud-shaped curtain.

All of the walls are covered with removable abstract stickers, so Jesse can redecorate her room any time she likes. She has a Japanese futon for her dolls, a large bean bag chair, and a shelf bursting with colorful picture books. Jill removed the door from the large closet and filled it with space organizers and shelf units which her husband bought at a local do-it-yourself store. (She put her Perfect husband in charge of that project!) One area is filled with building blocks, marble towers, and tinker toys. Another shelf holds board games. There's an entire art center with lots of messy things to do. Wouldn't you spend hours in a room like that?

ACCEPTING

The Popular woman lives by the maxim "live and let live." Since her primary life goals are having fun and being loved by everyone, she doesn't waste time evaluating what's wrong with the people she meets. She'd rather focus on what's *right* about people and about life. She accepts the fact that everyone has faults; everyone makes mistakes. She resists the eternal temptation to set herself up as judge and jury. And since no one likes to be judged, this characteristic goes a long way in promoting her personal popularity. This woman has many winsome qualities, but one of the most endearing is her childlike faith and trust in her fellow human beings. She always believes the best about others.

Although she likes to talk and may even engage in idle gossip, you'll rarely find her spreading vicious rumors. Even when someone *deserves*, by most standards, to be judged and censored, she'll resist the chorus of condemnation. Instead, she'll hold steadfastly to what is good in that person. More importantly, she willingly entrusts her life to the loving care of her heavenly Father. As a result, she is not plagued by worry and fear as other temperaments are. She takes each day as it comes, considering it a gift from God.

POPULAR WEAKNESSES

TOO TALKATIVE

The Popular woman often wonders why everyone else is so quiet all the time. She thinks to herself, "Oh how tragic: a world filled with painfully shy people. Well, thank God I'm here to fill all that dead airtime with captivating stories and irresistible jokes." But let me encourage you Popular women to conduct an experiment. See what happens if you keep quiet for more than five minutes. (Unless you are the Popular type, you have no idea how difficult it will be to conduct this experiment!) No doubt you'll discover that, oddly enough, all those painfully shy people suddenly have plenty to say.

Her tendency to talk too much, combined with her lack of attention to details, often leaves the Popular woman with a case of the dreaded "foot-in-mouth" disease. Because she doesn't pay attention to little details such as whom she's talking to, what that person's name is, or what's appropriate, yet feels compelled to say something, she may say the wrong thing. In the process, she embarrasses herself, her family, and the people around her.

I remember attending a funeral where such an event unfolded. I watched as a bright, bubbly Popular woman marched over to the next of kin and burst out with all the enthusiasm she could muster: "I'm so excited to be here." Oops. She had no idea what to say, but that didn't stop her from speaking up.

PERMISSIVE

Let's imagine you stop by to see the Popular woman one afternoon. You're trying to have a conversation with her and meanwhile, her kids are jumping up and down on the brand new couch and coloring the walls with permanent magic marker. She doesn't even seem to notice. After all, discipline? What's that?

Her kids don't take her seriously and she is permissive to the point that her kids become the terror of the church or neighborhood. She may wink and laugh and look the other way pretending not to notice, but if she doesn't rein in that little tribe soon, they might end up in serious trouble.

She's the eternal optimist and usually that's great; it can enable her to handle the hassles of today, knowing brighter days are ahead. But pushed to extremes, her optimism becomes denial. She may ignore issues or danger signs in her marriage with a shrug of her shoulders, "Well, things will get better." Or she may overlook behavior problems in her children, thinking, "I'll teach them to obey later." She may try to convince herself that it will be easier to discipline her children "next year" when they are a little older. Next year becomes next year becomes next year and the disciplining never gets easier. It only gets harder.

The Popular woman tends to avoid confrontation. Since her goal in life is to have fun, she puts off dealing with problems. A feisty six-year-old is problem enough, but if she doesn't find it within herself to confront that child and face the inevitable conflict, heaven help her when the teenage years hit.

FORGETFUL

Thus far, I've resisted the temptation to confess my own sins. But this Popular woman trait hits so close to home, I just had to share a personal story. This was the year, my husband declared, that we absolutely, positively wouldn't give in to the Halloween madness. "Well, we'll just have to come up with an alternative," I thought. So when I received a flyer from a huge local church advertising a fall festival, I thought, "Aha! We'll go have a blast. Then when the kids start moaning and groaning on Halloween, I'll remind them what a great time we had bobbing for apples and carving pumpkins at the church festival."

I woke up bright and early Saturday morning and began rallying the troops for the illustrious festival. How much better this would be than any dumb old trick-or-treat nonsense, I declared. Then the thought crossed my mind, "Gee, Donna, maybe you should double-check the time on that flyer."

Now, of course, there was one small problem. And you fellow Popular women already know what it was. I had absolutely no clue where I had put that flyer. It had entered my mind when I first read the flyer that I should write the information down on my handy-dandy "Busy Woman's Daily Planner." But I think it pretty much goes without saying that, at the time, I had absolutely no clue where my handy-dandy-guaranteed-to-get-you-organized organizer was.

As my dressed-and-ready-to-go gang anxiously awaited our impending departure, I ransacked my home office. After fifteen minutes of ripping through piles of papers, I called out triumphantly, "Here it is." A few seconds elapsed and I whispered sheepishly, "It was last night." It's funny on paper. But I can assure you, my heartbroken children weren't laughing.

By the way, when I noticed the date on the flyer, I realized I had also forgotten my niece's thirteenth birthday. I doubt she was laughing either. Forgetfulness is a real weakness for the Popular woman.

UNRELIABLE

The Popular woman is a big-picture person. She'll come up with a creative idea for a Christmas party and get all excited about the concept. Now, implementing the concept is a whole different story. Her battle cry is "Don't bore me with the details." She would never dream of doing things by the book. In fact, she couldn't be bothered even opening the book. Come to think of it, she probably couldn't even find the book!

This lack of attention to detail can get her into all kinds of minor mishaps and sometimes, serious trouble. Little stuff like forgetting to put gas in the car can lead to big stuff like breaking down with three children in the car. (Guess who that happened to?) She makes commitments without thinking through what it will actually take to follow through, and as a result, she may leave a trail of broken promises behind. If she's not careful, she can inadvertently cause resentment in her husband and children—all because she doesn't want to be bored with little things—like doing what she promised to do, when and how she promised to do it.

She loves to wing it and sometimes she creates fabulously fun meals, funky clothes, and nifty art projects. But quite often, her cavalier attitude leads to a great big mess and a final product that's far from what she hoped and promised to deliver. In short, she's unreliable.

FUSSY

If the Popular woman so much as loads the dishwasher, she's singing, "Nobody knows the trouble I've seen." She just can't seem to do a speck of work without fussin' and complainin'. She's driving to the grocery store a-fumin' and a-frettin' over traffic. Then she's a-grumblin' and a-groanin' about what's out of stock. She's shifting from hip to hip, tossing disapproving glances at the check-out clerk who's taking too long. She's in a big hurry to get home (an hour ago she was in a big hurry to *get out* of the house, now she's in a hurry to get *back in* the house). Every once in a while she'll stop and hear herself, and maybe she'll even realize what people around her may be thinking: "You're not very much fun to be with right now!"

There's one simple reason why the Popular woman does so much fussing and fretting: she just plain doesn't like to work. Let's face it: work is no fun! *Volunteering* for work is fun, but following through and actually *doing* the work is another gig entirely.

MESSY HOUSEKEEPER

Sometimes the Popular woman is so messy, she gets on her own nerves. She never seems to know where anything is! That's why leaving the house is such a huge ordeal for her. She loves *being* out of the house; it's *getting* out of the house that does her in.

First, she has to take a shower. That's a problem because she doesn't know where the towels are. Then she has to style her hair, which is a hassle because she doesn't know where her curlers are. Where could she have left her makeup bag? Of course, she rarely has anything clean and ironed to wear, but more about that in a minute. I think it pretty much goes without saying that she doesn't know where her keys are, and what about that diaper bag?

We've said the Popular woman can have a great time doing just about anything. Well, actually, there is *one* thing she doesn't have a good time doing: housecleaning. Her motto is, "If you came to see me, welcome. If you came to see my house, you're gonna need an appointment." I wish you could see my bathroom counter. Actually, I wish *I* could see my bathroom counter. I firmly believe it exists, but I haven't seen any evidence of it in lo, these many years. All my life, my living quarters have been a wreck. When I was a kid, my bedroom was always a wreck. I'll never forget the time when Larry, the boy of my elementary school dreams, came to spend the night with my brother, Danny. He was walking down the hallway, unbeknownst to me, when I made my fateful error: I opened my bedroom door. Well, if old Larry ever had any marriage intentions toward me, I could see by the look on his face that they had just evaporated.

My dorm room was a wreck. As I recall, the only way I could figure out which outfit I wanted to wear was by process of elimination. I'd try on every outfit in the closet, decide I didn't want to wear it and throw it on the floor. By the time I hit upon the outfit I did want to wear for the day, it looked like it had been raining skirts and scarves. My dorm room was so bad, my roommate started a home business selling tickets to view the spectacle: "Step right up, coeds. Come see for yourself. It's a miracle in progress: This girl lives like this and has not caught any communicable diseases."

When Cameron and I got married, our first apartment was a wreck. Our second apartment was a wreck. So was our third. Then we bought a house and my husband was *sure* I'd be transformed into a good steward over our only financial investment. Wrong. It was a wreck. Then we bought our second home in a fancy, schmancy neighborhood (well, fancy by *our* standards; our first home was actually a trailer), and my husband was confident the peer pressure from the surrounding "House Beautiful" women would be inspiration enough for me to get cracking. Nope. My house in the fancy schmancy neighborhood is a wreck.

I got a call from my teenager one Saturday afternoon, cautiously inquiring into the current condition of the house. She had cleaned the whole house on Thursday. (Thank God, she had misbehaved on Wednesday, so I could dole out punishment in the form of chores.) Anyway, we'd managed to hold ground on Friday so that when she left to spend the night at a friend's house around five o'clock, you could still see the floors. Now, she wanted to bring her friend to *our house* and wanted to know if it was safe.

"Well, remember that lesson we had on hospitality the other night. You know, how you shouldn't be so concerned about having a perfect house. How people actually feel more comfortable when your house isn't perfect?"

"Yeah," she remembered.

"Well, I think you have an exciting opportunity to make your girlfriend *very* comfortable if you bring her on home right about now."

OVERWHELMING

As you can imagine from the previous illustrations, not everyone thinks the Popular woman is adorable. In fact, some folks just can't stand her. Their number-one objection? She's too *overwhelming!* The husband of one of my best friends refers to me only as "That Partow Woman." This is no joke! I've only been in the man's presence on two very brief occasions, but I guess even that was a bit too much.

Another Popular woman, Sandy, tells the story of her first experience volunteering at her church, shortly after she became a Christian:

> I was so excited about serving God and sharing the things I was learning. But since I was young and inexperienced, they [the church staff] told me the only assignment I was qualified for was working as an assistant in the five-year-olds Sunday school class. Basically, I was in charge of supervising the cutting and pasting. It didn't matter to me, though. I loved having fun with the

children. The teacher was a stern old woman who had been teaching for many, many years. In fact, her granddaughter was in the class. When the little girl arrived each Sunday morning, she always ran past her grandmother, straight over to my table. It was awkward, but there wasn't much I could do about it. I truly adored all the children and enthusiastically showered them with affection, while the older woman never displayed any emotion. I always got the feeling that this woman didn't like me very much. Then one day, I received a four-page letter in the mail from my beloved colaborer in Christ, ripping me limb-from-limb. The final sentence (right before "Yours In Jesus' Name") was "You are the most OVERWHELMING person I have ever met." I never stepped into that classroom again.

The Popular woman can indeed overwhelm people when her strengths are carried to extremes.

SEEMS PHONY

Even when the Popular woman is at her best, other temperaments may misunderstand her motives. The following scenario reveals how the Popular woman can appear phony, even when her intentions are good. Rhonda was an outgoing and active member of her church. One day, she received a call from her pastor. "Rhonda," he said, "You are such an encouragement to my wife. I have a special assignment for you. I met a young pastor's wife who is about your age and she is struggling with depression. My wife and I thought perhaps you could attend her church on Sunday evenings and befriend her." She was thrilled with the assignment.

So off she went in hopes of cheering up the depressed pastor's wife. Rhonda recalls what happened.

I took one look around the church and thought, "Well, no wonder she's depressed. Everyone around here is so quiet." So I started talking nonstop, trying to fill the void. That didn't quite solve it. Then I thought, "Oh, I know what the problem is. Everyone around here is so serious. Just thinking about it has got me depressed." So I started cracking jokes. Well, she still seemed depressed and I finally figured out why. "No wonder she's down in the dumps, this place is so cold!" So I began giving out hugs and double-cheek kisses to everyone who would stand still long enough.

Then I got a phone call. . . .

The woman I was supposed to be helping apparently did not find any of these activities helpful or amusing. I couldn't believe how angry she was at me, and I'll never forget her words: "You are the biggest phony I have ever met in my life. Every time I see you hug someone, it makes me want to puke. You claim to love people. If you really loved as Jesus loved, you would be *ON TIME*."

Rhonda didn't realize that the woman she was dealing with was the Powerful woman. And, as you will soon discover, the Powerful woman is the last person on earth who wants to be hugged and kissed and made a spectacle of. And the kind of person who places a high priority on promptness, following through on commitments and doing things in the proper order, all of which were qualities which Rhonda admits she lacked. Looking back, Rhonda notes, "If only I had understood the temperaments back then, I could have been more sensitive to her needs. Now, when I deal with women who are the Powerful type, I make a special effort to be prompt, to deliberately speak more softly, and to respect their need for personal space."

What an illustration that story is of the clash of temperaments. God created one woman to dish out hugs and kisses just as he created the other to bring quiet beauty and order into the world. We need to be so careful before we cast judgment on another person. It could be that God created that person to touch lives in a way you never could. Remember, just because someone is different from you doesn't mean she's wrong. If you take away no other lesson from reading this book, I hope you'll take that one.

MAKING THE MOST OF YOUR TEMPERAMENT

Your first step toward making the most of your temperament is heeding the advice you've no doubt heard your whole life: talk less and listen more. It's corny, but true: God gave you two ears and one mouth. Try using them in that ratio. The Bible abounds with warnings about the dangers of the tongue. It says we're going to be held accountable for every word we speak. Can you imagine that? Some of us are going to stand there giving an account for a very long time.

Why not invest time reading and meditating on the book of James? It has much to say about the tongue, including this:

> When we put bits into the mouths of horses to make them obey us, we can turn the whole animal. Or take ships as an example. Although they are so large and are driven by strong winds, they are steered by a very small rudder wherever the pilot wants to go. Likewise the tongue is a small part of the body, but it makes great boasts. Consider what a great forest is set on fire by a small spark. The tongue also is a fire, a world of evil among the parts of the body. It corrupts the whole person, sets the whole course of his life on fire, and is itself set on fire by hell. All kinds of animals, birds, reptiles and creatures of the sea are being tamed and have been tamed by man, but no man can tame the tongue. It is a restless evil, full of deadly poison. (James 3:3–8)

Strong words, wouldn't you say? If your tongue is a serious battleground, you might consider undertaking the in-depth, inductive study titled *James: A Faith that Works* by Kay Arthur. It comes in a workbook format and is only available through Precept Ministries, P.O. Box 182218, Chattanooga, TN 37422, 615–892–6814. (In recent years, an increasing number of Kay Arthur's studies have become available in book form, so check with your local Christian bookstore first.)

Speaking of the tongue, you may also need to come to grips with the tendency to exaggerate. In reality, exaggeration is often nothing more than lying with a socially acceptable label attached. Suddenly, it's not such a cute little sin. Suddenly, it's on the list of the Ten Commandments. Is it possible that you have exaggerated some of your favorite stories so wildly for so long that you have actually started believing them yourself? A sobering experience might be to sit down and give an accurate account of what happened. You may realize how far the exaggeration game can take you from the truth.

Many Popular women tend to be self-centered and self-absorbed. Just as a small example, do you remember the names of new people you meet? Do you even listen for their names? Or do you figure, "Hey, they'll get to know me; that's all that matters"? As your heart condition improves, so will your ability to recall names. Wait and see!

Do you tend to forget everything? I have a terrible habit of jotting important information on slips of paper and promptly losing them. A woman recently left a message in my voice mail, saying she wanted to order twelve books (that's $120—money I could surely use). She said her name was Barb, indicated we had talked previously, and hung up. Now, I have no idea who Barb is or where I might have written her number. I spent an hour looking, but never found her phone number.

Some resources that have helped this woman get it together include *The Disciplines of the Beautiful Woman, Disciplines of the Heart,* and *Disciplines of the Home,* all three written by Ann Ortlund. Then you can check out books by Emilie Barnes, including *More Hours in My Day.* The latest Queen of Get-It-Together is Sandra Felton, best known for her book *The Messies Manual* and the sequels and spin-offs it has spawned. She has even written a book called *Living with a Messie,* which you might want to buy for your husband!

The most revolutionary change in my life came after reading *Disciplines of the Beautiful Woman,* which recommended carrying a personal notebook. I have been using one, to a greater or lesser extent, for the past sixteen years. The trick is finding a daily planner that's big enough to hold everything you want to organize, yet small and convenient enough that you'll actually carry it with you wherever you go. If you don't carry it everywhere, it's really no use at all.

Another revolution occurred in my life when I recognized the importance of spending time with people who were a positive influence, even if it meant scheduling them into my life. No matter how hectic things gets, I spend every Monday night with a group of godly women who challenge me to grow—as a Christian and as a mother. Let me urge those of you who share this temperament with me: be careful who you spend time with. Since you love approval, you tend to be more easily led astray than other temperaments. If you start hanging with the wrong group of women, they can definitely bring you down.

A great passage of the Bible for you to memorize is Psalm 1, substituting "she" for "he":

> Blessed is the woman who does not walk in the counsel of the wicked or stand in the way of sinners or sit in the seat of mockers. But her delight is in the law of the LORD, and on his law she meditates day and night. She is like a tree planted by streams of water, which yields its fruit in season and whose leaf does not wither. Whatever she does prospers. Not so the wicked! They are like chaff that the wind blows away. Therefore the wicked will not stand in the judgment, nor sinners in the assembly of the righteous. For the LORD watches over the way of the righteous, but the way of the wicked will perish.

Do you notice a progression in those verses? First, you're just walking by a tempting situation; then it gets your attention, so you stop and stand to take a closer look. Next thing you know, you're sitting down with mockers. Sounds like the lure of the television, doesn't it? Boy, that's another battleground! You're walking through the family room and a show catches your eye. You stand to watch it for a few minutes and the next thing you know you're plopped down on the couch. Four hours later, you've got a mind full of mush and not a drop of housework has been accomplished. Any temperament can struggle with the television, but certainly those of us who like to have a good time need to stay on guard.

One of the most unattractive habits shared by many Popular women is the seemingly irresistible urge to "one up" other people's stories. You may think that this is a way of connecting, a way of communicating "Hey, I can relate to what you are saying." But that's not the way others perceive it. Why not try a little experiment? For the next week or so, consciously stay alert to other people's perceptions of you. When you're in a group, your natural tendency is probably to shift into your performance mode and pay little attention to the nonverbal cues others send your way. In particular, learn the cues that indicate boredom: disconnecting eye contact, shifting from side to side, glancing at watches, looking around the room, and of course, yawning.

It may seem impossible to you that anyone would ever be bored by *your* stories, but at least remain open to the possibility. You might be unpleasantly surprised by the results. If your stories tend to drag on forever, learn to get to the point. Well, okay, learn to get there faster than you used to!

Do you often regret your words? Have you ever played that game where you see how long you can keep your mouth shut in class or Sunday school or whatever? Have you ever written little reminder notes to yourself about keeping quiet? And yet, in spite of all your efforts, you can never keep quiet for very long. Somehow, you still manage to say the wrong thing at the wrong time? Here are some Bible verses to ponder: Proverbs 4:23 says, "Above all else, guard your heart, for it is the wellspring of life." Matthew 12:35–37 notes, "The good man brings good things out of the good stored up in him, and the evil man brings evil things out of the evil stored up in him. But I tell you that men will have to give account on the day of judgment for every careless word they have spoken. For by your words you will be acquitted, and by your words you will be condemned." The problem isn't with your mouth; the problem is with your heart.

Perhaps you've never thought of it this way before, but the underlying issue is a low regard for other people. Chances are, you have a tough time listening because you don't genuinely care about what anyone else has to say. When someone else is talking, you're busy plotting your next sentence, or interrupting and finishing other people's sentences, even answering questions on their behalf. Do you, by any chance, answer questions directed at your husband and children? Admit it, now!

Pray that God will change your heart, giving you a genuine concern for the interests of others. As you do that, you'll find yourself more eager to listen and less eager to offer up pat answers or amusing stories.

Does that mean you should somehow force yourself to become introverted? Definitely not. God created you to be an extrovert and there's nothing inherently wrong with being an outgoing person. It only becomes a problem when our heart is not right before God. When your heart begins to overflow with the things of God—with love, joy, peace, patience, kindness, faithfulness, and self-control—your tongue won't get you into nearly as much trouble. In fact, your words will become a powerful tool for blessing the world around you.

Focus on your heart. As you prayerfully and practically work to make changes, remember that the goal is not to become someone you're not; the goal is to become the best possible YOU. Here are some quick tips to help you achieve that goal:

1. *Use your personal popularity for good.* With your winning smile, vibrant personality and natural charisma, you have tremendous potential to influence your world. So make a conscious decision about how you are going to use that influence. You might even sit down and complete the following sentence, "Because they know me, I want people to_____." Then fill in the blank describing the positive impact you want to have on people's lives.

2. *Throw parties for a cause.* Here again, you have a great opportunity to make a difference in your world, just by being you. I've always loved to throw parties, but rather than generic "stand around and goof off" parties, I host parties with a mission. I hosted a Nepali Festival, featuring slides and a message from an itinerant evangelist and food from that region of the world. When I hosted a Morroccon Festival, we removed the legs from our dining room table, put pillows around and we all sat on the floor to eat, while missionaries to that country shared their life and ministry with us. The truly brave among us even tried eating Morroccon style: with our bare hands! Then there was the Haitian Festival and, well, you get the idea. Why not party with a purpose?

3. *Spread your creativity.* I absolutely love speaking at women's retreats and I can always tell whether or not the Popular women of the church are using their gifts.

(Every church has their share of these creative women; the question is what role they are willing to play.) I've been to some churches where you would never even guess that a special event was underway. But at other churches—WOW. The creativity of the decorations are such a blessing to everyone. From the minute everyone arrives, we know something exciting is going to happen. We know *someone* cared enough to put their creativity to work. Don't let anyone tell you that your creative gifts are superfluous or unnecessary. Spread that creativity around and be a blessing!

4. *Reach out to the lonely.* Because you're such a natural people-person, you probably have no idea just how lonely some women are. Believe me, I meet them at every church and in every city in America. Women who are overlooked and left out, women who are never included on anyone's social calendar. If only you knew what a difference you could make just by making one phone call per day to women whose phones never ring. If only you knew what it would mean for them to feel included or just to hear a cheerful voice. Look around you: perhaps there are lonely widows or lonely stay-at-home moms in your church or neighborhood. Reach out and touch them. You can make a difference in their lives, just by being you.

5. *Be a motivator.* One of my neighbors, Ann, is a shining example of a motivator. When she started attending church a few years back, half the neighborhood followed her lead. When she decided to join a small group Bible study, suddenly it was the "thing to do." She is so excited about what God is doing in her life, and she shares it with such exuberance, that others can't help but get excited. You can do the same in your neighborhood!

3

Introducing the Perfect Woman

PERFECT STRENGTHS

METICULOUS HOUSEKEEPER

The Perfect woman is often seen with her beloved companion: her trusty feather duster. These are the women who put Martha Stewart to shame, but then again, they're also the women who keep Martha Stewart in business, so I guess it's okay. The Perfect woman loves creating and maintaining the ideal home. She's usually a fabulous decorator and gourmet cook. She approaches household chores in a well-organized and self-disciplined fashion. Her motto is "A place for everything and everything in its place."

I remember attending a full-day "home organization" seminar taught by Emilie Barnes, the Legendary Queen of Household Management. She absolutely captivated me with her ostrich feather duster, super-boxes, alphabetical card filing systems, and cleaning-supply apron. It was obvious that she truly had a passion for housework. I used to think those Perfect women were big phony balonies. "No one's *that* organized," I thought. "When no one's looking, I'll bet their houses are just as messy as mine. After all, even *I* clean up for company." (In fact, whenever I start cleaning, my kids invariably say, "So, who's

47

coming over?" The first time my daughter said that to me, she was only two years old. Just a toddler and she already had me figured out.)

But the Perfect woman is no phony. She doesn't wait until someone is coming over to clean. She genuinely takes great delight in keeping her surroundings in order. If one of your friends is this temperament, you can stop by her house at any given moment, day or night, and guess what? Everything will be absolutely, positively PERFECT.

Of course, there is one *major* problem with the Perfect woman. When she moves into the neighborhood, she makes the rest of us look bad! Our husbands start getting wild ideas like "home-cooked meals" or "ironed shirts." They want to know why *our* whites aren't whiter than white. (Just kidding, of course!) I have a girlfriend who is a Popular woman, and her mother-in-law is a Perfect woman. Her poor husband just can't understand why their house doesn't look like the one he grew up in. Based on what you've learned so far about the temperaments, what are the chances of a Popular woman's house ever looking anything remotely like the Perfect woman's house? The correct answer is nonexistent!

ORGANIZED

The Perfect woman's organizational skills extend beyond her home. If she works—whether it's in an office, running a home business, or volunteering at the church—her desk will be in perfect order. In fact, a surefire way to identify this temperament is to peek into drawers—the pens will be neatly lined up in one section, note paper stacked in a corner, you get the idea. Her entire approach to life is organized: she'll carry a daily planner, keep records of car repairs, invite you for dinner, wait for a return invitation, then invite you again.

She's the perfect person to turn to for advice on virtually any topic, from alphabetizing your spices to wallpapering the nursery, and everything in between. Chances are, she's got a shelf filled with how-to books and instructional videos covering do-it-yourself auto repair, cake decorating, constructing your dream home, you name it. She might even have a card catalog system to manage the whole thing. This is no joke; I actually know a Perfect woman with just such a system.

She also takes a systematic approach to her family's health. Although she's a gourmet cook and can serve up sugar-rich desserts with the best of them, chances are, she serves nutritious food for ordinary occasions. She may even be a health food advocate, who takes an interest in alternative/preventive medicine. No doubt, every family member takes their morning vitamins, individually selected to address their physical weaknesses. If your child isn't feeling well, call this woman for advice. For example, let's say your child has been coughing. The Perfect woman will have a fifty-point, color-coded checklist to determine the precise cause of the ailment. She may be able to suggest nutritional or herbal strategies for preliminary treatment. Not only that, with a flip of a page in her daily planner, she'll be able to give you the name and phone number for the city's leading medical specialist for its treatment.

PERFECTLY GROOMED

While the Popular woman always has that "just rolled out of bed" look, the Perfect woman always looks carefully put together. In fact, the easiest way to spot this temperament is to study her appearance: neat, fashionable, well-groomed. Many have short, sleek hairstyles. I've theorized that this is so they can look perfect—even in the shower! They'll also do their best to keep their small children looking perfect. One woman confided to me that she ironed her three-year-old son's playclothes each morning.

I'll never forget stopping by my friend Ruth's house in the middle of the afternoon one day, shortly after her second child was born. There she was, perfectly groomed and neatly dressed, from her head down to her feet. What stands out most in my memory was watching her change the baby's diaper and observing that her fingernails were perfectly manicured.

Before I understood the temperaments, I thought surely ALL women looked as ragged around the house as I do. (You know, funky old clothes, no make-up, hair in a ponytail—shower optional!) Well, I had never seen my neighbor, Gayle, looking anything less than perfect. So early one Saturday morning, for a joke,

I turned on my video camera and began walking toward her house, narrating the whole time: "Ladies and gentlemen, we are now approaching the home of Gayle. We are about to discover what she really looks like—without her hair styled, without makeup, without any manmade accoutrements. Here she comes, she's opening the door, and she looks . . . absolutely PERFECT." We've now been neighbors for four years and I have never once seen her without makeup. Gayle told me she never leaves her bedroom until she's showered, dressed, and fully groomed.

WONDERFUL HOSTESS

On yet another occasion, I stopped by my friend Jan's house on the day before her daughter's sixth birthday party. The theme was "The Little Mermaid" but there wasn't a pre-packaged Disney character in sight. No way! She was cutting out small white triangles and I asked what they were. "Shark's teeth," she replied casually. She had made a giant shark and planned to photograph each of the party attendees peeking out of the shark's mouth. To get just the right effect, she was cutting out individual shark teeth by hand and gluing them, one-by-one, onto the handmade shark. Does this boggle your mind?!

The party was, of course, fabulous. Jan handpainted fish cookies with frosting in tropical patterns. There was a home-made mermaid cake. Not the kind with little plastic characters you pick up at the local grocery store bakery. No, this had a beautiful mermaid doll protruding out of the center of the cake.

For the adults, she prepared gourmet foods ranging from chicken and wild rice to sautéed shrimp. When she discovered that Cameron and I had to leave early, she prepared special take-home plates for us before we left. There were all kinds of games for children and a luau, complete with hula dancing and limbo, for the adults.

The amazing part is, she entertains like this *on a regular basis.*

DETAIL-ORIENTED

The Perfect woman actually *reads* the instruction manuals that go with her appliances, which is why her appliances last so much longer than an ordinary woman's. She likes to do everything by the book and doesn't waste time reinventing the wheel. She wants to know the right way to do things and places great faith in what worked in the past. She's not the type to chase after every new innovation that comes down the pike, preferring to stick with the tried and true. In fact, the decor in her home is probably very classic and traditional.

When the Perfect woman brings this characteristic to bear on her devotional life, the results are marvelous. She becomes an avid student of the Bible, she devotes herself to a regularly scheduled daily quiet time, and she systemically cultivates the spiritual disciplines that lead to a deeper Christian life.

THOUGHTFUL

Though it's wonderful that the Perfect woman never overlooks a detail, what's even more important is the way her attention to details translates into thoughtfulness. She remembers birthdays and holidays with cards and gifts, and not the kind of gifts you grab off the shelf at K-mart at the last minute. No, she gives gifts that were carefully chosen and purchased weeks in advance.

Caroline is a great example. In our neighborhood, we have monthly dinner parties called "Dine with Friends," where five couples take turns hosting dinner in their home. I remember one occasion when the hostess had asked Caroline to share one of her legendary recipes. This is no minor thing, people. You have to attend a training class and become certified and even then, you've got to sign a release form before obtaining individual recipes. (Kidding!)

Anyway, wouldn't you know the hostess overmarinated the chicken? So, when her husband tried to put it on the grill, it went sopping through. When Caroline arrived on the scene early, in case her help was needed in the kitchen, she realized the hostess' dilemma and immediately sprang into action. She sent her husband to the nearest grocery store to buy chicken and gathered the ingredients to make a new marinade. She mixed it up and had it refrigerated for half an hour . . . all before I managed to *arrive* at the party.

When the hostess brought out the dinner plates (which Caroline had helped her arrange to look like something you'd be served in a gourmet restaurant), she reached to put a plate in front of me. Caroline softly whispered, "No, no, no. I've got Donna's plate right here. See, it doesn't have any mushrooms on it." I gave her a "How on earth did you know that?" glance and she explained: "You left your mushrooms on the plate last time."

Here is a woman who not only noticed that I didn't eat my mushrooms at another dinner party, she actually remembered it two months after the fact. More to the point, she cared enough to do something about it. Wow! That's what I call thoughtful.

FRUGAL

The Perfect woman is extremely frugal. It doesn't matter how much money she has, she wants to spend it wisely. She may have enough money in her child's college fund to cover four years at an Ivy League University, yet she will spend four hours every week clipping seventy-five-cent coupons and driving to five different grocery stores in hopes of saving twenty dollars.

Grocery stores aren't the only place she wants to save money. Just this morning, one of my friends called to let me know about a new consignment shop she had found. She was overjoyed to report that she had bought four beautiful party dresses for twenty dollars. Her husband is extremely successful and they could certainly afford to shop at the finest stores in town, but as she says, "I *hate* paying retail."

CAREFUL DECISION-MAKER

While some may consider the Perfect woman too slow in making decisions, she is simply cautious. She investigates every possible angle. If she wants to buy a new blender, she'll go to the library and research the various brands in *Consumer Reports* magazines. (Come to think of it, she might just have a subscription to *Consumer Reports*.) Often she can avoid problems the rest of us fall into, because she makes wise decisions in the first place and averts problems before they begin.

SOPHISTICATED

The Perfect woman is extremely sophisticated. Rather than Disney movies, she has her children watching classic films such as *National Velvet* and *Little Women*. She doesn't want her children reading *The Babysitters Club* or *Goosebumps*; instead, she'll provide them with a reading list of great literature. In fact, she'll probably invest in those leather-bound editions of the World's Greatest Books. While the rest of the women in the waiting room read *People* magazine, she takes out her *National Geographic*. When she needs decorating ideas, she doesn't turn to *Family Circle,* she turns to *Architectural Digest*. (Here's a little tip: If any of your friends subscribe to *Architectural Digest,* you should immediately be able to guess which temperament you're dealing with!) She takes her children to the ballet, to museums, to the symphony.

She wouldn't be caught dead hosting a potluck supper. Her idea of a simple dinner party is a five-course meal that always features stuffed mushrooms and various recipes from *Bon Appetit*. She orders her clothes from the Talbots catalog and children's play-clothes are direct from L.L. Bean. She wouldn't dream of sending her children to the local state college; the Ivy League is in their future.

PERFECT WEAKNESSES

PERFECTIONISTIC

Isn't it wonderful that the Perfect woman is so perfect? Wouldn't it be just dandy to have a wife or mother like that? Then your house would be perfect and everyone would be happy, right? Well, not necessarily. You see, all of this perfection can go too far and end up creating stress for her family. She sets unrealistically high standards for everything from household chores to academic and sports performance. She'll drive past ten gymnastic studios to get to the right one, even if it's thirty miles away. She'll hire the right coach and make sure her kids get the right teacher at the right school. In theory, that sounds wonderful. In reality, it creates an incredible amount of stress. Some women maintain homes that are so neat and clean, people are afraid to breathe. This can be a very stifling environment for a child, especially a Popular or Peaceful child.

Have you ever watched an event like the following unfold? You are attending a social gathering in the home of a Perfect woman. The food, the decor, the ambiance—everything is perfect. Even the white carpet looks perfect, until that fateful moment when someone spills a bit of punch. Now, it doesn't have to be a glass full of punch, just a little *bit* of punch. What happens next? With great fanfare, the hostess runs to get out her bottle of carpet cleaning solution and spends ten minutes on her hands and knees cleaning up every microscopic trace of punch. It's like watching her perform surgery. In fact, all other conversations cease as the unfolding drama becomes the talk of the party. ("What's she doing?" "Oh, really, who spilled it?")

It's nice that the Perfect woman wants her carpet to look great. The problem is that she seems to care more about the condition of her carpet than the feelings of her guest. That's perfection run amok.

UNPOPULAR

Since the Perfect woman is very quiet and thoughtful, she can come across as cold and distant, which can make her quite unpopular. The reality is that she may simply be shy or fearful. Chances are, she has been hurt by disappointing friendships in the past and wants to guard her heart. She works tirelessly to ensure that everything in her life—her home, her family, her career or ministry—appears absolutely perfect. And it usually does from a distance. She doesn't want you to get close to her, for fear you might figure out she's not quite as perfect as she wants you to believe. She is often very guarded with her personal life and her emotions.

She's cautious in making new friends. After all, the perfect friend is not easy to come by. Should she allow you the privilege of becoming her friend, get ready for a package of E-X-P-E-C-T-A-T-I-O-N-S that Dale Carnegie himself couldn't live up to. She will expect you to listen to her endless tales of woe, told with painstaking detail. She'll expect you to know when and why she's depressed. When she's mad at you, she'll expect you to figure out why with hardly a clue from her. She'll expect you to remember her birthday and give her the kind of thoughtful gift she prides herself in giving. When you don't live up to her expectations (and the truth is, no mere mortal will ever be perfect enough for her taste), she can become extremely bitter.

RIGID

The Perfect woman can be quite rigid in demanding adherence to her many, many, *many* rules. She's got a rule for everything from the mundane to the sublime. From "always put the spices back on the shelf in alphabetical order" to "always load all the glasses in the dishwasher before you begin loading the cups and saucers" to "always give solid evidence that you planned your wife's anniversary gift at least three months in advance." There's only one right way to do everything, and she sincerely believes she knows what it is.

Once the Perfect woman sets the rules, she considers them set in stone. She can be a tough taskmaster toward her children, her husband, and even her friends. Unfortunately, she sometimes gets so busy orchestrating life that she forgets to live life.

The Perfect woman lives by the letter of the law, not the spirit. I recently put up a notice at a senior citizen's center that I was looking for a grandma "to hold my baby" while I tried to get some work done. Well, I got one response and it was a Perfect grandma. She came to work for me and guess what she did? She held the baby. Period. She didn't wash the baby bottles. One day she came to me and said, "There are no clean bottles." I responded that I'd been too exhausted (from writing this book) to catch up on dishes. She said calmly, "I'll just have to give her jar food then." And that's what she did.

It goes without saying that she didn't help with the baby's laundry or keep the nursery in order. I thought all of these things were "implied" but I didn't bother to enumerate them. From her perspective, doing any of those other things might have involved putting the baby down for a moment; and the sign said she was supposed to *hold* the baby. What I meant to say was that I was looking for someone who would take care of all things concerning the baby. But not being detail-oriented, I scribbled a very vague notice and tacked it up without thinking it through. The sign said, "Hold the baby" so that's what she did. She did it quite marvelously, I might add.

PRONE TO THE BLUES

The Perfect woman will schedule her day down to half-hour increments and see that everything looks great on paper. However, when her day doesn't work out the way her planner said it would, she often becomes frustrated and discouraged. Now imagine any mother of preschoolers plotting out her day and expecting it to go as planned! Basically, this woman is setting herself up for depression. And unless she can find a way to lower her expectations, she can make herself and everyone around her miserable.

She has to find a way to live with the unexpected, because life is full of unexpected twists, turns, and yes, disappointments. If she doesn't, her emotional life will present an ongoing struggle. More than any other temperament, the Perfect woman is prone to the blues. Some are even given to despair, feeling that if life can't be as perfect as they dreamed it would be, they may as well check out early. Although no one has tracked suicide by temperament, I believe it's safe to assume that this temperament has the highest rate. The alarming number of artists, musicians, philosophers, and other creative geniuses who have taken their own lives bears this out.

Understanding this fact has made me much more sensitive to my Perfect friends. I even have a fresh example to offer. For the past several weeks, I've bumped into Martha on a half dozen occasions. Each time, I felt like she snubbed me and I began feeling slighted. I started thinking, "What's up with her? Is she too good for me? Why is she mad at me?" Then an unusual thought entered my mind: "Donna, maybe it has absolutely nothing to do with you." As someone who has always believed the universe revolved around me, this was a very novel concept. But I began to entertain the idea and it eventually took hold.

Sure enough, when I gave her a call, I discovered she had been depressed for some time. Unfortunately, I hadn't bothered to notice. Like most Popular types, I'm often self-absorbed.

Anyway, I talked with her for an hour and let her express her frustrations. I tried to offer her hope and encouragement that maybe there were some solutions, after all. Mostly, though, I offered a listening ear and that's what she needed.

I had another Perfect friend I hadn't heard from in a few months. I've been "too busy" to call her. When we finally did get together, she confided that she, too, had been struggling with depression for several months. Please be sensitive to this tendency in your Perfect friend. If you don't hear from her, take the initiative to reach out and give her a call. When she doesn't ask for help or attention, that's the very moment she needs you most.

UNFORGIVING

In the same way she remembers every little detail about decorating and cooking, she remembers every little detail about what you've done wrong. More specifically, how you and the rest of the world have done *her* wrong. This is the type of wife who says to her husband, "Oh yeah, how about the time on July 9, 1973 when you . . ." and then goes into elaborate and accurate detail about the offense.

As a matter of fact (which, by the way, is a favorite Perfect woman phrase), she keeps a permanent mental record of wrongs, cross-referenced by offending party, type of offense, and date of occurrence. I actually read about one woman who kept a written record of everyone who had offended her. Can you imagine? Not only that, some women secretly like being wronged, because it gives them the opportunity to shift into the martyr role, which happens to be a role they relish playing. Unfortunately, it's not a role many folks like being an audience to.

I once read a poem that shook me to the core, and I'll never forget one line in particular. It read: "A bitter old person is one of the crowning works of the devil." Doesn't that alarm you? That your life could become a living testament to the power of evil and all you'd have to do is become *bitter*? Perfect women in particular need to guard against giving the devil a foothold in their lives, by making a conscious effort to forgive and forget.

CHEAPSKATE

On another occasion, I spent the night in a Perfect woman's home—a home worth more than a million dollars, filled with hundreds of thousands of dollars in furnishings from around the world. "Perfect" doesn't quite capture it. What a lovely, enjoyable experience, right? Not exactly. The place was absolutely freezing. And when I had to use the potty in the middle of the night, I was literally terror-stricken. (I can still hear my heart beating wildly.) Why? There was not a speck of light anywhere in this huge mansion. Earlier in the evening, the husband and wife argued in front of us because someone left on the hall light for two minutes longer than necessary. (My husband and I just looked at each other and felt like we'd entered the *Twilight Zone*.) Little did I know, they *never* thought turning on lights was necessary. I'm talking total darkness, here, people. I had to feel my way along the pitch-dark hallway, praying I'd stumble on a door handle before I stumbled down a flight of stairs and killed myself. Only a certified cheapskate wouldn't think to leave the light on for guests.

MAKING THE MOST OF YOUR TEMPERAMENT

If I were a Perfect woman (and Lord knows I'm not!), the question I'd want to ask myself would be, "Why do I need everything to be so doggone perfect?" As you work toward becoming the best possible you, ironically, your first step is lowering your standards. That probably sounds contradictory, but it's not. In order to bring balance into your life, you'll need to come to grips with the fact that this is an imperfect world, where things won't always turn out the way you planned. Learning to accept imperfection from yourself and especially from your husband and children will liberate you from the bondage of perfectionism.

As you prayerfully examine your life, perhaps you'll discover that your greatest need is to cultivate a heart of grace and mercy. You might also ponder the implications of this verse:

> Why do you look at the speck of sawdust in your brother's
> eye and pay no attention to the plank in your own eye?
> How can you say to your brother, "Let me take the speck

out of your eye," when all the time there is a plank in your own eye? You hypocrite, first take the plank out of your own eye, and then you will see clearly to remove the speck from your brother's eye. (Matthew 7:3–5)

Keep in mind that the "plank" in your eye may be your tendency to look for the speck in everyone else's eyes.

Romans 12:3 and 14:4 state this even more forcefully:

For by the grace given me I say to every one of you: Do not think of yourself more highly than you ought, but rather think of yourself with sober judgment, in accordance with the measure of faith God has given you. Who are you to judge someone else's servant? To his own master he stands or falls. And he will stand, for the Lord is able to make him stand.

In case we missed it, God reminds us again in James 4:12: "There is only one Lawgiver and Judge, the one who is able to save and destroy. But you—who are you to judge your neighbor?"

Although God didn't create you to become a stand-up comedian, you may find your relationships enriched as you develop your sense of humor. It's sad but true: no one likes people who are deadly serious all the time. Your family and friends love you, but you sometimes make it hard for them to like you. Your toughest battle, after perfectionism, may be against depression. Perhaps the following suggestions will prove helpful as you seek to make the most of your temperament.

TAKE CARE OF YOUR BODY

Okay, I realize that for many of you, this is like preaching to the choir. You already eat right and exercise, so this section is just a reinforcement of what you're already doing; but perhaps others *need* to hear this. "Do you not know that your body is a temple of the Holy Spirit, who is in you, whom you have received from God? You are not your own; you were bought at a price. Therefore honor God with your body" (1 Corinthians 6:19–20). Romans 12:1 takes it a step further: "Therefore, I urge you, brothers, in view of God's mercy, to offer your bodies as living sacrifices,

holy and pleasing to God—this is your spiritual act of worship."
Treat your body like the temple of the Holy Spirit, not a trash can!
Specifically, eat plenty of fruits and vegetables and drink all the
water you possibly can. Read *Fit for Life* by Harvey and Marilyn
Diamond (available at most libraries and bookstores). Although
it's difficult, try to incorporate the dietary guidelines as far as possible. David and Anne Fraham write good nutritional books from
a Christian perspective. I suspect that, once you throw yourself
into this endeavor, you'll become a nutrition aficionado, to the
benefit of yourself and your loved ones.

MEDITATE ON GOD'S WORD
AND PRAY DAILY

Begin with Psalms, especially Psalm 119:27: "Let me
understand the teaching of your precepts; then I will meditate
on your wonders. My soul is weary with sorrow; strengthen me
according to your word."

COUNT YOUR BLESSINGS

Take out a piece of paper and list twenty blessings or
powerful answers to prayer. Keep it in the front of your Bible and
frequently update it as you experience God's miracles and even
his small gifts. Review it daily until your heart begins to overflow
with thankfulness and joy. "Give thanks in all circumstances, for
this is God's will for you in Christ Jesus" (1 Thessalonians 5:18).

BOOST YOUR SELF-IMAGE
BY PONDERING ALL THE TRUTHS ABOUT
WHO YOU ARE IN CHRIST

Neil T. Anderson covers this extensively in his writings,
particularly *The Bondage Breaker*. Don't believe your feelings;
believe the truth. For example, did you know that you are a
princess? Consider Romans 8:17: "Now if we are children, then
we are heirs—heirs of God and co-heirs with Christ, if indeed we
share in his sufferings in order that we may also share in his
glory." If God, the King of the Universe, is your Father, that

makes you a daughter of the King—a princess. Pretty hard to get down on yourself in view of that truth, isn't it?

SET YOURSELF FREE

Make a conscious decision to forgive those who have offended you, realizing that forgiving doesn't make their position right; forgiving sets you free.

"Forgive us our debts, as we also have forgiven our debtors. And lead us not into temptation, but deliver us from the evil one." For if you forgive men when they sin against you, your heavenly Father will also forgive you. But if you do not forgive men their sins, your Father will not forgive your sins. (Matthew 6:12–16)

Bear with each other and forgive whatever grievances you may have against one another. Forgive as the Lord forgave you. And over all these virtues put on love, which binds them all together in perfect unity. Let the peace of Christ rule in your hearts, since as members of one body you were called to peace. And be thankful. (Colossians 3:13–15)

STOP LOOKING FOR THE GRAY CLOUD
IN THE SILVER LINING

Choose to focus your attention on what's right in the world, rather than what's wrong.

Do not be anxious about anything, but in everything, by prayer and petition, with thanksgiving, present your requests to God. And the peace of God, which transcends all understanding, will guard your hearts and your minds in Christ Jesus. Finally, brothers, whatever is true, whatever is noble, whatever is right, whatever is pure, whatever is lovely, whatever is admirable—if anything is excellent or praiseworthy—think about such things. (Philippians 4:6–8)

REALIZE THAT DEPRESSION IS FREQUENTLY BIOCHEMICAL

Depression is not a reflection of weak character or a lack of faith, so don't beat yourself up about it. It may be a symptom of inadequate thiamine, biotin, B_3, B_6, B_{12} or other vitamins and minerals. Take a high-potency vitamin and at least two to three times the RDA of B-complex vitamins. Some physicians also recommend L-phenylalanine and potassium/magnesium aspartate (1000 mg each per day). We all have our physical weaknesses, because we dwell in jars of clay. "But we have this treasure in jars of clay to show that this all-surpassing power is from God and not from us" (2 Corinthians 4:7). Just think, someday God will deliver us from these imperfect bodies! In the meantime, we have to work with what we've got.

Consult your physician. If he or she prescribes medication, by all means, take it. Chronic depression and manic depression are serious diseases and should be treated just as you would treat cancer, leukemia, or diabetes.

BE REALISTIC

Let go of unrealistic expectations. Realize they only lead to disappointment, bitterness, and anger. This is an imperfect world filled with imperfect people. "For all have sinned and fall short of the glory of God" (Romans 3:23). The good news is that we "are justified freely by his grace through the redemption that came by Christ Jesus" (Romans 3:24). And since God has justified, we have no right to condemn. Jesus warned us not to expect our lives to be heaven on earth, but he also offers reassurance: "I have told you these things, so that in me you may have peace. In this world you will have trouble. But take heart! I have overcome the world" (John 16:33).

Pray the following prayer daily. Perhaps even commit it to memory.

SEVENTEENTH-CENTURY NUN'S PRAYER

Lord, you know better than I know myself that I am growing older and will someday be old. Keep me from the

*fatal habit of thinking I must say something in every sub-
ject and on every occasion. Release me from the craving to
straighten out everybody's affairs. Make me thoughtful, but
not moody. Helpful, but not bossy. With my vast store of
wisdom, it seems a pity not to use it all, but You know,
Lord, that I want a few friends at the end.*

*Keep my mind free from the endless recital of details;
give me wings to get to the point. Seal my lips on my aches
and pains. They are increasing, and love of rehearsing them
is becoming sweeter as the years go by. I dare not ask for
grace enough to enjoy the tales of others' pains, but help
me to endure them with patience.*

*I dare not ask for improved memory, but for a grow-
ing humility and a lessening cocksureness when my memory seems to clash with the memories of others. Teach me
the glorious lesson that occasionally . . . I may be mistaken.*

*Keep me reasonably sweet. I do not want to be a
saint—some of them are so hard to live with—but a bitter
old person is one of the crowning works of the devil. Give
me the ability to see good things in unexpected places, and
talents in unexpected people. And give me, Lord, the grace
to tell them so. Amen.*

Introducing the Powerful Woman

POWERFUL STRENGTHS

TAKE-CHARGE WOMAN

I've got to tell you right off the bat: I think this temperament tends to get a bum rap in many books. In listing strengths, the best one book could come up with was stuff like "puts projects before people," "doesn't consult spouse before making life-changing decisions," "doesn't take time for real conversation" and "is easily threatened by questions." These are the strengths? I was afraid to get to the part about weaknesses.

I may as well admit to having a personal stake in presenting the true strengths of the Powerful woman, because I am an even mix of Powerful and Popular. And as much as I love to have a good time and enjoy life, I am thankful God gave me the Powerful drive and determination to make a real difference in this world. If it weren't for my Powerful side, there's no way I could have written this or any other book. Books which, I hope and pray, have changed many lives for the better.

Women with this temperament do, in fact, have many wonderful strengths. Without further ado, let me introduce you to the Powerful woman. Here she is with her commander's baton, telling everybody else what to do! (Hey, wait a minute, that *is* a strength. Some people need to be told what to do!)

She is a "shake things up, make things happen" kind of woman. She is very energetic and outgoing, and she's always up to something new. As I've traveled around the country offering women's retreats, I've noticed that almost all of them are planned and coordinated by a Powerful woman. And I always quip "I will personally guarantee that there are women in this room today who are here for one reason and one reason only: they were *told* they were going to be here." That always generates a good amount of laughter because it's so true.

Isn't it interesting that a Powerful *man* is praised to the high heavens for his leadership abilities, but when a Powerful *woman* demonstrates those same traits, she gets accused of being bossy, overly aggressive, and domineering? So often men consider her a threat, while she is resented and judged by other women. Rather than supporting the woman who takes the lead, other women want to "cut her down to size." I've seen this happen time and time again, in my own life and in the lives of women I greatly admire. A famous Christian author with extraordinary leadership skills once told me that I shouldn't even *bother* trying to play a vital role in my local church, because the chances of my ever being accepted were virtually nonexistent. She said this based on thirty years of ministry experience, during which she had rarely seen a Powerful woman who didn't encounter constant opposition as she tried to exercise her leadership skills. You might think her words discouraged me. Quite the contrary! They were among the most liberating I had ever heard! They assured me that the opposition I was facing wasn't *personal;* but indeed, was virtually *universal.* What a sad commentary.

Powerful women, take heart. You are not alone. And the rest of you ladies, listen up: Support the Powerful woman who's willing to lead. Be thankful she takes the initiative to get the ball rolling. Otherwise, most of you would be sitting home with nowhere to go and nothing to do. Thank God for these take-charge women!

COURAGEOUS

This is a lady with plenty of what New Yorkers call "chutzpah." If you invite her to go skiing with you, she'll head right for the expert slopes. It doesn't matter that she's never been skiing before. She figures, if she sets her mind to it, she can do it. And very often, she can. Her motto is, "Often wrong, but never in doubt!"

Some might say derogatorily, "She's got her nerve." Well, they can use whatever tone of voice they like, this lady does indeed have plenty of nerve, which can be used in powerful ways for good. When a Powerful woman turns her life over to God, he can accomplish extraordinary things through her. No matter what needs to be accomplished, no matter what the obstacles, she will hold firmly to her belief that she can do it with God's help.

One of my favorite movies is "The Inn of the Sixth Happiness" starring Ingrid Bergman. It's based on the true life story of Gladys Aylward, a British house servant who approached the China Inland Mission in 1930 about serving God as an overseas missionary. They turned her down flat because she was not properly educated and didn't have any impressive credentials. But she believed God had called her and wasn't easily deterred.

She began saving every penny she earned and depositing it with the ticket agent at the railway station. She began reading all she could about missions in China and learned of an elderly widow, Jeannie Lawson, who was eager for someone to come assist with her ministry. Finally, she had enough to purchase a ticket from London, through Europe and the Soviet Union, on to China. If this sounds daring now, imagine what nerve it took for a woman to travel alone to China sixty years ago. Men did not dare go to the mission field without a mission society backing and supporting them. Even today, few missionaries would consider leaving home without a sending agency and without having their full support raised. This lady had chutzpah by the ton.

In 1940, when the Japanese began bombing the village where she lived and worked, she led a group of one hundred children on a harrowing journey over rugged terrain to safety in another Chinese city. Let me tell you, there's not a Popular type on the planet who could survive in such a challenging environment. The Perfect types would have gotten too depressed to move forward when things didn't turn out perfectly from the start. And as you'll soon find out, the Peaceful type would never be caught dead bucking the system. When the mission society said no she would have gone back to housecleaning and never uttered a word of complaint. But the Powerful type has the courage of her convictions.

DETERMINED

The surest way to motivate the Powerful woman is to tell her "It can't be done!" Then watch her fly into action as she rises to meet the challenge. She views life as a series of problems to solve or challenges to overcome. When I was rising to the challenge of encouraging women to form mothers' networks in their communities using my book, *No More Lone Ranger Moms*, I would often tell my audiences: "If you want to see a mothers' network formed in your church or neighborhood but don't have the gumption to do it yourself, here's what you should do. Walk up to a Powerful woman, holding a copy of *No More Lone Ranger Moms* in your hand, and say, 'I don't think anyone could organize something like this in our church.' The gauntlet will have been thrown. She'll have that mothers' network whipped into shape in no time. You'll have a logo and letterhead and a board of directors elected, with her as the president."

This determined woman thrives on challenges. Whereas most people will mutter, "If it ain't broke, don't fix it." She will shout, "Hey, if it ain't broke, let's break it and see what happens!" She lives from battle to battle, from conquest to conquest. That's why she often struggles after leaving the workplace to stay home with her children. There's nothing specific to accomplish; nothing is ever finished. I mean, as moms, wouldn't it be nice to be able to say, just once, "Yes, the work has been completed. The laundry has been finished once and for all." Let's face it, that just isn't going to happen. Although I have said to my family a few times, "I *am* finished."

CRUSADER

The Powerful woman not only notices the wrongs and injustices of life (which puts her ahead of two temperaments already), she is compelled to set things right (which puts her ahead of *all* the other temperaments!). She is the one who crusades for change. Powerful moms can be found protesting outside of abortion clinics, walking a picket line outside of a convenience store that carries pornography, or serving as chairperson for a local charity.

Some women run home businesses AND crusade. Like me, for example! During the last week of August 1995, I received a call on the church prayer chain about a twelve-year-old girl named Nikki, who had been left homeless when both of her parents were sent off to prison. Her relatives had all been contacted and not one of them was willing to take her in. She was desperately in need of a home. It was a Thursday afternoon. The Child Protective Services officials had agreed to give our church until Monday to find a suitable home for her or she would be taken into custody.

I immediately called the pastor and told him we would consider taking her into our home. This girl had been wrongly abandoned and I felt compelled to make it right. I remember saying to my husband, "I can't sleep at night in a world where children are treated like that. What kind of people have we become when an innocent child can be completely unloved and unwanted?" That was two years ago. Nikki still lives with us and has become a lovely, godly young lady. Like I said, the Powerful crusader must correct wrongs.

PRODUCTIVE

Since Powerful women are so hard-working, goal-oriented, and energetic, they tend to lead exceptionally productive lives. Many have successful, high-powered careers. As mentioned above, many—even those who believe strongly in the importance of being a stay-at-home mom—will crave more than "just" motherhood. I did. That's why I launched a home business and later, a speaking and writing ministry. Our need for a second income was the deciding factor, but even if we didn't absolutely need the money, I know that sooner or later I would have pursued outside interests.

I meet many women with this temperament who run successful home businesses or who head up various ministries.

There's no reason to feel guilty about this, although some people who don't understand temperaments will try to make you feel guilty. Don't give in to them. That's how God wired you. He created you to thrive on getting things done.

My only word of caution to Powerful moms (including myself) is to be sure to listen to your heavenly Father's voice, so you accomplish what he has in mind for your life. And here's a great rule to follow: If the work you're doing is from God, you should be able to accomplish it in a reasonable amount of time without neglecting your family. If your work is not from God, no amount of effort on your part will be enough to bring the success and fulfillment you're longing for. Believe me, I've learned this lesson the hard way.

Recently I met a Powerful woman in Texas who organized her church's annual ladies retreat, for which I was the speaker. What a dynamo this lady was! And wow, what an incredible retreat! What a blessing to the hundreds of women who attended! At the closing, she spent twenty minutes thanking each of the women who played a part in making the retreat possible. She described what they contributed, called them to the front of the room, and presented them with gifts she had made herself. Then she made a comment that really grabbed my attention:

"God gave me a vision and heart for women's ministry many years ago. But it's taken a long time for me to learn to *trust other women* to do their part. I used to feel like I had to do everything myself if I wanted it done right. Now I know to just call the right woman and let her go. Let her do it however she feels is best and it'll all come together." That's a hard lesson for many Powerful women (I know I'm not there yet!), but once they learn it, there's literally no limit to what God can accomplish in and through their lives.

OPEN AND HONEST

You never have to wonder what the Powerful woman is really thinking or feeling. That's because she'll let you know, right up front, whether you want to know or not. She is the most open and honest of all the temperaments. Now, not everyone *likes* hearing the truth, but that's more their problem than hers.

Often she has excellent insight that is ignored because someone didn't like the way it was presented. I think that's really a shame, don't you? The Bible says we should speak the truth *in love*. So, perhaps we Powerful women could benefit from reading books such as *How to Win Friends and Influence People*, to learn how to communicate more tactfully. Tact, by the way, is the art of making a point without making an enemy.

Interestingly enough, while the Powerful woman might get under your skin when she tells you what she really thinks one-to-one, I'll bet you love her when she says it from the podium or in the pages of her books. In fact, the vast majority of today's popular Christian speakers are this temperament. Believe me, I've met a lot of them! And most of them made me look—and feel—like a quiet little church mouse. Usually they are a combination of Powerful-Popular or, hold onto your seats: Powerful-Perfect. Imagine a woman who not only wants it done her way NOW but wants it done PERFECTLY.

Anyway, I'm always amused when I get letters from women around the country saying how much they wish they lived near me and what great friends we would be, and so on and so on. Here's how Becky Freeman, author of *Worms in My Tea and Other Mixed Blessings*, put it when she wrote an endorsement for one of my books:

> I wish Donna Partow lived next door! Not because she has it all together—oh no—but because she is refreshingly, gut-wrenchingly honest. She minces no words, cuts straight through the masks, and opens her soul.

Becky and I have since developed a wonderful long-distance friendship, regularly exchanging email and occasionally talking by phone. We have a lot in common and have developed a mutual admiration society. Nevertheless, I have a feeling my "refreshing, gut-wrenching honesty" would eventually get on dear Becky's nerves if she lived in my neck o' the woods. Is that the roar of my neighbors cheering "amen" in the background? Powerful women, keep in mind that "open and honest" is indeed a strength, but pushed to an extreme, it can become a severe weakness.

EFFECTIVE DISCIPLINARIAN

The Powerful mom will carefully discipline her children, who are usually exceptionally well behaved. She spells out exactly what she expects and carries herself with an air of confident authority that children inherently respect. My good friend, Jaime, is a shining example of a woman who has her children under loving control. She has two daughters who are only eleven months apart, and they are the most well-behaved little girls you will ever meet.

She recently related this story to me:

> When the girls were two and three years old, their absolute favorite thing was going to the library. Then we'd go home and I would read to them for hours and hours. On the way to the library on this particular day, I explained to them very carefully that they were not to run away from me. They were not to run around at all. A library is for being quiet. I told them that if they disobeyed, we would not be able to take any library books home. I made sure they understood exactly what I was talking about.
>
> Well, we spent at least an hour carefully picking out thirty books and the girls were wonderful. But then, just as we were ready to leave, they began running up and down the stacks of books. The librarian had just finished checking out all the books. I called the girls over and said, "Unfortunately, you disobeyed Mommy, so we won't be able to take any of these books home with us." I didn't raise my voice at all. I calmly walked over to the book return and stood there while they put every single book back. The librarian stood there in shock. The girls cried the whole way home, but they have never misbehaved at the library again.

I once asked Jaime what her secret was, how she got her children to behave so beautifully. She said simply, "I never give any warnings. I tell them the rules clearly. Then the minute they disobey, I nail them. It may seem harsh, but it's actually the most loving thing. When you give the kids warning after warning, or you don't consistently enforce the rules you've set, what you're really doing is training them to be disobedient. Then you end up angry and harsh because they become what you've trained them to be."

Well, Jaime, you are absolutely right. Of course, knowing that the Powerful woman is right (as she almost always is) and having the internal fortitude to apply her disciplinary techniques are two different things entirely. Just ask the Popular moms!

POWERFUL WEAKNESSES

UNPOPULAR

As you may have noticed, the Powerful woman has many wonderful, admirable strengths. But they aren't the kind of strengths that endear her to the folks around her. Instead, she has the kind of strengths that are admired when she's dead and gone. While the Popular woman is making everyone laugh (so her friends love her) and the Perfect woman is maintaining a wonderful home (so her family loves her), the Powerful woman is busy saving the world (and who loves you for that?). Unfortunately, such grandiose activities do not often lead to personal popularity. In fact, she may be greatly admired at a distance, but despised by people around her. That's why it's not uncommon for the Powerful woman to be among the least popular women in her church or community.

MEAN

We're not pulling any punches here: the Powerful woman can wallop a mean punch. To others, she may appear angry, distant, and unapproachable, even when she's not in a particularly bad mood. She may just be so preoccupied with her own agenda that frankly, she doesn't even notice you. When she *is* in a bad mood, boy, will you know it. And if it's you who put her in the aforementioned bad mood, look out!

When things don't play out according to her glorious vision, her temper can explode, wreaking havoc in its wake. She can be mean to her husband, her children, and even total strangers. These are the women honking their horns and balling out the cashiers at the local grocery store. They think the planet is populated by incompetent fools, whom they merely tolerate at best. This is a woman who can literally frighten people with her seething rage and bullying tactics.

She'll strike out and hurt other people's feelings with tough language and a harsh, unloving attitude. She will often try to control her children by fear and intimidation. Now, there's a place for a healthy fear of parental authority, just as we need a healthy fear of the Lord. But many Powerful moms strike an unhealthy fear in their children's hearts. One women confided in me: "Outwardly, my kids obey my every word, but I know their hearts are far from me. The sad truth is, my own kids are terrified of me." She may also use her mean streak to control her husband, especially if she married a mild-mannered Peaceful man, which is extremely common.

Unfortunately, fear drives out love. "There is no fear in love. But perfect love drives out fear, because fear has to do with punishment. The one who fears is not made perfect in love" (1 John 4:18).

If you are a Powerful woman, you need to realize you are in danger of winning every battle, but losing the war for your family. Take heed and try not to be such a big meanie.

SELF-CENTERED

Have you ever been around a person who was interested in one topic—herself? I remember doing a large conference where the other speaker was a prominent radio personality. Having listened to her show, I knew she was definitely the Powerful type. All the speakers and behind-the-scenes workers gathered for a special luncheon and this woman didn't say a single word. Not a peep! I couldn't believe it. The topics ranged from Kentucky Fried Chicken to world peace, yet this woman didn't comment on any of it.

Then it happened: someone asked her a question about a truly fascinating topic: herself. That was all it took. For the next hour, she talked nonstop about herself and bragged about her various accomplishments. No one else could get a word in edgewise. It was the old "Well, enough about me, let's hear about you. What do *you* think about me?" routine. It wasn't pretty. As Christians, we are to "Do nothing out of selfish ambition or vain conceit, but in humility consider others better than [ourselves]. Each of you should look not only to your own interests, but also to the interests of others" (Philippians 2:3–4).

USES PEOPLE

When it comes to friendship, frankly, the Powerful woman doesn't have the time. It's not that she's incapable of being friendly, it's just that she isn't all that interested in the two-way give-and-take required to maintain a long-term friendship. She has her projects and her accomplishments and that keeps her busy enough. Although, she doesn't mind leading a group (translation: telling everyone else what to do) or getting things organized and headed in the right direction (translation: telling everyone else what to do).

Notice we didn't say she doesn't have time for friendship; she doesn't have time for friends. There's a difference. She'll be only too happy for you to help her: she'll borrow stuff, ask for favors galore, and most of all, she'll call you to report her various accomplishments and expect you to make a big production over each one. The truth is, she tends to use people, viewing them as tools to accomplish her goals and objectives. In her mind, projects are more important than people—especially when they are *her* pet projects. This attitude inevitably leads to conflict. Here's how the Bible puts it:

> What causes fights and quarrels among you? Don't they come from your desires that battle within you? You want something but don't get it. You kill and covet, but you cannot have what you want. You quarrel and fight. You do not have, because you do not ask God. When you ask, you do not receive, because you ask with wrong motives, that you may spend what you get on your pleasures. (James 4:1–3)

IMPULSIVE

The Powerful woman's ability to get things done is the envy of everyone in the neighborhood. That's because she won't hesitate to take strong action to get the results she's after. Unfortunately, she's often too impulsive in pursuing results. Let me give you an example. She'll wake up one morning and decide the living room needs expansion. Without any hesitation whatsoever, she'll march straight to the garage, take out a chain saw, and knock that wall down. When dear sweet hubby gets home, "Surprise!" Of course, if he's been married to her for any length of time, he's pretty much used to it. Now mind you, we didn't say she finished the project, she just started the project. Lest you think I exaggerate, I actually know the woman who did this!

WORKAHOLIC

In case this tendency to leave projects left unfinished gives you the impression that this woman is lazy, let's set the record straight. Absolutely nothing could be further from the truth. Many are, in fact, workaholics. I'd better go ahead and 'fess up right now: "Hi, my name is Donna and I am a workaholic." When I worked in corporate America, I worked an average of sixty hours per week, even when I had the lowest job on the totem pole that paid zilch. Then I launched my own home business in 1989 and really began putting in the hours. It wasn't unusual for me to work ten to twelve hours a day, six days a week. I remember one week in particular I worked more than one hundred hours. On another occasion, I worked virtually around-the-clock for four straight days. I wrote almost the entire first draft of *Becoming a Vessel God Can Use* over a four-day period, working eighteen hours per day. Like I told you, I am a workaholic. And when I relax, I feel guilty.

One day, my daughter Leah and I were listening to a Christian children's tape. A little boy was sweetly singing, "Talk to me, show me that you care. Talk to me, listen to what I say." Leah turned to me and said, "Mommy, I wish you did that." Well, I knew she wasn't referring to *singing*. My kids beg me not to sing. So I said, "What, dear? You wish Mommy did what?" And she replied, "You know, talk to me." I said, "Leah, we HOME SCHOOL. I talk to you all the time!"

But she didn't believe a word of it. "Mommy, all you ever talk about is school and work. That doesn't count. You just want to work on your computer all day."

She was absolutely right. I spent all my time working and if she wanted something, I'd say, "Not now, Mommy's busy." Then I'd take a break to "do school" and I'd constantly rush her along to get her work finished. Even when I was spending focused time with her, which was extremely rare, the unspoken message was always, "Mommy is in a hurry to get back to work, so let's wrap this up quickly." I'm half-convinced that the only reason I started home schooling is because I didn't want to waste time playing with my children. I wanted to accomplish something, so I turned play time into school time.

The one thing I was willing to "waste time" doing with Leah was coloring. Then finally I hit upon a way to turn even that activity into work. I convinced her to launch her own home business selling her colorings at my speeches for twenty-five cents a piece. Now, mind you, I didn't consciously set out to ruin her fun. In fact, she thinks coloring is even *more* fun, now that it earns her money. The point is, *that's the way the Powerful woman automatically thinks.* She's constantly asking herself on a sub-conscious—and often conscious level—"How can I turn this into a productive use of my time?"

Here's another thing I've realized about myself and maybe some of you can relate to this: When I am not in my frenzied working mode, I drift into my coma state, conserving my strength for the big moment when I will be working again. Before I understood that I was "conserving my energy for impor-tant work," my own behavior baffled me and my family. On the one hand, I was obviously a workaholic. Yet when it came to housework and the more mundane tasks of life and mother-hood, I suddenly behaved like a sluggard.

In their book on temperaments, *The Two Sides of Love,* John Trent and Gary Smalley refer to this temperament as the Lion. Interestingly enough, real lions sleep twenty hours per day. Did you know that? But when they *are* awake, look out. They spring into action and get so much done in those short four hours, that they are considered the king of the jungle. What a picture of the Powerful woman!

Nevertherless, the Powerful woman needs to realize that much of life consists of the mundane. I love the way Oswald Chambers puts it:

We do not need the grace of God to stand crises, human nature and pride are sufficient, we can face the strain magnificently; but it does require the supernatural grace of God to live twenty-four hours in every day as a saint, to go through drudgery as a disciple, to live an ordinary, unobserved, ignored existence as a disciple of Jesus. It is inbred in us that we have to do exceptional things for God; but we have not. We have to be exceptional in the ordinary things, to be holy in mean streets, among mean people, and this is not learned in five minutes.[1]

BOSSY

Because of my writing and speaking ministry, I get lots of letters. I get crazy letters. I get heart-wrenching letters. I get wonderfully uplifting letters. And sometimes, I get letters filled with correction and instruction from bossy know-it-alls. One of my favorites was from an elderly woman who opened her letter with the following:

"We were assigned to read your book for Sunday school class. As soon as I opened it, I turned to the woman next to me and said, 'This book is no good. See, she used the wrong Bible.'"

She then went on to critique my book, by page and paragraph number, pointing out everything she knew was wrong with it. From my spelling and grammar to my theology, she set me straight. Then at the bottom of the letter, in bold, block letters, she wrote a command (no time to even write the letters P.S.): "DON'T ATTEND A CHURCH THAT HAS THE PROMISE KEEPERS."

We had never even met, but here she was taking charge of everything from which Bible I read to which preachers I listened to on the radio to which church I should attend. And why? Because she knew it all. If you are this temperament, be alert to the fact that you can come across as the bossiest, most annoying know-it-all on the planet.

USUALLY RIGHT, BUT OFTEN REJECTED

Few books have affected me like *Give Me This Mountain* by Helen Roseveare (InterVarsity). I still remember the day I read it.

I was home from work, sick in bed, and plucked it off the bookshelf. I literally couldn't put it down. It recounts her experiences as a medical missionary to the Congo in Central Africa. I remember at various points shouting with joy and at others, weeping uncontrollably. (This book is out of print. Check your church or public library for a copy.)

Now here's what's truly interesting. A year or so later, I read a third-party analysis of her life and ministry in Ruth Tucker's book, *From Jerusalem to Irian Jaya*. It talked about how much conflict and opposition Helen faced:

> Instead of establishing a regional medical center where a doctor worked around the clock and still fell short of meeting the needs of the sick, she envisioned a training center where nurses would be taught the Bible and basic medicine and then sent back to their villages to handle routine cases, teach preventive medicine, and serve as lay evangelists. It was a far-reaching plan, but from the start Helen was blocked at every turn by her colleagues, who believed that a mission had no business involving itself in training the nationals in such fields as medicine.[2]

Call me crazy, but it sure sounds to me like Helen had a brilliant idea. Nevertheless, she was opposed every step of the way by her colaborers. Actually, that's quite typical for this temperament. Very often, they have brilliant ideas and are absolutely right when they propose solutions to problems, but people don't want to listen to them or implement their ideas. Not only that, people often delight in actively opposing their plans.

Frankly, I think that's pretty sad, don't you? Okay, so some folks thought she was too pushy "for a woman." All I know is, she made an extraordinary contribution through her life's work. I wonder how much the world misses out on because the idea was proposed by a Powerful person and actively opposed?

Perhaps the most significant observation to make about the Powerful woman is that God chooses to use her in powerful ways.

> Despite her remarkable sacrifice and great accomplishments ... Helen left Africa in 1973 broken in spirit. It was a tragedy, at least in human terms, that her twenty years

of service in Africa ended that way. [Nevertheless,] . . .
instead of bitterness there was a new spirit of humility and
a new appreciation for what Jesus had done for her on the
cross. God was molding her for an even greater ministry—
one of which she herself could never have dreamed. In the
years that followed she became a much sought after inter-
nationally acclaimed spokesperson for Christian missions.
She continues today to write and speak from the heart,
and **her honest forthrightness** [emphasis added] has
been a refreshing breeze in a profession that too long has
been stifled by its image of supersainthood.[3]

Powerful women, take heart. Though you may not be Miss
Popularity, you're pretty popular with the God of the Universe.
How's that for a trade-off? According to the Bible, no Christian
should be surprised if the world despises him or her. To be
unpopular for the right reasons is, in God's sight, a virtue.
Nevertheless, being right is not the highest virtue; being loving
is. Make a conscious effort, before expressing your viewpoint, to
ask yourself not only "Am I right?" but "Is this a loving thing to
say and a kind way to say it?"

MAKING THE MOST OF YOUR TEMPERAMENT

If you want to make the most of your temperament, your
top priority should be coming to grips with whatever is driving
your need for control. Did you grow up in a home where life was
out of control? Perhaps you had an alcoholic parent? Pray that
you will discover, deep within, that it's okay to admit you have
faults and that you aren't always right. People don't like know-it-
alls, so why waste your time and energy trying to pretend you
know it all? Only God knows all and he's not telling. Instead,

Your attitude should be the same as that of Christ Jesus:
Who, being in very nature God, did not consider equal-
ity with God something to be grasped, but made himself
nothing, taking the very nature of a servant, being made
in human likeness. And being found in appearance as a
man, he humbled himself and became obedient to
death—even death on a cross! (Philippians 2:5–8)

Although our culture extols workaholism, it is, nevertheless, an "a-holism." It is not commendable. It is an addiction. Here's a little test you can take: "Would you rather work than anything else? If you won the lottery, would you keep on working?" If you are out of control, you need to come back to center.

Let me give you an illustration that I hope will really touch your heart, as it has touched mine. The city of Phoenix, where I live, recently introduced a new technological breakthrough called photo radar. Here's how this little device works. If you violate the speed limit, it photographs your license plate, sends the data through a centralized computer and then—get ready for this—they actually *mail* you the ticket. Now let's imagine you wake up one morning and realize you are late for an important appointment. You hop into the car and start driving like a maniac. You know the drill: as you travel down the road, you're digging through your purse for makeup. You put on your blush on the on-ramp. Then you get brave and try to navigate potholes and put on mascara at the same time. You've got places to go, things to do, people to see! You do not have time to get bogged down in little details like obeying the speed limit.

Well, let's imagine you make it to your destination, then return home later in the day. All is well in the universe . . . until that fateful day when the ticket arrives in the mail. The point of the story is this: you thought you had gotten away with something, but you really didn't. You did what seemed expedient at the time and you had no idea what it cost you until the ticket came due.

Friend, you might achieve all of your goals and not know how much it cost you until the ticket comes due. Like when your kids rebel because you were too preoccupied to give them the love and nurture they needed. Or like when you stand before God and give an account for how you invested your life. Not only do you need to slow down and smell the roses, you need to stop pushing everyone around you to work as hard as you do. Learn to relax. You can start by reading the book, *When I Relax I Feel Guilty* by Tim Hansel (David C. Cook, 1979).

Acknowledge the truth that you are not in control of the universe. Be willing to relinquish your need to control everything. Let God be God. And while you are on this earth, you must also be willing to submit to the leadership of others. Your natural inclination is to look down on all the "dummies" out there, but maybe it's time to admit that other people have gotten to positions of authority over you because (1) they deserve to be in a position over you and (2) God placed them there.

While I'm on a roll here (and I'm mostly preaching to myself, by the way, but I hope you're listening in), stop using people. You may think you are getting away with it, but people eventually realize that you are manipulating them for your own purposes and they will begin to resent you. Realize that you are not naturally a people-person and make a decision to consciously work on it. Read Dale Carnegie's book, *How to Win Friends and Influence People*, but don't use the "techniques" for further manipulation; really learn to value others above yourself, as the Bible says we should. Part of valuing other people is withholding your advice until you are asked. Most people don't appreciate your advice because they don't like being told what to do by you or anyone else.

Florence Littauer surveyed her audiences about what one quality they most disliked in others. Guess what topped the list? BOSSY. Then in a second survey, not one person in the audience admitted being bossy. That's because we Powerful types fancy ourselves as being helpful. Here's how Florence explains it: "Because the Powerful thinks so quickly and knows what's right, he says what comes to his mind, without worrying about how people will take it. He is more concerned with getting things done than with the feelings of others. He feels he's helping the cause, but those in his way may look at him as bossy." [4]

Stop arguing and stirring up trouble.

But if you harbor bitter envy and selfish ambition in your hearts, do not boast about it or deny the truth. Such "wisdom" does not come down from heaven but is earthly, unspiritual, of the devil. For where you have envy and selfish ambition, there you find disorder and every evil practice. But the wisdom that comes from heaven is first of all pure; then peace-loving, considerate, submissive, full of mercy and good fruit, impartial and sincere. Peacemakers who sow in peace raise a harvest of righteousness. (James 3:14–18)

Again, Florence Littauer says it best: "Cholerics love controversy and arguments and whether they play it for fun or for serious, this stirring up problems is an extremely negative characteristic."[5] Feel free to let someone else be right once in a while, and always remember: it's possible to be one hundred percent right, but still be extremely unpopular. So take your pick: do you want to be right or loved? It's up to you.

Your aim should be to cultivate a heart of humility:

All of you, clothe yourselves with humility toward one another, because, "God opposes the proud but gives grace to the humble." Humble yourselves, therefore, under God's mighty hand, that he may lift you up in due time. (1 Peter 5:5–6)

Read Andrew Murray's book, *Humility*. In fact, anything by this wonderful nineteenth-century devotional writer should prove helpful. Consider the following gem of wisdom:

It is easy to think we humble ourselves before God. Yet, humility toward men will be the only sufficient proof that our humility before God is real. It will be the only proof that humility has taken up its abode in us, and become our very nature.... When in the presence of God lowliness of heart has become, not a posture we assume for a time when we think of Him, or pray to Him, but the very spirit of our life, it will manifest itself in all our bearing toward our brethren. The lesson is one of deep importance. The only humility that is really ours is not that which we try to show before God . . . but that which we carry with us, and carry out, in our ordinary conduct. It is in our most unguarded moments that we really show and see what we are.[6]

As you cultivate that heart of humility, you'll have increasing opportunities to put your many talents to work. Here are just a few ideas:

1. *Take charge of a fledgling concern and provide the loving leadership needed to turn things around—or be bold enough to create something out of nothing!* You have incredible vision and energy, so put them to work to make a difference in this world! Perhaps you can jump-start the women's ministry at your local church or launch a women's support network in your neighborhood. Where others see only obstacles, you have the power to see opportunity. Communicate that hope and enthusiasm to those around you. Let God do his work through you. I promise nothing in this world can bring you more joy and fulfillment that exercising your gifts in the center of God's will.

2. *Be courageous!* Even if you face opposition—as you undoubtedly will—you have a great opportunity to be a living example of courage and grace under pressure. As long as you are following where God leads and doing what he has called you to do, press on. In the words of the schoolmaster in the movie *Chariots of Fire*: "Discover where your true chance of greatness lies. Seize that chance and let no power or persuasion deter you from your task." Show the world what the word "determination" means!

3. *Crusade for a cause.* Even if there are no leadership opportunitites open to you, you can still make a difference by crusading for a cause. Perhaps you can become active in the pro-life movement or serve as chairman for a charity fund-raiser. Pray first, then pick a cause you believe in and pour your energy into it.

4. *Stay productive.* Just because some women get tired just *thinking* about all that you can accomplish, don't be deterred. Take care of first things first on the homefront, but if God has equipped you with extra energy, there's no need to apologize for leading an exceptionally productive life. Go for it! Change the world!

5. *Remain open and honest.* Here again, cultivating that heart of humility will enable you to be the best possible you. As you live your life openly and honestly before a

watching world, not everyone will understand. Some will be intimidated; others will pass judgment. It doesn't matter. As long as your heart is right before God, I promise your openness and honesty *will* make an eternal difference. A verse that's greatly encouraged me is 1 Peter 2:23: "When they hurled their insults at him, he did not retaliate; when he suffered, he made no threats. Instead, he entrusted himself to him who judges justly." Isn't that beautiful? Don't worry about whether or not others misjudge you. Instead, entrust yourself to God, who always judges justly.

5

Introducing the Peaceful Woman

A nd now I'd like to introduce you to a very special woman. The Peaceful woman doesn't draw *attention* to herself; but she does draw *hurting people* to herelf. That's because hurting people sense that, in her, they've found a safe, listening ear. Even total strangers tend to open up with the Peaceful woman, telling her about their problems and being comforted by her.

PEACEFUL STRENGTHS

COMFORTING

When the Peaceful woman says, "I feeeeeeeeel your pain," she actually *means* it. You're apt to find her with her ever-present box of tissues, comforting the afflicted: "Oh, you poor thing. I've been so worried about you. You seem kinda down lately."

She's the type of friend who will call you, just to check in and see if everything's going okay. And if you ever need a friend to talk to, this is the woman to call. She's a very sympathetic listener, with a genuine concern for other people. She'll listen to your tales of woe for hours on end, without ever trying to fix you or top your story. She takes sincere delight in ministering to people's deepest, heartfelt needs.

My good friend Denise is like that. She calls me at least once a week to ask how she can pray for me and to make sure

I haven't had a nervous breakdown since her last phone call. (She knows me well enough to know *it could happen!*) Whenever I'm at the end of my rope and feel the weight of all my commitments crashing in, I invite myself over to Denise's house. I sit on her back porch swing, gazing at her flower garden, while she makes me a cup of herb tea. If she knows I'm coming over, sometimes she'll prepare my favorite treat: raspberry shortbread cookies. What on earth would I do without this woman?

To tell you the truth, almost every one of my closest friends is this temperament. If you look in the acknowledgments section of any of my books, you'll see their names time and again. These women are the wind beneath my wings. Thanks to their quiet love, support, and devotion, I'm able to run around the country "doing great things for God." I'm so thankful for friends who aren't the least bit impressed with "great" things. Instead, they love me enough to look me in the eye and ask how faithful I'm being in the small things. What a blessing!

THOUGHTFUL

The Peaceful woman lives by the motto, "It's *all* small stuff." And oh, how right she is! When my daughter, Taraneh, was about eight weeks old, I got a call from a Peaceful woman in my neighborhood. She offered to drive my older daughter, Leah, to and from vacation Bible school for the week. As she explained it, "I remember the hardest time for me was when my babies were right around two months old. That's when the casseroles have stopped coming and the sleep deprivation starts to kick in."

Another Peaceful woman recently called to say, "My daughter has outgrown her warm school clothes. I thought of Leah right away. Would you like to stop over tomorrow and pick them up?" Not so long ago, the same woman had called to say, "I'll bet Tara is just about old enough to sit in a walker now. Would you like to borrow mine? My baby's too old for it, and it's still in great condition." You see, the Peaceful woman is always thinking about other people and what they might need.

Just before my baby arrived, my devoted band of Peaceful women really came to my rescue. One wanted to know if I was in need of a baby swing and car seat. Yep, I was. Another heard I was on bed rest, so she came over to clean my house and wouldn't take no for an answer.

As you can see, these are marvelous women to have on hand when a new baby is on the way. They are so wonderful at bequeathing you the necessities. By way of contrast, the Popular woman has *no idea* what she did with her old baby stuff. The Perfect woman isn't going to lend you her stuff because she wants to keep it in perfect condition in case she has another child or to preserve for her grandchildren. The Powerful woman is, as always, too preoccupied with her own projects to give much thought to your needs.

ATTENTIVE

Another one of this mom's specialties is notecards. How she loves sending note cards! These are the women who keep the Current catalog in business. (The Powerful women are asking themselves "What on earth is the Current catalog?") They'll not only send you birthday and anniversary cards; they'll send you Thanksgiving and Easter cards. And cards when you sang a beautiful solo at church. Come to think of it, they'll even send you one if you *bomb* that solo. Cards when your child starred as the shepherd in the Christmas pageant. Cards just because she's thinking of you. In short, cards, cards, cards.

Here's one of my favorites, which I've kept for years. It was sent by the mother of two girls who were in my Sunday school class:

Dear Donna:

Just wanted to tell you that Julie and Kristi were very moved by your testimony in Sunday school. It's great for them to hear of the reality of life without Christ and the power of God to change people. . . .

It might be good if you could work out a way to have a confidential talk with Julie sometime. She had a bad "test" this summer—she failed. She's been weighed down about it. She just recently told me the truth. A talk

with you might help deal more completely with it all.
Would you be game for a talk with her?
You are much loved by us all at [the church].

XO
Joan

Notice that she's encouraging me for what I've already done. But she's also hoping I'll go "comfort the afflicted," which is actually a Peaceful woman specialty.

LOYAL

She's a very loyal friend. Once she's yours, she's yours for keeps. Janet was born nine months after me, to a family down the street. We were neighbors for eighteen years, playing with all the same kids, traveling in all the same circles. Today, we both live in Phoenix. She talked me into it, in the quiet, persistent way that Peaceful women specialize in. What I think is fascinating is that people from our hometown—people whose names and faces I have long since forgotten—fly thousands of miles to spend time with their old friend, Janet. These are the same people who don't even send me a Christmas card. (Of course, I don't send *anyone* a Christmas card because I can never quite get my act together on time. I've been meaning to send a "Partow Family Update" letter to our friends back East since we moved to Arizona. That was five years ago! If you're an old friend of ours, rest assured, we're doing okay. Hey, come visit *us* once in a while!)

You see, that's the difference between a so-called Popular type and the Peaceful type. While I've gone on to have hundreds of friends (which, I must admit, were really just acquaintances), Janet has steadfastly maintained deep, abiding relationships with a small circle of childhood friends.

At times, the Peaceful woman can grow discouraged, feeling that others don't reciprocate in friendship. Her Powerful friends are too preoccupied with their projects to give the kind of thoughtful attention she yearns for. Wouldn't you know, my best friend—a Peaceful woman—turned fifty last month. Ever since her forty-ninth birthday, I kept telling myself I'd make a big fuss: throw her a surprise party, invite all her old friends, shop ahead for a thoughtful gift. SURPRISE! I completely forgot . . . until a few weeks ago. I was too busy writing this book to look at my calendar. Still haven't gotten to the store to buy that birthday gift. . . .

Meanwhile, her Perfect friends will remember her birthday, of course, and give her the perfect gift in honor of the occasion. But they are too emotionally reserved to truly meet her need for close companionship. And it goes without saying that her Popular Friends are too busy running off with the "friend of the week" to maintain a long-term commitment.

So Peaceful women, you may need to find women who share your temperament to meet your need for lifelong friendship.

PEACEMAKER

One of the reasons the Peaceful woman can maintain such long-term relationships is because she rarely gets bogged down in interpersonal conflict. She thrives on harmony and will do whatever she can to maintain it. She's quick to adjust herself to the people around her and never insists on having things go her way. It is her sincere desire to please others. And not in the same way the Popular woman wants to please (that is, as a means to earn your applause and approval). The Peaceful woman is not thinking about herself at all. Quite the opposite, she's thinking of you and how much she genuinely wants you to be happy. Who wouldn't want to be lifelong friends with a person like that?

Often, when I speak at churches around the country, I'll be approached by a very low-key woman who is concerned about some conflict or another within her congregation. (All churches have conflict, you know.) Interestingly enough, while the Peaceful woman will not deliberately stir up conflict and will, in fact, avoid it whenever possible, she often feels compelled to act once she recognizes that's the best hope for seeing a peaceful resolution. She has a wonderful ability to see every side of an issue and to help others see their opponent's perspective. Her mediation skills are not only valued in the church or on the job, but in the neighborhood, at the playground, and on the homefront.

DEPENDABLE

The Peaceful woman is one-hundred-percent dependable. If she says she'll take care of something, it is as good as done. She's always there when everyone needs her, even though others aren't always as quick to meet her needs. In need of a babysitter? Count on her! Sick and in need of a casserole? She'll be on your doorstep with her chicken-rice specialty. This quality is particularly valued by her husband and children. They know, without a doubt, that she will be there during the tough times.

My friend Terri recalls,

> When I was a senior in high school, I felt like my whole world turned upside down. My dad got a job transfer and all of a sudden, we were living on the other side of the country. I had no friends and I just couldn't get excited about making new friends, knowing that I would be going away to college in a year. The school was totally different—ten times the size of the school I had attended. I remember so clearly how my mom came to my room every night to see how things were going. And I do mean *every* night, without fail. She'd just sit there and listen. She must have gotten sick of my complaining, but she never let on that she did. When nothing else made sense, I knew I could depend on my mom to be there at the end of the day.

PROTECTIVE

This is the kind of woman who sneaks into her children's rooms in the middle of the night, just to make sure they are sleeping okay. During waking hours, she likes to keep her child on her lap, if at all possible. I don't care if he's leaving for college! If she can get him on her lap, great. But she definitely keeps him within eyesight, that's for sure. I've noticed that many women with this temperament choose home schooling so they can keep those kids in the nest and under their protective wings as long as possible. (The other type that home schools are the Powerful women who want to whip those kids into shape and take charge of their education.)

If she does put her child into school, she'll volunteer to be in the classroom as often as she can. Why? Just to make sure her children are getting enough attention. When my daughter attended first grade at the local school, whenever I dropped by, I could count on the same group of women to be there. And let's not forget that poor overworked teacher—better bring her an apple. But if that teacher is smart, she won't dare criticize the children of the Peaceful woman. This mild-mannered lady can get pretty excited when it comes to defending her family.

TAKES TIME FOR THE CHILDREN

Many of my Peaceful friends have large families. Barb has five; Sue has five; Denise has four of her own, plus her three-year-old grandson; Christine has three but plans to have more. These are women who *take time* for their children; who sit and read for hours; who are not in a big hurry to go do something supposedly more important. These are the kind of women who resist the temptation to constantly utter my favorite phrase, "Not now, Mommy's busy." Three of them home school, which of course, is just about the ultimate time commitment a mother can make. Barb's children came of age before home schooling did. Otherwise, I suspect she might have joined the movement. Instead, she kept her children in Christian school, at great financial hardship, and always played an active role in their education.

The Peaceful woman is willing to chauffeur her children around town. Sue, for one, amazes me. She wakes up at 5 o'clock and starts getting the kids ready. She drives past the local public school on her way to a charter school, twelve miles from her home. There she drops two of her children. She turns around and drops off her teenage daughter at a top-notch junior high school, which she had to obtain "boundary exception" to enroll in. She returns home and begins home schooling her oldest daughter. At 2 o'clock, she again drives past her local public school to take her oldest daughter to the "boundary exception" school for photography class. Soon it's time to reverse the drop-off schedule, play pick-up kids, and head home.

Most of us would never do that much driving around, but this woman gladly will. (Incidentally, I've noticed that this temperament actually enjoys driving around. It's, well, peaceful.) Sue explains, "I just want the best for my children." She sure does. And she's willing to work sacrificially, day and night, to see that they get it.

PATIENT

If I spent that much time in the car with my kids, I'd be yelling at the other drivers all day long. You cut me off, I get mad. Period. And I'd probably be yelling at the kids, too. But the Peaceful woman is not easily angered. She doesn't even get mad when people commit the ultimate crime: obeying the speed limit. She's content to mosey her way through life, in no particular hurry. She's willing to go with the flow and doesn't insist that things go her way. In fact, she'll quickly adapt her schedule to suit the people around her. "It doesn't really matter to me" is a common Peaceful saying.

FAITHFUL

I never met Patsy Cline, the 1950s crooner who sang "Stand by Your Man," but I can guess her temperament. The Peaceful woman is loyal to the bitter end. Loyalty is her hallmark and the chief characteristic of her relational style. She has an exceptional ability to absorb emotional pain and still maintain her commitment to another person.

She will stick with a difficult marriage long after most of us would have given up. I know women whose husbands were no-good bums—drinking, gambling, and womanizing—but the wives put up with it, year after year after year. As you'll see in a moment, Peaceful women often marry Popular Men, who are the most prone to infidelity. She'll forgive and hold the pain inside. Now, faithfulness can go too far and turn into codependence, but we'll save the weaknesses for the following section.

Part of the reason she puts up with so much is because she is a peacemaker who wants to avoid conflict at all cost. In addition, she doesn't expect people to be perfect and is tolerant of human frailties in others. Which isn't to say she doesn't have her limits! When she makes up her mind that it's over, brother, it is OVER. Period, final, end of story.

Kathy put up with all kinds of garbage from her husband for twenty years. Finally, she caught him red-handed in an affair. She pointed to the door and didn't listen to a single word of his protests. She had the divorce papers finalized within a matter of weeks and moved on with her life. Enough was enough.

DEVOTED CARE-GIVERS

It's not unusual to discover Peaceful women in the caring professions: teaching, nursing, lay counseling. I've also noticed a good number of them leading women's Bible studies or women's ministries. She won't be as splashy as the Popular temperament in leadership positions, but a faithful following will gather around her and she'll have a highly effective ministry. Even if it's not a paid position, she finds satisfaction and fulfillment taking care of a sick spouse or children. She wants to please others, not as a people-pleaser but out of a genuine motivation and a heart that's willing to set aside her own needs to serve others. She follows through on her commitments, as well. These are the women who will care for sickly relatives for years and years, and never consider putting them in a nursing care situation, even if a doctor pleads with them to do so.

I recently met the mother-in-law of just such a woman. At twenty-two years of age, her husband Heethe was severely injured in a fifteen-foot fall. He had to learn to walk and talk all over again. The doctor told her that ninety-nine percent of marriages hit with a medical crisis of this magnitude end in divorce. She quietly replied, "This is one that won't." Heethe's mother, Neicy, told me that she has rarely seen such loyalty, faithfulness, and dedication. "She's completely calm even when he loses his cool from frustration. She never utters a word of complaint as she bathes and cares for him. She has told me that the thought of leaving him has never even entered her mind."

The other person who has stood with Heethe throughout this ordeal is his brother, Jett, who is also the Peaceful temperament. (We'll be getting to the male temperaments in action shortly, but I couldn't resist sharing this here!) He was about to enter his senior year of college on a baseball scholarship, but he gave it up to stay home and help out any way he could. He quietly but firmly declared, "I'm not going back." Everyone was completely shocked, because they knew the incredible sacrifice he was making. A writer for *Guideposts* magazine called to interview him and he was dumbfounded. He honestly didn't think it was any big deal. What a beautiful picture of the Peaceful temperament in action.

PEACEFUL WEAKNESSES

UNENTHUSIASTIC

Believe it or not, this devoted, kind-hearted woman actually does have a few faults. Although it certainly doesn't seem like a weakness to her, I believe the most annoying of the Peaceful mom's traits is her lack of enthusiasm. You can turn to her and say, "I climbed Mount Everest this past weekend," and she'll say, "That's nice." And you're thinking, "She didn't get it." So you repeat with greater emphasis, "I CLIMBED MOUNT EVEREST." You can emphasize all you want. You're not going to generate much excitement. Her goal is to conserve her limited supply of energy. She's not about to squander it getting worked up about your latest exploits.

It took me quite a while to figure this one out, even though I have many friends with this temperament. I can remember several occasions of taking one of my books hot off the press to my Peaceful friends to show them that their names were on the acknowledgments page. Now if someone put *my* name on the first page of a book, I would be strutting around, bragging as if I wrote the book myself: "Yeah, guess she figures she owes it all to me. What can I say? I taught her everything she knows."

Guess what? Not one of my friends responded as I had hoped. None of them! They just looked at their name, looked at me, and mumbled, "oh ..." I was shocked and thought, "WHAT'S WRONG WITH THESE PEOPLE? Don't they know how exciting this is? Don't they even love me anymore?" Gradually the conservation of energy theory dawned on me and it's been proven, time and again. I still put their names in the front of my books. However, I no longer look for "the BIG reaction" ... at least not from my Peaceful friends.

Now, this may seem like a small weakness. Some may not even consider it a weakness at all. But to those of us pouring our hearts out and striving around the clock to get things done, such reactions are like buckets of cold water in the face. It's like the proverbial rain on the parade. This lack of enthusiasm can cause significant conflict in her relationships with friends and family members who have either the Powerful or Popular temperament. They may interpret her lack of enthusiasm as a lack of love and concern, which can actually result in emotional damage to her children.

Here's a little P.S. After I wrote this section, I called and read it to one of my Peaceful friends, who explained: "We don't mean to be unenthusiastic. It's just that we're embarrassed. We don't want to draw attention to ourselves; we're *background* people!"

UNINVOLVED

Background people, eh? I can understand that, but Peaceful women tend to be too uninvolved. Yes, our families need to come first, but *something* should come second. Unfortunately, some women actually hide behind motherhood and use it as a justification for their lack of involvement. No matter what anyone asks her to do, the answer is "No, I just don't see how I could." She enrolls her children in the local school, but doesn't want to volunteer for any fund-raising committees. Or she homeschools her kids, but doesn't want to participate in the local support group. She'll attend church on Sunday morning, but that's the extent of her involvement. She doesn't want to join a small group or attend the women's Bible study. Trying to get her involved is like pulling teeth! Whether it's a hobby, a political cause, a volunteer position, or a ministry, if you're a Peaceful woman, you might do well to reach out beyond the four walls of your house on occasion. Find something to devote yourself to and do it with gusto: Do as the Bible says: "Whatever you do, work at it with all your heart, as working for the Lord, not for men, since you know that you will receive an inheritance from the Lord as a reward. It is the Lord Christ you are serving" (Colossians 3:23–24).

FEARFUL

Part of the reason this woman hesitates to get involved is because she's fearful. She's plagued by "what ifs." What if I volunteer to make a cake and it doesn't turn out right? What if I join the Bible study and I can't keep up with the lessons? Or what if the leader calls on me and I don't know what to say? What if I join this committee and people realize I don't know what I'm doing? What if it leads to conflict? What if some people in the church don't approve of the new ideas we propose? What if, what if, what if? It's possible to actually be paralyzed by fears and insecurities, to the point that you never try anything new, never risk anything. Sure, it's safe, but it's no way to live. The Bible says, "For God did not give us a spirit of timidity [fear], but a spirit of power, of love and of self-discipline" (2 Timothy 1:7).

Other verses which should be of special encouragement to you, as you seek to overcome that "spirit of fear":

> Strengthen the feeble hands, steady the knees that give way; say to those with fearful hearts, "Be strong, do not fear; your God will come." (Isaiah 35:3–4)

> So do not fear, for I am with you; do not be dismayed, for I am your God. I will strengthen you and help you; I will uphold you with my righteous right hand. (Isaiah 41:10)

> But even if you should suffer for what is right, you are blessed. "Do not fear what they fear; do not be frightened." But in your hearts set apart Christ as Lord. Always be prepared to give an answer to everyone who asks you to give the reason for the hope that you have. (1 Peter 3:14–15)

SLUGGISH

The other reason the Peaceful woman is reluctant to get involved is because it sounds too much like work, and she is not very big on work! She's inclined to evaluate a situation based on the answer to this question: "What's the bare minimum I can do and still get away with it?" Then she'll do the bare minimum and not a drop more. If you stop by her house, you'll often find it not only disorganized (as the Popular mom's house usually is) but deep-down dirty. The oven has never been cleaned, because who looks in there, anyway? The bathrooms have never been scrubbed, because that would require applying serious elbow grease. The dishes lie around for ages and the countertops are eternally cluttered, because she's lounging on the couch watching TV.

In fact, TV is her major downfall. She loves soap operas because she gets to experience life vicariously—all the romance and excitement without exerting a drop of energy. She loves game shows because she can imagine winning prizes without studying to learn any of the answers. And she loves the trashy talk shows because they lend an air of excitement to her otherwise dull life.

This sluggish lifestyle may lead to excessive weight gain, which may slow her down even more. Then the mere thought of getting up off the couch and back into life will become so overwhelming, she won't even try. I've known women who've fallen into this vicious cycle. Eventually, they became so sluggish and gained so much weight, they basically dropped out of life. Don't let that happen to you. Throw that TV away and set yourself free from its enslaving influence. Get up and get back into life!

COMPROMISING

Her noble desire to avoid conflict coupled with her sluggish nature may lead to some ignoble ends. For example, her inclination toward soap opera addiction will undoubtedly compromise her mental purity. She's a follower by nature and tends to compromise her standards to suit whomever she spends the most time with. If she's surrounded by dynamic, godly women and follows the crowd, she'll do well. By it's not likely that many dynamic, godly women are lounging around in this woman's living room every day, sitting idly by while she stares at the tube. With that type of lifestyle, she's inclined to attract the wrong type of friends—friends who drag her down rather than challenge her to grow mentally and spiritually. Maybe her soap opera buddies will introduce her to racy romance novels and she'll become addicted to those, as well. Or maybe they'll encourage her to gossip or speak ill of her husband (see 2 Thessalonians 3:10–12).

Recognize that you are a follower and put that trait to work in your favor. Make it your primary mission to surround yourself with the type of women you hope to become, then follow their lead. I think you and your family will be glad you did. It will involve getting up off the couch and taking some risks, but it will be worth it!

ENABLER

Another one of the Peaceful woman's positive traits that can go too far and create problems is her faithfulness. (As with all the temperaments, her weaknesses are merely strengths carried to extremes.) It's difficult to say exactly when being loyal turns into being a doormat, but most of us recognize it when we hear the war stories. The words "enabler" and "codependent" became buzzwords in the 1980s, as we realized that certain people actually make it easier for alcoholics, drug addicts, and abusers to lead their dysfunctional lifestyles.

Although anyone can fall into the role of enabler, the Peaceful woman is the most likely to do so. I realize the following example may seem extreme, but you might be amazed at the stories I hear from Christian women around the country. One woman told me she had become a go-go dancer because her husband thought it was "exciting" to watch her entice other men. She knew it was wrong, but she didn't want to argue with her husband. To avoid conflict and in the name of submission, she publicly humiliated herself. She finally drew the line when he invited men from the bar home and told her to have sex with them so he could watch. This man was an *elder* in the local church.

Perhaps you're thinking, "Well, my husband isn't an alcoholic and I'm certainly not a go-go dancer," so this doesn't apply to me. Maybe not, but I would encourage you to examine your relationships with your husband and children to see in what ways you might be making it easy for them to behave irresponsibly. Then lovingly, but firmly, back away and let them reap the logical consequences of their choices.

MAKING THE MOST OF YOUR TEMPERAMENT

Okay, Peaceful woman, I may as well admit how partial I am to you. My husband and virtually all of my closest friends share your temperament. But friends must be tough sometimes, so I'm going to lay it on the line for you here. Girl, you need to drum up some enthusiasm! You can be so smug sometimes! You may not be considered a controlling person, but you've certainly learned how to control others with your lack of enthusiasm. Florence Littuaer observes: "Once [Peaceful women] find they can upset others by their refusal to get enthused, they use this ability as a quiet form of control and chuckle under their breath at the antics the rest of us go through, trying to elicit excitement."[1] As the frequent victim of this game, I don't think it's very funny.

How about this idea: Try something new. Anything new. Even if it's just going to a different restaurant or sitting in a different pew at church or ordering a different flavor ice cream. Go somewhere you've never been before, just because you've never been there before.

Perhaps you've felt that you were better than the other temperaments because you don't have glaring weaknesses, but you should realize that laziness is strongly condemned in the Bible. Read through the book of Proverbs and note how many places it condemns the "sluggard" or lazy person, while extolling the virtues of hard work. And in the New Testament, Paul writes:

> For even when we were with you, we gave you this rule: "If a man will not work, he shall not eat." We hear that some among you are idle. They are not busy; they are busybodies. Such people we command and urge in the Lord Jesus Christ to settle down and earn the bread they eat. (2 Thessalonians 3:10–12)

Sure, laziness is an inoffensive sin—the proverbial victimless crime—but it's a serious one in God's eyes. Check out the Parable of the Talents in Matthew 25 and notice Christ's anger toward the "wicked, lazy servant" (v. 26). God has given you time and talents to invest. He doesn't want you to bury them in a napkin!

Find some ways to motivate yourself. Maybe set some goals and ask one of your Powerful friends to torment you day and night until you achieve one. Hey, that's the kind of assignment they relish.

One can hardly write a Christian book for women without referencing the dreaded Proverbs 31 woman *somewhere*. And guess what? It's going right here at the end of your chapter! Why? When I read this passage, what stands out in my mind is how busy and active this woman is. Yes, it mentions her inner qualities, but the vast majority of the verses focus on how incredibly hardworking she is. That's because hard work builds character. Just for fun, why not go through the entire passage and highlight all of the action words. God's ideal woman is busy, active, hardworking—you should be, too. A friend of mine in college had a saying you might do well to adopt: LIFE—Be in it!

A wife of noble character who can find? She is worth far more than rubies. Her husband has full confidence in her and lacks nothing of value. She brings him good, not harm, all the days of her life. She selects wool and flax and works with eager hands. She is like the merchant ships, bringing her food from afar. She gets up while it is still dark; she provides food for her family and portions for her servant girls. She considers a field and buys it; out of her earnings she plants a vineyard. She sets about her work vigorously; her arms are strong for her tasks. She sees that her trading is profitable, and her lamp does not go out at night. In her hand she holds the distaff and grasps the spindle with her fingers. She opens her arms to the poor and extends her hands to the needy. When it snows, she has no fear for her household; for all of them are clothed in scarlet. She makes coverings for her bed; she is clothed in fine linen and purple. Her husband is respected at the city gate, where he takes his seat among the elders of the land. She makes linen garments and sells them, and supplies the merchants with sashes. She is clothed with strength and dignity; she can laugh at the days to come. She speaks with wisdom, and faithful instruction is on her tongue. She watches over the affairs of her household and does not eat the bread of idleness. Her children arise and call her blessed; her husband also, and he praises her: "Many women do noble things, but you surpass them all." Charm is deceptive, and beauty is fleeting; but a woman who fears the LORD is to be praised. Give her the reward she has earned, and let her works bring her praise at the city gate. (Proverbs 31:10–31)

As you seek to "get in the game of life," let me offer you some quick practical tips, as I've done for the other three temperaments:

1. *Actively seek to comfort those around you.* You have such an incredible gift for comforting; don't allow your natural retiscence to prevent you from using it to the full. There are so many hurting people out there and you can make a tremendous difference in their lives just by being you. Ask your pastor if your church has a Stephens Ministry. If so, find out how you can become trained as a Stephens minister. If not, encourage your pastor to find out more about this wonderful cross-denominational ministry, which trains lay people to comfort others in times of need, especially during sickness and grief.

2. *Translate your thoughts into action.* It's wonderful that you automatically think of other peoples' needs, but don't stop at thinking. If you think of someone who may need a casserole, *bake it and bring it over.* If you realize a pregnant woman is probably in need of rest, take the initiative to help out with child care or housecleaning. Another ministry opportunity might be connecting women in need with those who are able to help out. In other words, you don't have to meet all the needs yourself. You'd be totally exhausted if you tried. Instead, when you notice a need—**and I believe that God enables you to see needs that other people don't even notice**—bring it to the attention of those who can help. You might notify the pastor or women's ministry leader. Or you might compile a list of women who say, "Yeah, I

can make a meal once in a while." You could even do it informally: "Barb, did you know that Susan's doctor has put her on bedrest? I'm planning to take a meal; would you be able to, as well?" Choose whichever option suits your lifestyle best!

3. *Get on the mailing list for the Current catalog,* which features notecards for every occasion: get well, happy birthday, sympathy, thinking-of-you and lots of all-purpose blank notecards. Again, I believe God will bring to your attention those who need a word of encouragement. *This is one of your special gifts.* Don't assume others will send cards if you don't take the time. Chances are, they won't. So have a supply of cards on hand and you'll be a real blessing to others in your own, quiet way.

4. *Maintain old friendships.* Here is another of your special gifts and another opportunity for you to be a quiet blessing, just by being who God created you to be. Even if others don't always express how much it means to them, persevere in maintaining those old friendships. In a world that's always changing, folks are surely thankful for anything that remains constant: especially if it's the steadfast love of a faithful friend.

5. *Be a peacemaker.* Although you are probably reluctant to "jump into the fray" when there's a conflict in your church or among your friends, recognize that you have a unique ability to bring peace. No other temperament possesses your ability to see every side of the issue and to remain calm in the heat of the battle. You can ask anyone in church leadership and they will tell you how desperately needed your mediation skills are. Pray about it and ask God to show you how he wants to use you as you "MAKE EVERY EFFORT to keep the unity of the Spirit through the bond of peace" (Ephesians 4:3, emphasis added).

Part 2

Understand Your Man

6

The Male Temperaments
in Action

If you're reading this book, chances are you have a husband. And chances are, he drives you nuts at least part of the time. In Part 3, we'll talk specifically about marriage—why problems arise and how you can make yours better. But first I'd like to take a brief look at how the temperaments look when demonstrated by the men in our lives. Obviously, the underlying characteristics are the same, but I hope that seeing the male temperaments in action will give you a clearer idea of what to expect from your other half. I firmly believe that understanding your man will do more than virtually anything else to bring peace to your life. I endured much inner turmoil before I understood the implications of my husband's temperament. Now I am not only a better wife, I rest easier knowing that he is not intentionally frustrating me. (He's frustrating me... but it's *not* intentional!)

I thought the best way to illustrate this was to bring you along on a recent trip, during which I encountered each of these men in action. Our family was traveling from our home in Arizona to a home business conference in California, where my husband, Cameron, and I were to speak. We brought along the children, Nikki (13), Leah (6), and baby Taraneh, so we could all visit Cameron's sister after the conference.

The tale begins on Thursday night, when Cameron laid out our plan of action. He informed me of my responsibilities for the next day and told me to get everything done and be ready by 3:15. The kids and I spent the day running around like a band of lunatics. I had deadlines to meet, places to go, things to do. I did not have time for his trivial little list of unimportant stuff like . . . uh, *packing*, for example.

Anyway, Cameron pulled in at exactly 3:15 and walked in the house expectantly. After fifteen years of marriage, for some mysterious reason my husband actually believed that THIS time I'd be dressed, packed, ready, and waiting. Based on what you've heard about the temperaments so far, what do you think were the chances of that happening? There I stood with soaking wet hair, talking on the phone to a church in Pittsburgh. Leah was running around trying to find her missing shoe. The suit-cases—which he'd given me specific instructions were to be lined up in the downstairs hallway by the garage door—were still strewn around the upstairs bedrooms. Each time I'd go by, I'd casually toss something else in.

We managed to get out of the house forty-five minutes behind my husband's carefully written-out schedule and arrived at the airport with just enough time for him to park the car in the long-term parking lot to save money. (In case you haven't guessed, my husband has a touch of the Perfect in his tempera-ment!) The kids and I went running through the airport, with me using the stroller like a deadly weapon.

We arrived at the gate and I plopped down about twenty pounds of gear. I had a diaper bag, my daughter's backpack with colored pictures hanging out the top, my speaking notebook, my prop and prize bag, Leah's sweater, and some baby blankets in case it got cold on the plane, plus my purse and daily planner. As the line progressed, I used my foot to kick the pile forward in front of me.

All of a sudden, without a word of greeting, a well-dressed man walked over, pointed to the huge pile of stuff in front of me, and said firmly, "What you need to do is take all of this and put it over there. You'll still be able to see it. If you keep pushing it along like this, you're gonna be worn out before you ever board the plane." He put his hand on his hip and waited for me to take action. Anyone standing in line probably thought the guy was my domineering husband, but here he was a total stranger barking out instructions on how I should wait in line at the airport. Have you guessed which temperament he was? The Powerful man! Here's the funny part: I sprang into action and did exactly as I was told, even though airport personnel get very nervous when bags have no obvious people attached to them.

The next morning, we awoke in our hotel room to discover the baby had red dots all over her face, hands, and feet. I had a good idea what they were because I had been listening all the night before to zzzzzz. And besides, my legs and arms were covered with mosquito bites. I pronounced my diagnosis and announced that the show must go on. But Cameron was not about to accept the off-the-cuff diagnosis of a Popular woman. Instead, he was determined to get her to a doctor as soon as possible.

Rather than coming to the seminar with me, my husband took her to the emergency room. Four hours and fifty-five dollars later, he returned to report that they had no idea what those mysterious red bumps were. Although he hadn't obtained a definitive answer from the doctors, and even though he actually missed the portion of the seminar he was supposed to teach, Cameron felt he had made the right decision. Attending to the baby was far more important to my husband than getting the job done. As you might have guessed based on your study of the temperament types, my husband is a combination of the Perfect and Peaceful temperaments.

While my husband was at the emergency room, I got a glimpse of another temperament in action when the pastor got up to introduce me. Now, a Perfect pastor would have typed up a detailed overview of my credentials to present to the audience. A Powerful pastor would have commanded them to "Pay attention to the important things this woman has to say so you, too, can get something accomplished." A Peaceful pastor would have dispensed with the introduction and led the group in a time of prayer for my baby's well-being.

But this was a Popular pastor. So he did what this temperament usually does. Two seconds before he got up, he turned to me and asked, "Is there anything in particular you want me to mention when I introduce you?" I shook my head. He leaped to his feet and started talking: "Well, one day I was sitting at my desk. You know, my desk right down the hall here. The one with that big black scuff mark on it. Anyway, there was a magazine. Usually I don't read magazines, because I don't have time, but I felt like God told me to read this one. So I read it and there was this article about Donna Partow. And I thought, maybe I'll give her a call. I did and I couldn't believe she answered her own phone." Well, you get the idea. The brief introduction lasted about fifteen minutes. And all the while I was sitting there thinking, "Hey, he's cutting into MY talking time."

The seminar got underway. When we got to the first question and answer section, some audience member had the nerve to ask me some legal mumbo-jumbo question, which of course I didn't know the answer to. So I made something up. I mean, hey, it's only the IRS. (Just kidding, folks!) Little did I know the next person I called on was going to be a Perfect type. He proceeded to explain that my answer was wrong and then gave a blow-by-blow description of how he had applied for the needed license and gave the exact name of the government agency and where it was located. The next thing I knew, he was taking out his Day-Timer to give the phone number to call for the right information. (It was obvious to him that I didn't have the right information.) As the day progressed, any time he didn't think I gave the right answer, his hand would go up.

When Cameron finally returned from his mission of mercy, midway through the lunch break, I told him the seminar was going terribly. I could tell the audience just hated me, because they all sat there staring at me with blank looks. When I called for audience feedback, they either ignored me or gave the wrong answer. Later in the afternoon, when we got to the portion of the seminar on temperaments, eighty percent of the participants were the Peaceful type. I thought, "Mystery solved." These folks make it a policy not to get too excited about anything. At the end of the seminar, the pastor asked everyone to complete evaluation forms and they all gave me glowing reports. My Peaceful husband explained, "They were enjoying the seminar *on the inside*."

Well, we left the seminar and all the Peaceful seminar attendees and headed for a visit with Cameron's sister and her family. The highlight of our stay was a tennis match featuring his fifteen-year-old nephew, Ali, where, among other things, we encountered a variety of dad types. We arrived at the tennis club to discover a perfectly dressed man quietly taking notes while his son played on the near court. He had a little yellow tablet and black fine-point pen and was marking every double fault, every winning or losing volley, and every unforced error. Could he be a Perfect dad?

We watched for a few minutes, when suddenly a man in a bold, bright-colored shirt walked up and barked at my sister-in-law: "That's my seat." She instantly leaped off the bench, and he promptly sat down as if he owned the place. When we recovered from the shock wave, we realized that Ali was scheduled to play against this Powerful dad's son on the far court. (Incidentally, the surest way to know you're dealing with a Powerful type is by the intensity in the air that surrounds them.) With this guy for a dad, I felt sorry for the competition and almost hoped he would win. And in fact, it looked like he would win, until Ali's dad arrived midway into the deciding set of the match. Oblivious to the fact that he had arrived almost an hour late, he immediately started clapping and cheering. (If you guessed Popular dad, you're right!)

The Powerful and Perfect dads threw disapproving glances his way. After all, their sons were on the court trying to concentrate on their respective matches. Undeterred, Ali's father rounded all of us up and led us on an expedition that involved walking around the courts, climbing up a steep, rugged hill, then back down through eighteen-inch high weeds, so we could sit in the dirt behind the tennis court, shouting words of encouragement to Ali. From the moment his dad arrived, Ali didn't let his opponent win a single point.

Well, you can imagine what happened to the Powerful dad's kid when the match was up with no trophy to take home. While we cheered and slapped Ali on the back, that dad immediately began bawling his son out, telling him everything he did wrong. I couldn't resist turning around and offering the boy a word of encouragement about his backhand.

Well, that's just one Saturday afternoon with the dad types! Now let's take a closer look at each.

He's the Popular Man

When I fired up my computer this morning and saw the blank page with the chapter title "He's the Popular Man" at the top, I knew exactly what I had to do. I called David. He picked up the phone and cheered enthusiastically, "Hi, Donna! What can I do for you?" I have no doubt that he subscribed to the phone company's "caller ID" service just for the sheer joy of doing *that* to whoever calls his house. The Popular man loves to brighten people's day.

You just can't miss David. He's out in the street playing with the kids, talking to everyone—and I do mean everyone, from little kids to grandmas—who passes by, laughing and joking, and always, always telling stories. There are some folks whose temperaments are hard to read. But you can spot the Popular man a mile away. First, he's loud. He has a loud voice and he wears loud clothes. Even if he's required to wear a blue suit to work, he'll don Mickey Mouse suspenders underneath. Second, he's open. His mouth is open; his arms are open to give out a bear hug or a back clasp; and his *life* is an open book. He'll tell you more than you ever wanted to know about his wife, his kids, his career, his childhood and, of course, his favorite sports teams.

POPULAR STRENGTHS

FIRES UP THE TROOPS

The first thing you notice about the Popular man is that he just oozes enthusiasm. It doesn't matter if he's psyched up about taking out the garbage, he'll have all the men in the neighborhood convinced that trash day is the event of the season. If it's something genuinely exciting, look out! David relates how he fired up the neighborhood troops to attend a major men's conference:

Life was good in 1994. No particular problems. I had a great marriage and a great family. I had a great job. But I still felt like something was missing. I heard about Promise Keepers and it sounded interesting. I remember walking into the stadium on Friday night and seeing 60,000 other men. That says it all. Wow. We were all there for the same reason. We want to get better. It was incredible to see all the men going forward on the alter call. It was engulfing. [I realized] I'm not the only guy who wants to be a better dad, a better husband.

I came back all fired up and called my pastor. "Man, I've got to tell you about this." So on Sunday morning, he let me get up and tell the whole congregation. I said, "We ought to get together and start a men's group right here in the church." Next thing, everybody's coming up to me after church.

We planned to meet at IHOP [International House of Pancakes] the next Friday morning. Five guys showed up that first morning. The next week we had ten. The next week we were at fifteen. I just kept telling everyone, "You've got to come." Pretty soon, we had so many people, we had to divide into two groups.

Then I hooked up with my neighbor, Bob. We both knew what a difference accountability had made in our lives and wanted to get more men involved. Bob owns an RV [recreational vehicle] dealership, and he came up with the idea of getting a bunch of guys together in the RVs and driving to the next men's conference in Los Angeles. We just talked it up wherever we went. I made a list of guys I thought might want to go. Some I called. Others I watched for opportunities to bring it up.

In 1995, thirty men from David's neighborhood went to a men's conference in four RVs. It was the talk of the town. One woman, who didn't normally attend church commented, "I don't know what your church is teaching, but my husband's been sweeping the floor every night. I think I like your church!" In 1996, thirty-eight men went, and they are hoping for even more next year.

Thank heaven, the Popular man can fire up the troops.

GREAT SALESMAN

Not surprisingly, David also happens to be one of the top sales representatives for his company. David couldn't resist telling me a couple of stories, which I can't resist telling you. For Halloween, he sends his customers a "boo bucket" full of candy with a note reading, "I'm trying to scare up some sales." On other occasions, "Just out of the blue," as he puts it, he sends customers a bucket filled with jelly beans and a note: "I hope your sales have BEAN good." Get it?

David's networking savvy also explains why everyone in the neighborhood wears his company's brand of shoes. I remember the most recent occasion when I realized the Partow clan was in need of new sneakers. I called David and asked if I could "come shopping" from his garage supply. "Sure, come on over at 9:30. Trudy and her kids are coming, too."

Well, we had a good time trying on sneakers in his living room, with David cracking jokes and chasing the kids around the whole time. I asked him how a particular pair of sneakers looked on me and he exclaimed: "You look ten pounds lighter and two inches taller!" I bought them. This guy could sell heaters in Phoenix . . . in August.

GREAT FAMILY MOTIVATOR

Another of my favorite Popular men is my Iranian brother-in-law, Roohy. I mentioned how his arrival at the tennis court was enough to turn the entire match around for his son. He does an extraordinary job of motivating and encouraging his children. He is, quite simply, the most wonderful dad I've ever seen in action. He is so loving, affectionate, and affirming. There's not a shadow of a doubt in his kids' minds that their dad thinks they are the most talented, wonderful people in the whole world. And I guess that explains where his kids are today.

When they came to the United States from Iran in 1985, the children were four, six, and seven. They didn't speak a word of English and they lived in absolute poverty. They suffered severe financial hardships, year after year. But do you think they sat around with glum faces, feeling sorry for themselves? Do you think they sat around looking for someone to blame or pleading for government assistance? Not at all! They were the richest family I've ever known—if you measure riches in love and laughter. Rather than the hard times driving them apart, it pulled them closer together.

Each night after school, Roohy would literally cheer the children on toward excellence in their homework. Did you ever hear someone cheering about Algebra? It's quite amusing! He couldn't land a nine-to-five job so he constantly thought up money-making ideas. (The Popular man makes a great entrepreneur-salesperson and likes to hop from job to job.) Since he loved having a good time, he decided to become a disc jockey. And he was so excited about having his own business and being a DJ, that the *kids* got excited about having their own business and being DJs.

Today, the children are nineteen, eighteen, and sixteen. They work side-by-side with their dad in the DJ business on the weekends. The two oldest are now launching out and doing their own gigs for school events. All three are at the top of their class in one of California's finest high schools. The oldest son, Dean, was just awarded a full college scholarship to study pre-med. They've recently bought a house and their future looks bright. I give plenty of credit to my incredibly hard-working sister-in-law, Jaleh. She worked day and night to keep the family afloat financially. But it was Roohy who kept the children's spirits alive and motivated them to believe that "In America, you can become whatever you want."

The Popular man motivates and inspires his family.

POPULAR WEAKNESSES

HAPHAZARD

When it comes to home improvements—or anything else requiring attention to detail or God forbid, reading an instruction manual—this man is in a heap o' trouble. This is a serious deficit on Christmas Eve when you're confronted with all those toys labeled "some assembly required." I mentioned this little weakness to David and he immediately launched into the following story:

> We had these tannish brown light socket things. I guess they're called outlets or something. I wanted to change them all to white. Not exactly a big deal. Unscrew a few screws. I figured I could handle this project. Of course, I had to turn all the electricity off first. On one of them, I didn't exactly hook it back up correctly. I went to turn the power back on and it shorted out the electricity in the entire house.

Then he added very casually, " . . . and it was on Thanksgiving."

I just about fell off of my chair. Of *course* the Popular man would pull this stunt on Thanksgiving! When else? The saga continues:

> We were having company. And, I don't know if you know this or not, but not many electricians work on Thanksgiving. So there we were: No heat, no Thanksgiving dinner, and company a comin'. The worst part was that not even the porch light worked. I mean I really blew the whole thing out. We were afraid people couldn't find our house, 'cause you couldn't see the house number. It was starting to get cold in the house. I walked up and down the street and asked every neighbor what they knew about electricity. It turned out that the uncle of a cousin's something or another had missed his flight. He wasn't even supposed to be there. Thank God he was.

Meanwhile, back at the house, you can imagine that his wife was dying. So I asked David what on earth possessed him to undertake this home improvement project in the midst of preparing for Thanksgiving dinner guests. To which he replied, quite predictably, "Oh, I had some free time on my hands. Hey, I had the day off. I wanted to do a project."

Ladies, I did not put a single word in that man's mouth. No wonder *Home Improvement* is such a hit show.

POOR MONEY MANAGER

Although the Popular man is usually lots of laughs, you might not be laughing on your way to the bank, as you try to cover yet another series of bounced checks. I asked Dan, another of my favorite Popular men, if he ever gets into trouble for spending money and he said, "OH, YEAH! On a daily basis. But I usually have a good explanation."

It's quite likely that your husband spends money like it's going out of style. He may even drive the poor family into bankruptcy, but on the bright side, he can provide free entertainment in the midst of it. If your husband is this temperament and if you haven't done so already: TAKE THE CREDIT CARDS AWAY FROM THAT MAN! And take over the checkbook while you're at it. May as well take over paying those bills, too, if you expect them to be paid on time. Although there are certainly exceptions, most Popular men are terrible money managers.

Part of the problem is that he's just lousy at details. Stuff like math makes his head spin. Besides, money management just isn't that much fun. And part of it is that he loves to dress stylishly, drive a flashy car, and have all the right sports gear — all of which costs money, which he may or may not have. Unfortunately, he's not about to let a little detail like lack of funds stand in the way of his good time.

As one Popular man put it: "My wife thinks I'm crazy for spending sixty dollars on NFL jerseys for the kids, when we could get sweatshirts at K-Mart for ten dollars. But I figure, 'Hey, the kids have to look good.'"

He tends to be an impulse buyer and likes to buy double of what's needed in the toy department. If his wife sends him to buy a Hot Wheels car, he'll come back with a six pack of Hot Wheels and a track. And not just any old track, but the one with the big loop-de-loop. One man admitted, "Just the other day, my wife calculated that I've spent over seven hundred dollars on Thomas the Tank Engine trains. I told her I bought the entire set because one day it may be a collector's item, but I actually didn't think that much about it at the time."

He may also give way to impulse spending on large-ticket toys, like cars, trucks, and boats. My friend Diane recently traveled for five days to visit her sister. When she returned, there was a brand-new truck in the driveway. Her husband, who has been out of work for nearly a year, just happened to be driving by the car dealership and the next thing he knew, he was the proud owner of the latest make and model. The truck was eventually repossessed because they couldn't make the monthly payments.

[Note: I recognize that some Christian marriage counselors insist that the husband must handle the family finances, regardless of temperament. I totally disagree. Whichever partner is best suited to the task should handle it. The fact that a woman writes checks and balances a checkbook does not mean she's usurping her husband's authority. It simply means she is helping him *and the family* by using her God-given talents.]

POOR JUDGE OF CHARACTER

Because the Popular man is an eternal optimist, who always expects the best of people, he tends to be a poor judge of character. There is nothing false in him, so he doesn't see through the false masks of pretenders. As a result, he can get taken in by con men, false teachers, and other unscrupulous people. I'm convinced that the Popular types of our nation single-handedly keep the late-night infomercial business booming.

Jake was extremely devoted to his church and especially to its dynamic pastor. He served as a deacon and spent many long hours serving alongside his pastor. He trusted him. He believed in him. Then one day, the pastor ran off with the piano player. Jake was shattered. He'd been raised in a Jewish home and I'll never forget what he said to me: "I attended synagogue for forty years, and the rabbi never ran off with anyone. I still believe Jesus is the Messiah, but I don't want anything to do with the church."

Like most Popular types, Jake didn't remain discouraged permanently. As a natural-born optimist, he was able to find a new church and after a period of healing, became just as enthusiastic about his new pastor as he had been about his unfaithful leader. However, it is possible for these men to get burned so many times, they end up cynical. Nothing could be more unfortunate. You see, if he gives way to cynicism, he will lose the very quality—that winsome, trusting nature—that attracts people to him and makes him unique.

PRONE TO WANDER

People often wonder why we hear so many stories about the pastor running off with the piano player. It's almost cliché. However, once you understand the temperaments, you'll see that it's not surprising at all.

It all begins when a dynamic, entertaining young man (obviously the Popular type) realizes his story-telling flair enables him to make the Bible come to life. People flock to attend his Sunday school class or small group to be entertained by him. He decides to become a pastor and attracts a large congregation with his lively, inspiring sermons. Life is fun and all is well. He marries the Perfect wife and it's even better.

Then the burden of actually *running a church* begins to weigh down on him. It requires attention to details. It requires listening endlessly to people's problems. It requires mediating conflicts and sitting in on long, dull meetings. Not one of these things is within his realm of strengths. The pressure begins to mount. This isn't what he thought being a pastor would be all about. He feels like a failure. Meanwhile, his Perfect wife is perfectly miserable with this flake of a husband she married. She criticizes him day and night. Life isn't fun anymore. No one appreciates him. No one accepts him for who he is . . . except, of course, the piano player.

More than any other temperament, the Popular husband is prone to wander. The following section explains why.

WHAT YOUR POPULAR HUSBAND NEEDS MOST FROM YOU

As if you don't know this already, your husband's battle cry is "Let's Do it the Fun Way." What you may not realize are his greatest emotional needs, which are for attention, affection, approval, and acceptance.[1] When he doesn't have his needs met, this normally fun-loving guy can become severely depressed. Here are some ways you can be sensitive to his needs.

ATTENTION

Your husband has a burning need to be the center of attention. He wants you to listen to his stories and laugh along, even if you've heard them a million times before. When he gets home from work, he wants to tell you all the incredible things that happened that day. Incredible stuff always happens to the Popular man. He's an "odd experiences" magnet. If you want him to feel loved, take time to sit down and listen.

In addition to desiring his wife's attention, he actively seeks to draw outsiders' attention to himself. If you constantly criticize him for telling stories, exaggerating too much or whatever, you may eventually wear down his natural optimism and take the wind out of his sails. You may think, "Oh great, he's finally getting serious and quieting down a bit" and you'll feel like you have finally fixed him. But you'll be in for a very disappointing surprise. Rather than developing the strengths of the other temperaments (which all your criticism is intended to do), he will develop the weaknesses of the other temperaments.

Depending on which way you try to push him, he may become negative and depressed like the Perfect man, unmotivated like the Peaceful man, or an unavailable workaholic like the Powerful man.

Rather than trying to get your husband to become something he is not, accept him for who he is. Yes, he is disorganized and loud and gullible. Yes, he is too trusting and yes, it would be just dandy if he could get organized and pay attention to details. But if you keep beating up on him, I promise that you will not like the results.

For years, Joanna worked relentlessly to get her husband, Dan, to sit down and shut up. She constantly reminded him of verses in the Bible about controlling his tongue. When they returned from a social event where Dan had been the life of the party, Joanna would punish him with disapproval and silence. Eventually, he learned to force himself to keep quiet when he had something *nice* to say. In those instances, Dan discovered he really could manage to hold his tongue. But when he had something negative or thoughtless to say, he still couldn't hold his tongue.

Think about the implications of this for a minute. Previously, Dan talked *all* the time. He told lots of funny stories and jokes and was tons of fun to be around. Sure, once in a while, he'd put his foot in his mouth or say something people didn't appreciate hearing. But people forgave his little slipups because all the cute, endearing things he said counterbalanced the bad.

What happened when Dan stopped telling jokes and stories and only spoke up when he absolutely couldn't hold his tongue another minute? The only thing people ever heard him say were the little slipups. As a result, he gradually became extremely unpopular. Now, for the Popular type, this is a fate worse than death. The change took place gradually, over the course of several years. By the end of that time, he was a withdrawn, angry person. The once buoyant, self-confident man had become socially insecure. The former party-goer now holed up in his office day after day, working around the clock. A family that previously hosted guests in their home at least twice a week now never opened their doors to show hospitality.

The truth finally dawned on this couple when they took the Personality Test and Dan revealed almost all of the weaknesses of the Perfect man: bashful, unforgiving, resentful, insecure, unpopular, pessimistic, alienated, withdrawn, depressed, loner, and so forth. They couldn't believe it! He had none of the strengths, and they both knew he was not a Perfect type. In short, his personality had been seriously damaged.

This couple is now working to rebuild Dan's personal confidence and to piece the fragments of his God-given personality back together. At least part of this emotional damage was caused by a wife who constantly beat up on her husband, demanding that he shape up and shut up. Please don't do this to your husband. Instead, focus on his strengths, pray daily that God will help him overcome his weaknesses and strive to meet his heartfelt need for attention.

Am I saying these problems are all the wife's fault and the husband is just a poor, helpless victim of this awful woman?

Definitely not. He's an adult, capable of making his own choices. Nor do I want to discount the fact that his behavior was genuinely offensive to her. If I were writing a book for men, I'd be coming down hard on his tendency to embarrass his wife and run roughshod over her needs for stability and dignity. But, ladies, I'm writing to you! You may not be able to change your husband into the person you want him to be (Lord knows, we've all tried, haven't we?), but with the power of God on your side, you can work prayerfully to bring about changes in your own heart and mind.

AFFECTION

This need should not require much amplification! Your husband needs lots of hugs and kisses. This can be a problem since he usually marries a Perfect wife who is not naturally affectionate. Well, start with cheek kisses! Even if it will mean smudging your makeup or rumpling your perfectly ironed clothes, give that man a hug!

APPROVAL

If your husband landed in a sales job, he's probably quite successful. But if he is in a job that requires attention to detail or other technical skills he lacks, he may be feeling like a failure. Even if he's not the president of the company, he wants to know you approve of his career and his accomplishments. Praise him for closing the sale or maybe just for bringing home the paycheck week after week.

If you withhold your approval, your husband will find people who will approve of him, even if that means giving in to office peer pressures, to which he is extremely susceptible anyway. He'll become "one of the guys" even if it means drinking and flirting with the women in the office. He'll become the kind of man who praises the Lord enthusiastically at church (because that's what brings approval), then spews out profanities at the office (because that's what brings approval). By giving him your approval, you'll be helping him overcome those weaknesses.

ACCEPTANCE

This is, by far, your husband's deepest need. He absolutely, positively needs to know you accept him, warts and all. Rather than criticizing him and judging him for his weaknesses, *help him*. Help him organize the garage and his closets. Go into his office on the weekend (maybe once a quarter) and help him organize his work, as well. Keep a copy of his calendar at home and call him with reminders, if he'd like you to.

Now, if you do this with a servant's heart rather than a nagging voice, he will love you all the more for it. He will realize how much he needs you and how lucky he is to have you. Like my husband always says, though, the key is to "help in a helpful way." If he feels like you are bossing him around, you can bet he won't appreciate it. But if he sees that you accept him for who he is and just want to help him out, your efforts will endear you to him.

If he doesn't get acceptance from you, don't be surprised if he looks for it elsewhere. He might just spend all his time at work or playing basketball with his buddies. He may even hang out at the local bar "where everybody knows his name." Of course, if you and your husband are both Christians and he is hanging out at the bar, naturally a red flag will go up. But remember to look for more subtle indications that your husband's needs are being met outside the home. For example, if he spends an inordinate percentage of his free time volunteering at the church or being scout master extraordinaire, he may not be getting enough of your attention, approval, or acceptance. If your husband constantly looks for excuses to be anywhere but home with you, take time to reflect on your relationship. Is it possible that he feels you don't truly accept him as he is?

I don't want to alarm you unnecessarily and I certainly don't mean to imply that every Popular husband in America is rushing headlong into adultery. However, I think it would be irresponsible of me *not* to put you on guard to a significant emotional need your husband has. I've counseled with enough hurting women to know that it's not uncommon for an emotionally hurting Popular man to turn to another woman who will give him the attention, affection, approval, and acceptance he longs for.

Of course, you should encourage him to grow—mentally, spiritually, and relationally. You love him too much to let him settle for the status quo. You want him to be the best he can be *for his own sake,* but you accept him as he is and assure him that you love him in spite of his imperfections. You've married a fun guy, so enjoy your life together!

8

He's the Perfect Man

Do you have a husband oozing with talent? A very sensitive, self-sacrificing man? A faithful friend who never pushes his way into the limelight, but allows others to shine? A perfectionist, who appreciates the fine arts? If you've married a Perfect type, you've formed a partnership with an extraordinary man. In fact, virtually all of the world's great artists, composers, philosophers, inventors, and theoreticians share this temperament. The Bible is just bursting with Perfect men, including Jacob, Moses, Solomon, Elijah, Elisha, Jeremiah, Isaiah, Daniel, Ezekiel, Obadiah, Jonah, John the Baptist, and the apostles John and Thomas. Quite a hall of fame, wouldn't you say?

The Perfect man is the second most obvious to spot in a crowd, but not because he's loud. Quite the contrary: he's very quiet. He speaks softly, because he doesn't want to draw attention to himself. He may even speak so softly that you have to ask him to repeat what he said. His clothing is "quiet" as well: he'll choose low-key, traditional styles and colors like navy and gray. These are the men with twenty gray suits in the closet and when you ask what they want for Christmas they respond, "a gray suit." While the Popular man is open, the Perfect man is "closed." He has a closed mouth, operating on what's commonly called "a need-to-know basis." He won't tell you stories; he'll tell you the facts. His body language is also closed, with his hands held close to his side and gestures kept to a minimum. And, finally, he has a closed life. Not only will he resist sharing intimate details of his life with strangers, he'll resist sharing intimate details of his life with his *own wife.*

PERFECT STRENGTHS

EXTREMELY ORGANIZED

A surefire way to quickly determine whether or not your husband fits this temperament is by looking at his personal space: his car, his office, his closet, and so forth. If it's neat and orderly, you've married a Perfect type. Here's the quickest way: Look at the garage. If it looks better than your living room, you know you're onto something. Just for fun, I've been wandering the neighborhood and peeking into garages every chance I get. The Perfect man's garages are often open because Mr. Perfect is in their putzing around. (See the next section to learn why!) I spotted one garage with wall-to-wall carpeting, beautifully-framed pictures on the walls and *curtains* on the windows. The screw drivers and other hand tools were lined up in size order on a white pegboard. One side of the garage had floor to ceiling white storage cabinets, while the other two sides had elevated shelves for storing boxes. You can bet those boxes are neatly packed, labeled, and numbered, with a cross-reference system so that he can immediately put his hands on any item in any of the fifty-seven boxes. There was even a wash basin so he could clean his hands before going back into the house.

By the way, we keep our garage door closed at all times because we are so embarrassed by it. The irony is that we don't have nearly as much stuff to store as most of our neighbors, but we have made absolutely no provision for storing what we do have. It's just thrown in heaps on the garage floor. My husband and I are both very ashamed of this, but not ashamed enough to actually get up and do something about it. Which brings me to an important point: my husband is Perfect *at work,* but one-hundred-percent Peaceful *at home.* His work office is neat and organized, but his home office is a catastrophe. The Perfect-Peaceful husband returns home from work completely depleted of energy. He's the classic couch potato. He can't understand men who run giant corporations all day, then come home and play tennis. (Only Powerful men can do that!) If you've got a Perfect-Peaceful husband, I'll bet you've observed the same tendencies.

PRACTICAL

The Perfect man is the original Mr. Fix-It. One of my neighbors is an attorney, but I often see him in his perfect garage with his power tools making bookshelves and cabinets and such. This is the ideal person to have on hand come Christmas Eve or when you buy a new computer. In fact, any time instruction manuals rear their ugly heads, you'd better find yourself a Perfect man. He's the only one who will actually read them. In fact, he *likes* reading instruction manuals. My friend Joan told me that when they bought a new car, her husband sat down and read the entire owner's manual *before anyone was allowed to drive the car.*

This guy loves charts. When our neighbors Bob and Debbie brought their first child home from the hospital, Bob made a chart to keep track of the baby's every move, from number of hours sleeping and crying to the number of wet and messy diapers changed each day. Debbie reports that he has a giant white board in their bedroom, where he keeps track of their investments and liabilities and the progress they are making toward digging out of debt. Whenever they have to make a family decision, he breaks out his clipboard and makes a pros-and-cons chart.

The Perfect man almost always carries a Day-Timer, where he keeps careful track of his business expenses, mileage, even grocery items he notices are out of stock, and anything else you can list or chart.

SELF-SACRIFICING

Many Perfect men are "give"-aholics. They'll work around the clock to provide the very best for their families — only the finest clothes, the finest schools, and so forth. They'll shower their wives with fine jewelry, presented while enjoying fine dining. They not only give sacrificially to their family, but to friends, as well. I mentioned earlier that one of our neighbors, a Perfect type, owns a very successful RV dealership. One day, out of the clear blue sky, his wife called to tell us he thought we might need a free vacation using one of his RVs. When we went to pick up the $150,000 vehicle, not only would he not accept a penny, he insisted on filling the gas tank. He has extended this gesture to many couples in the neighborhood.

When the church ran out of space for Sunday school, this man faithfully drove RVs to the church parking lot early Sunday morning and allowed them to be used as classrooms. When another friend faced a family crisis, he paid for a Christian counselor to help her work it through. In fact, whenever a need in the church or neighborhood arises, he is first in line with a donation and offer of assistance. He is just about the most self-sacrificing person I know.

In his book, *Transformed Temperaments,* Dr. Tim LaHaye explains this tendency: "It seems easier for a [Perfect] person to see through the sham and the shallow material rewards this world offers and to rightly evaluate eternal things. I have observed that many missionaries going to the foreign field have a higher-than-average degree of [Perfect] temperament. This characteristic accounts for the fact that many gifted missionaries are willing to renounce the pleasures and possessions of this life to serve Jesus Christ."[1]

SOLID CHRISTIAN

Once a Perfect man commits his life to Christ, he usually becomes a pillar of the church. Just as he studies other instruction manuals, he devotes himself to studying the ultimate instruction manual: the Bible. Our friend Jack became a Christian during his retirement years. We bought him a Bible and when we saw him a week later, he had already read from Genesis to 2 Samuel. The Perfect man knows his Bible inside out; his theology is flawless. Before long, he'll be teaching adult Sunday school classes. He may even decide to attend seminary to deepen his understanding of God's Word or to become a pastor.

PERFECT WEAKNESSES

INTIMIDATING

Can I let you in on the inner workings of writing a book? I was just breezing through this book, coming up with great stories (well, I hope you like them!) and typing one hundred words per minute. I was having lots of fun, and frankly, it was almost too easy. Then I got to this chapter on the Perfect man and the whole thing fell apart. I haven't worked on the manuscript in weeks. Why? Because not one of the women I know who are married to Perfect men would talk to me about their husbands.

Now maybe you can understand a wife not wanting to talk about her husband's weaknesses, but I couldn't even get these women to talk about their husband's strengths. I was baffled. Then one woman explained it this way: "If I talk about my husband's strengths and say that he fits in this category, then it will be implied that he also has the weaknesses."

"So?" said I.

"So," said she, "he doesn't want to be associated in any way with weaknesses. He thinks he needs to be perfect and worries that anything less is not good enough."

"Oh," I responded, although I still couldn't quite relate. In my mind, we *all* have weaknesses and it's no big deal. But then it began to register: to the Perfect type, weaknesses—in fact, anything less than perfection—is a very big deal. In fact, it's enough to get downright depressed about. Enough to make a guy resentful, revengeful, and withdrawn.

The fear of their husband someday stumbling upon this book *for women*, picking it up, and reading far enough to uncover a positive comment remotely linked to a negative characteristic they *might* have was enough to make these normally talkative women fall silent. I couldn't help thinking, "Gee, I'm so glad my husband's Perfect side is more than overcompensated for by his gentle Peaceful side."

Because of their perfectionistic tendencies, these men can be extremely difficult to live with. Perfect types think perfectionism should be listed in the strengths column. It certainly can be a strength. However, those who have to live with them know that when perfectionism is pushed to an extreme, as it frequently is, it belongs right here in the weaknesses column.

PESSIMISTIC

"No" seems to be this man's favorite word. He's also a big fan of "No way. That's impossible. It'll never work. What a dumb thing to say. How on earth could you think that? Of all the crazy ideas."

Well, you get the picture. For every brilliant suggestion you make, he's got a dozen reasons why it's actually a stupid suggestion. The eternal pessimist, he views the world through gray-colored glasses.

You married him because he was the strong, silent type. But now you realize, "Hey, that man doesn't talk to me." The deafening silence is not as romantic as it seemed in those old John Wayne movies. In real life, he's not quite so strong: in fact, he's the *sullen,* silent type. His constant dark moods seem to reveal a deep inner weakness masquerading as strength.

He dreams of having the perfect family and the perfect job. Then when life doesn't turn out perfectly, or doesn't measure up to his ideal, he churns it around inside, becoming withdrawn, resentful, and increasingly pessimistic. Yet, when you ask him what's wrong, you always get the same reply: "Nothing." You can't help wondering, "Gee, if nothing's wrong, why does he have that miserable look on his face?" Since he often marries the Popular type, life for her becomes neither perfect nor fun.

CRITICAL

How would you like to have a man who criticized everything you did? A man who made sure you knew nothing you ever did was quite good enough, never quite up to his standards. Pretty demoralizing, wouldn't you think?

If the Perfect man isn't careful, he can actually crush his child's spirit with his constant criticism and drive for perfection. Interestingly enough, the Perfect man can dish it out, but he can't take it. He wants to criticize everyone else, but when you criticize him, he shuts down and drops out of sight. He can become, in short, an emotional bully.

Living with a Perfect man is like living with a film critic who thinks your entire life is a movie. Unfortunately, no one in his family *ever* rates "two thumbs up." Instead, all he does is criticize, criticize, criticize. As one woman noted, "He constantly criticizes my housekeeping, but he won't lift a finger himself. He just sits back and evaluates my work and points out everything I'm doing wrong."

He is extremely hard on his wife. Her housecleaning isn't good enough. Her childrearing techniques aren't good enough.

Her cooking isn't good enough. She doesn't spend money wisely enough. The list goes on and on. Day after day, on subject after subject, he makes sure his wife knows that she just doesn't measure up. In the same way these men keep track of the details on the job, they keep track of the details at home. They are especially adept at keeping track of everyone else's shortcomings.

HYPOCHONDRIAC

As you can imagine, all this stored up resentment, bitterness, and anger can churn around inside the Perfect man and begin to take a toll on his health. Add to that his attention to detail and you can end up with a man obsessed with the functioning of his body. He's constantly studying himself to see if anything's wrong. Under those circumstances, you can bet that plenty will go wrong. "Honey, can you look at this?" "Honey, I think I may be dying." It can really wear a woman down after awhile—a very *short* while I would imagine!

WHAT YOUR PERFECT HUSBAND NEEDS MOST FROM YOU

By now, we all know your husband's battle cry is "Let's do it the right way." Although his most obvious need is to have everything done perfectly, he has some emotional needs you should recognize, as well. He needs a "sense of stability, space, silence, and sensitivity."[2] Let's look at each in turn.

STABILITY

Your husband's need for stability often shows itself in his passion for organization and schedules. He wants to see things done a certain way, at a certain time, every day. For him, that creates a stable life. You've probably noticed that his biggest thrill comes from analyzing something and then creating a system to make it run smoother. That's why he's constantly on a mission to get *you* organized. That's why he reorganizes the kitchen and types up index cards that show which shelf everything belongs on (or tries to persuade you that all would be well in the universe if only *you* would undertake such a project).

Although it's hard to be treated like a project, try not to take it to heart. It's not that he doesn't love you, it's just that he craves stability. And a woman with a fly-by-the-seat-of-your-pants approach to life and household management makes him crazy.

Chances are, you crave the opposite. You crave change. And I'll bet you're even tempted to sneak up some change on that dear, dull man, who always does things the same old way. Ho hum. Well, resist the temptation. He likes to do things the proven way. If you want a happy honey, try your best to create a stable home life.

SPACE

Your husband needs some space. A place that is exclusively his. A place that is strictly off-limits to you and the kids. Perhaps you have a small house and carving out such a place would be a great sacrifice.

GOOD.

Huh?

You heard me right. I said, "GOOD." That way, you'll have to think and plan and pray and work twice as hard as a woman with a great big house. When your husband sees you going above and beyond to meet his need for space, it will be that much more meaningful to him.

It may mean sacrificing your *only* storage closet. Or you may have to sew a fabric partition for the corner of your living room or bedroom. One option you might consider is buying an old cubicle from an office liquidator. Look in the yellow pages for used furniture and you'll discover that there are huge warehouses filled with used office equipment. (There's one in every city and many larger towns.) In addition to partitions of every style and color, they carry desks, swivel chairs, bookshelves, filing cabinets. You name it. Some of it will be in great condition; some not so great, but all dirt cheap. You should be able to find a partition or cubicle for about $50–$100.

I bought just such a cubicle for my daughter Leah's loft bedroom. Then I bought some straw hats for a dollar each, decorated them with ribbons, and pinned them all over the cubicle. My neighbor was throwing away her old living room curtains, so I snatched those up and draped them around the outside, as well. It actually looks darling! Your husband probably wouldn't appreciate "darling straw hats" but I'll bet you could come up with some design that would make him quite happy.

Once he's got his own space, what's he going to do in there? Why, enjoy the silence, of course.

SILENCE

Generally speaking, most women are generally speaking. And generally speaking, it's driving their husbands insane! Now, I know you love to talk, talk, talk. So do I. But could you possibly give your honey one *quiet* evening a week? One night when you take the phone off the hook. (Sounds like blasphemy, doesn't it? What if someone is hit with a crisis? What if you suddenly remember you *had* a crisis and there's one woman left you haven't filled in on all the details? Think about this: when tough times come, we can either take it to the phone or take it to the THRONE. I suggest you tell God your troubles. He's the only one with the power to actually *do* something about them, anyway.)

Silence means no television playing anywhere in the house. How about that? By the way, if you have more than one television, shame on you! Sell it and use the proceeds to finance your husband's quiet space. See how bossy I can be? I'll bet you're even having second thoughts about wishing I lived in your neighborhood.

Silence means no screaming kids. Put them to bed early or instruct them to play quietly in their rooms. If your kids can't quietly entertain themselves one evening per week, you've got a real problem on your hands.

Now, here's sacrilege, especially coming from me, a woman who serves on the board of advisors for a Christian radio station. Quiet may even mean no music—not even Christian music. Or your husband may enjoy quiet background music. Ask him.

Now you're thinking, "Oh, how dull! An evening with no TV, no phone calls, no screaming kids, and none of my fascinating stories." Think about this instead: Is it really so much to ask? One night out of seven to give your husband the peace and quiet he truly needs? I don't think it is. Besides, you might just discover some unexpected blessings in the solitude.

If I may be so bold as to take charge of your family life (!) may I suggest you consider making Sunday your quiet evening? Perhaps you can even provide your family with tools (such as my Weekly Evaluation Worksheet, found in *Becoming a Vessel God Can Use*) for making the most of the opportunity to reflect on the prior week and plan for the week to come. I think you'll find it a blessing to your husband—and your entire family.

SENSITIVITY

If there's one thing that absolutely drives your husband crazy, it's insensitive, disorganized, forgetful, superficial, unpredictable people who can't show up *on time*. People like *you*, perchance? The reason these characteristics bother him so much is because of his deep need for stability. So realize that he's not picking on you (well, it is that, too, but . . .). It grates against the very fiber of his being when you waltz in an hour late with some story about running into the neighbor at the grocery store, and her brother-in-law's sister's cousin's nephew is graduating from Harvard. You just *couldn't* break away from a conversation of such importance to get home on time for his annual company Christmas dinner. The truth is (and he knows this full well) you *completely forgot* about the Christmas dinner. What's more, the only appropriate dress you own is either curled up in a heap on the closet floor or at the dry cleaner, where it's been since *last year's* Christmas party. Then you try to crack jokes and pretend, "Hey, it's no big deal."

The truth is, you were insensitive to your husband and the things that matter to him. If you ever hope to regain some of that perfect marital bliss you dreamed of, make every effort to give your husband the stability, space, silence, and sensitivity he yearns for. Lest you think I'm coming down too hard on you, I am well aware of just how cold and hurtful your husband can be. But as we advise the wives of the other temperaments, you can't change your husband, no matter how hard you try. You can pray for him, encourage him, refuse to "enable" him, but you can't change him. What you can do, by the power of God, is accept him and learn to live with him, faults and all.

9

He's the Powerful Man

The Powerful man is a bundle of energy and enthusiasm, charging through life with grand schemes for changing the world and everybody in it. In fact, like I said earlier, the quickest way to spot this temperament is to gauge the intensity in the air when he enters the room. (You can tell he's coming because the whole house vibrates when he walks!) The minute he walks in, you know he's there. Now, if your relationship is positive, he'll bring excitement and electricity. If your relationship is in trouble, you and the kids may be having the most wonderful day of your lives, but as soon as he walks in the door, the house will be filled with stress. If your husband's mere presence is enough to transform the atmosphere in your home, you're probably married to this temperament.

Another way to spot this temperament is by his gestures. Does your husband put his hands on his hips and lecture you? Does he pound his fist on the table to make a point? Does he point in your face? Is he the reason the phrase "in your face" was coined? This temperament is the worst invader of personal space. He'll get in your face; you back up. He takes a step forward; you back up. The next thing you know, your cowering in a corner with his finger two inches from your nose!

If this sounds like your husband, read on.

POWERFUL STRENGTHS

BORN LEADER

If you married a Powerful man, you know you married a born leader. He's never bored, because he constantly dreams up new ideas, plans, goals, and ambitions. Not that he's a pie-in-the-sky idealist; far from it. His feet are firmly rooted on terra firma. His sharp mind focuses its considerable intellectual prowess on the practical, rather than the theoretical.

There's not a company, organization, or church on the planet that he can't run with the utmost of confidence and skill. It doesn't matter if he has absolutely no idea what the organization does, he can rule it better than the bozos who are currently in charge. All the great crusaders against social injustice and most of the world's high-powered corporate and political leaders are, not surprisingly, this temperament. If you study the lives of history's great generals and world rulers, you'll discover the same has been true from the beginning of human civilization. It's the Powerful types who shake things up and change the world in the process.

Chances are, your husband drives around in a big, fancy sedan or a flashy sports car and carries his cellular phone with him wherever he goes. He has natural entrepreneurial tendencies and may well operate his own business. He might not run it for very long, though, because he quickly becomes bored and moves to another project. Researchers interviewed a panel of self-made millionaires, looking for some trait they might have in common. They examined upbringing, education, and job experience and found nothing. Finally, they hit upon one common denominator: they each had started, on average, eighteen different businesses. While other men would be discouraged in the face of failure, the Powerful man's motto is "You haven't really failed unless you refuse to get back up." Now there's a classic Powerful line, don't you think?

Stan was a pillar in a church we once attended. One day, he came home early from work and announced that he had been fired. His wife wasn't too surprised. Powerful people get fired all the time because they don't hesitate to tell the boss what they really think. (And it's never anything complimentary, you can be sure of that! Here's another hint: if your husband's been fired from every job he's ever had because of conflicts with the boss, he's definitely a Powerful type!) In Stan's case, he had told his boss in no uncertain terms that he knew a better way to run the business and, before firing him, the boss said something to the effect of,

"Oh, yeah, try it." Dumb thing to say! He asked his wife if she would support him in the decision he had made on the drive home: to take their life savings (a few hundred dollars) and invest it in a business that would compete with his former employer.

She agreed.

Smart lady.

Within months, the business was turning a profit. Within a few years, he was a self-made millionaire. With the proceeds of the business, he almost single-handedly financed the building of a gorgeous new church facility. He thought the old one was too dull and unworthy of God's glory; the new sanctuary is stunning—fit for a King, if you will! His take-charge style wasn't everyone's cup of tea, but he sure got the job done.

DECISIVE

As you can see from the above illustration, the Powerful man is extremely decisive. He's not one for making charts and endlessly analyzing data. He can't stand committee meetings or anything else he feels is a waste of his valuable time. His decisions are based on instinct, and he places great value on what his gut tells him. While others may dispute how he arrives at his decisions or try to "confuse him with the facts," the bottom line is: he's almost always right. He does indeed have extraordinary instinct and an innate sense of what will work in any given situation.

I once had a boss like that when I worked for a computer manufacturing company. He, too, was an entrepreneur and self-made millionaire. The engineering or accounting staff would agonize over data and present him with recommendations based on hours of careful analysis. He would listen for a few minutes then rapidly pronounce his judgment. The employees would walk out mumbling about how it'd never work and how they "ran the numbers" or "tested the prototype." In the end, his decisions were almost invariably proven right.

PURPOSEFUL

Part of the reason the Powerful man enjoys so much success in life is that he lives with a constant sense of mission. He always keeps at the forefront of his mind a clear purpose and knows exactly what he wants to accomplish each day. He is not easily distracted like the Popular man. He doesn't make lists for lists' sake as the Perfect man does; he makes lists of things he intends to accomplish. And then he very quickly sets about getting them done. He doesn't waste time agonizing over minor details; once it's good enough to achieve his purpose, he moves on to the next conquest. And unlike the Peaceful man, he has an unlimited supply of energy.

DOER

Your husband loves to "do"—especially to compete. The only potential problem is that he may push his sons to win, win, win. (But we're not to his weaknesses yet, so let's look at the positive side of his competitive spirit!) Your husband likes to win, to be the best, and he wants your family to be the best, too. Whether he's playing softball with the guys or Yahtzee with the kids, he likes to win.

The Powerful man will do more than watch your son play Little League—he'll coach the team. He'll do more than sit in the church pew, he'll take charge of the expansion program. (Powerful men absolutely LOVE church expansion programs, because they can see tangible evidence of their actions.) Even on vacation, he wants to accomplish things, which can actually be a really neat quality if not taken to extremes. You won't find this man lounging around on a beach or relaxing on some boring cruise ship. No way! He craves adventure. He wants to take active, challenging vacations. Our friends David and Cindy take the most incredible vacations, thanks to David's determination to actively DO something with his time off. They've taken a three-week hiking trip across New Zealand, traveled throughout Indonesia and Irian Jaya using every mode of transportation imaginable from jeeps to dug-out canoes. The last we heard, they were planning an African safari. (As you've probably guessed, David is another of those self-made millionaires. He has to be to afford these lavish trips. Best of all, he doesn't have to plead with the boss for time off. He IS the boss.)

What's really exciting, though, is that they've taken their children along on trips like llama trekking in Oregon and white-water rafting in Colorado. These kids would be bored stiff at something as tame as Disneyland, which I think is a very good sign.

PRINCIPLED

Bob, a top sales executive for a local computer company recently told me, "If you don't do the right thing and stand your ground, you could easily become corrupt in this business. I believe in telling the truth, no matter what, with no shades of gray. Whether its good or bad, I tell it like it is. In the short run, maybe it has cost me a few sales, but over the long-term I know it will help me."

A few months ago, Bob was offered a huge promotion, which is usually irresistible to the ambitious Powerful man. The money would have been double and the position would have brought incredible status. Accepting the position, however, would have meant uprooting his family, leaving his church and his friends, and moving to Los Angeles. Bob said, "Forget it." His colleagues were shocked.

POWERFUL WEAKNESSES

EMBARRASSING SCENES

Linda loves her Powerful husband, but she says she's fed up with him constantly causing embarrassing scenes.

> We're not welcome at neighborhood parties anymore because of the way my husband always stirs up controversies. He thinks it's fun and flatters himself that he's getting the conversation going. But no one else enjoys it. We'll be in a group of twelve people and Bob will be the only one talking for hours. Not just talking, though, stating his controversial opinions in a very argumentative tone of voice. I plead with him not to, but he can't seem to control himself.
>
> When we get home, I'll say something like, "You really ought to give other people a chance to talk once in

a while." And he'll argue that no one else had anything to say. He doesn't realize the effect his behavior has on other people. I can tell by their faces, they are so frustrated and fed up, they don't want to say anything for fear they might add fuel to the flame. I'm constantly embarrassed by his displays.

DEMANDS RESPECT FOR HIS RIGHTS

The Powerful man is big on his rights and when he feels they haven't been respected, he's not afraid to speak up. He has a very short fuse! I think Linda's husband is a bit extreme, but I've met enough men like him to know he's not as uncommon as we might hope. She continues:

> The other thing he does is fight with sales clerks, waitresses, teachers, you name it. Whenever we go out, I'm always afraid it's gonna end in a fight. More often than not, he sees "injustice" and he has to fight to make it right. The waitress took too long, so he'll fight with her and not leave a tip. Or the food isn't hot enough, so he'll demand a discount. Or our flight will be delayed a half hour, so he'll put up a big stink with the stewardess and demand credit toward future flights. Sometimes he actually does get his money back or freebies, but it's hardly worth the hassle and humiliation.

> No one is ever good enough for Bob. He thought our daughter's kindergarten teacher was incompetent, so he demanded that our daughter be put into a different class with the "top" teacher. Within a matter of weeks, he had a litany of complaints against the new teacher. He started hinting around that I should home school, but I have no doubt I wouldn't measure up either.

WORKAHOLIC

Susan shared her frustration with her husband, Jim: "He spends all day in his home office, working around the clock. If he takes a break, he feels guilty, no matter how many hours he has put in. It's totally obvious to me that his work means more to him than I do. He's a giver of *things,* but I'm not a collector of things. I didn't marry him so I'd have someone to take charge of my business affairs; I married him to have and *to hold.*"

Unfortunately, the Powerful type who aggressively pursed his wife before the wedding, may want little to do with her after the wedding. He has conquered her and now is ready for new conquests. It's not unusual for him to turn to his work as a source of challenge, perhaps working sixty hours per week and more. He can turn into the absentee husband and father, bringing home lots of money, but very little of himself.

PROJECT- NOT PEOPLE-ORIENTED

The Powerful man cares about projects, about what needs to be done, and in his mind, everything needs to be done right NOW. Susan gives an example.

My husband and I were put in charge of organizing our neighborhood's informal welcome wagon. It wasn't the world's most exciting organization, but they did a pretty good job. Well, within days of taking over the reigns, Jim had this brilliant idea—from some seminar he'd attended at work—about giving everyone a sense of ownership. I guess in the solitude of his home office it seemed like a great idea. Without consulting me or anyone else in the group, he conjured up a grand vision and put together an elaborate plan of action to bring it about. Over the course of about a week, he called and recruited various individuals to fill new staff positions he had single-handedly created. Then he sent out a newsletter announcing the reorganization and revealing his personal selections for each of the newly created jobs. As you can imagine, people hit the roof! Especially the people who formerly controlled the group, whom he conveniently left out of his grand scheme. To this day, some of the neighbors still harbor hard feelings toward Jim. But in his mind, it was a project. He didn't stop to think about the people involved or how they might feel about the changes. He saw a problem, found a solution, and implemented it without consulting anyone else.

The Powerful man needs to allow people to give input on decisions that affect them and realize that, except in the case of extreme emergencies, nothing needs to be implemented right NOW.

MATTER-OF-FACT

The Powerful man doesn't care for small talk; he only wants to talk about important things. And of course, he alone is capable of determining which topics are important enough to justify his attention. Whether he's talking to an employee, his wife, or his children, he wants to know, bottom-line, what's the problem to be solved? He'll never sit and listen for the sake of listening. He listens so he can then tell you what to do to "fix it." No matter how complex the problem, no matter how deep the emotional wound, his advice is the same: fix it and move on.

You may have noticed that he speaks in very short sentences, loaded with action words. And he doesn't like people who go off on tangents; he wants to stick to the issue at hand. He frequently interrupts others and finishes their sentences for them. Rather than actively listening, he'll be busy jumping in to offer a plan of action.

Susan reports that Jim never gives her an opportunity to talk about her feelings. "He is emotionally unavailable. He doesn't want to get close to me and he won't let me get close to him. When I had a miscarriage earlier this year, after six years of waiting for a baby, I desperately needed to talk about what I was going through. His attitude was 'Let's just forget about it. There's nothing we can do to change the situation, so what's the point of talking? Talking won't change anything.' He just couldn't understand that talking was part of the healing process. It was very devastating for me."

In dealing with the children, this dad will rarely play with them for the sake of playing and spending time together. As always, they have to be accomplishing something. Susan reports, "Jim worked with the boys to build a tree fort and that was great. But once the tree fort was finished, the boys wanted him to sit in it with them and goof off. Well, Jim wanted to conquer the next project. I think the boys were hurt; they had hoped the togetherness they enjoyed during the building process would continue. It didn't."

DEFENSIVE

As I mentioned when I introduced you to the Powerful woman, one popular book on temperaments actually lists this quality under the "strengths" category. But I think it's pretty obvious that this is a weakness. The Powerful man gets defensive easily. If you ask him a question, he views it as a challenge to his authority. Of course, if you're married to a Powerful type, you're probably a temperament that likes to ask tons of questions (Peaceful or Perfect).

You need to be particularly on guard in the area of child-rearing. Remind your husband that just because your children are asking questions doesn't mean they are defying him or challenging his authority. Children genuinely need clarification; they need to ask questions. If he closes the door to them, he will exasperate his children—something the Bible specifically warns fathers *not* to do.

WHAT YOUR POWERFUL HUSBAND NEEDS MOST FROM YOU

Your husband storms through life announcing, "Let's do it MY way." He loves to shake things up and make things happen. Which is great. Unless of course, it's *your* house he's shaking up. If you want to find contentment in your marriage to the Big Boss-Man, you would do well to keep in mind his deepest, heartfelt needs. Now, I know what you're mumbling: "My husband doesn't have a heart." Yes, he does. And the best way for you to reach that heart is by providing him with the following emotional food: a sense of obedience and appreciation for accomplishments.[1] Here are some suggestions to help you do just that:

SENSE OF OBEDIENCE

Gee, just typing that word "obey" gave me the heebie-jeebies. But, hey, remember the traditional marriage vows: "To love, honor and o-o-o-o- (did you choke on it? I did) o-BEY." Well, this man actually expects you to follow through on that commitment. Imagine the nerve? Seriously. I know how bossy, domineering, and tyrannical these guys can be, but if you can show him you really are trying to obey (ouch, there's that awful word again) he will rest securely in your love. Proverbs 31:11 says, "Her husband has full confidence in her."

Here's how the Littauers put it in their book *Personality Puzzle*: The Powerful type likes people who "are supportive and submissive, see things their way, cooperate quickly, and let them take credit" and they dislike people who "are lazy and not interested in working constantly, who buck their authority, get independent, or aren't loyal."[2] Does that mean you should blindly follow wherever he leads? Should you let him storm through life like the proverbial bull in a china shop, treating you, your children, and everyone else as nothing more than obstacles to his goals? Definitely not. That's not good for any of you, least of all him. You have a right to express your concerns and your viewpoint. You have a right to let your husband know exactly where you stand and when *he's standing on your toes*. But once you've clearly communicated with him, try backing off and praying. There's power in prayer—put it to work for you. Pray daily that God will change your husband. He's God enough to do it! One thing's for sure, constant nagging won't do a bit of good and may, in fact, make your husband more intractable.

Now the upside of all this is, the guy is almost always right. Which, you protest, is actually one of his most annoying qualities. Nevertheless, the sooner you recognize that your husband has extraordinary instincts and a natural flair for leadership, the easier it will become for you to follow his lead.

APPRECIATION FOR ACCOMPLISHMENTS

He'll come home with tales of how hard he's working and complaints about the long hours and the stress and the sacrifice, and so forth. And you'll be inclined to say something like, "Oh, honey, don't work so hard." Wrong sentence, ladies. What he wants you to say is, "Wow! No one on earth can work as hard as you. You are amazing. I mean, you are a one-man working machine. What you can accomplish is unbelievable. I stand in awe of you."

Now I know you were just trying to encourage him when you told him to stop working so hard. But the reality is that he lives for accomplishments. Telling him to stop accomplishing is about as encouraging as telling a world-renowned pianist to stop performing. Besides, he doesn't want your advice. (If he wants your advice, he'll give it to you.) What he wants is recognition.

If you'll allow me to digress from Powerful husbands to Powerful wives for a minute, I think we're about to come up with an important point. I've been thinking a lot about this issue lately. So often my husband says, "Oh, Donna, I wish you didn't work so hard. I feel so bad for you." And I mutter, "Oh, isn't it awful that I have absolutely no choice but to work day and night, night and day."

Well, now we've gotten enough financial stability (after facing near bankruptcy) that we can afford for either my husband or me to quit work. We've laid it out before the Lord and said, "If you bless Donna's ministry over the next two years, Cameron will quit his job and come on staff full-time. If not, Donna will give up her ministry to become a full-time mom." People say to me, "Wow, won't it be nice not having to work all the time." (They say this because I complain so much about working all the time.) The correct response, of course, is "Oh, yes, I can't wait to devote myself completely to the task of mothering." I know that's the culturally correct answer, but in my heart I know the truth: I love to *work*. I thrive on getting things done. For all my moaning and groaning, work—and more specifically, accomplishing something—fulfills a need deep inside of me.

Now here's the point I promised: If you're married to a Powerful man, he has that same burning need. Again, this doesn't mean you sit in silence while your husband abandons the family in headlong pursuit of his projects. No. You ask him to meet you halfway. You sit down and hammer out a compromise everyone can live with. If he's unwilling to yield, you pray like crazy and refuse to "enable" him when his behavior is unhealthy or out-of-bounds.

You have married a wonderful, Powerful man. Be thankful for all of his good qualities. Rather than fretting over his "challenging" characteristics, pray to the God who can change both your husband and your heart. I would strongly encourage you to get *The Power of a Praying Wife* by Stormie Omartian (Harvest House). It's been a life-changing book for me. I highly recommend this book to all wives, but it's a *must have* for you who are married to Powerful men!

10

He's the Peaceful Man

We've looked at the three other male temperaments in action, and if none of them sounded like your husband, he's probably the Peaceful type. And believe it or not, that's often the only way to identify this temperament: by process of elimination! While the Popular type is extremely loud, the Perfect type is extremely organized, and the Powerful type is extremely forceful, the Peaceful type is extremely anything. He has a chameleon-like ability to be all things to all people as the need arises. He has a dry wit and can be lots of fun like the Popular type. He enjoys routines, which may make him seem as organized as the Perfect type, and because he never gets into any conflict on the job, he'll stay with the same company for twenty years and end up the head of a department. And he can fulfill the role of "boss" even better than the bossy Powerful type.

There are some visual clues to look for, chief of which is his casual appearance. This guy will almost always wear the most casual outfit the occasion demands. He'd rather wear a two-piece than a three-piece suit; he'd rather wear slacks and a sports jacket than a suit; and he'd rather wear khaki shorts and a T-shirt than just about anything else in his wardrobe. His clothes are usually wrinkled. It doesn't matter how much starch his wife uses, his clothes will be a rumpled mess by the end of the day. That's because he lives by the motto: "Why stand when you can sit? Why sit when you can lie down?" (And when sitting, sit as close to reclining as you possibly can!)

When your husband comes home, you may not even notice for an hour or so! If you're working upstairs, he'll come in quietly and sit down on the couch. He may pick up a newspaper, but more likely, he'll pick up the channel surfer. But he won't scream, "Honey, I'm home." He'll patiently wait for you to come on down. If anything, his presence will have a calming effect on the atmosphere of the home.

PEACEFUL STRENGTHS

NICE GUY

The Peaceful man is, without a doubt, the nicest man in town. I think Dr. Tim LaHaye sums up this man perfectly in his book *Transformed Temperaments*: "The easiest people to get along with in life are Phlegmatics [Peaceful types]. Their calm, easygoing nature makes them well liked by others, and their clever wit and dry humor makes them a joy to have around. They qualify for the 'Mr. Nice Guy' label wherever they go. In fact, Phlegmatics are usually such good people that they act more like Christians before their salvation than other temperament types afterward."[1]

He's nice to be around because he's always the same no matter what the circumstances. He's the same yesterday, today, and forever, even if the whole world seems to be falling apart. When you can't count on anything else, you can count on the Peaceful man to remain unchanged. This is in sharp contrast to the Popular man whose mood is up one minute and down the next or the Perfect man who can slip into deep depressions or the Powerful man who might explode at the slightest provocation. Kids—and adults—find comfort and reassurance spending time with this steady, lovable man.

GREAT LISTENER

Peaceful dads are great listeners, both at home and on the job. When my husband Cameron announced that he was quitting his job to join me full-time in ministry, one of his coworkers broke down and cried. Her husband had recently left her with three small children and she had apparently come to rely on Cameron. He couldn't believe how strongly she reacted, "What did I ever do for you?" he asked. "You're the kindest person I've ever known," came the reply. And all he had done was listen to her.

You see, all three of the other temperaments have to jump in when someone else is talking. The Popular man constantly interrupts because he thinks he has something funnier or more interesting to say. Or he wants to top your story with one of his own. The Perfect man wants to give you detailed advice on how to make everything right. The Powerful man wants to dish out some orders about what you need to do right now to take charge of the situation. Not the Peaceful man. He's content to sit quietly and listen.

When my husband worked in corporate America, people would come from all parts of the building to sit in his cubicle and tell him their tales of woe. We're talking about people he hardly even knew. Somehow, they found out that here was a man with a listening ear. And so a never-ending stream of people came, not to seek his brilliant advice or to receive a battle plan on how to make it right. They didn't even want someone to crack jokes and cheer them up. They wanted a listening ear.

On the homefront, the wife of the Peaceful man often gets frustrated with him because he "wastes time" sitting around with the kids, doing nothing. Such wives would do well to take note of how, in the midst of all that "wasted" time, her husband manages to find out what their children are really thinking and feeling.

DIPLOMATIC

The Peaceful man believes everything should be done properly and with absolute dignity. He never, ever raises his voice in public. He is constantly mindful of everything he does and would rather die than draw attention to himself. He considers politeness a top priority and carefully weighs every word he speaks, for fear he might inadvertently offend someone. As you might guess, he is an extremely pleasant, enjoyable person to be around. And because of his inner drive to maintain peace and harmony in relationships, he has an extraordinary ability to mediate problems—whether sibling rivalry or warring nations. He also performs well under pressure, because he can almost always remain calm, even when everyone around him loses their cool. That's why many diplomats and high government officials have this temperament.

I think diplomacy even plays a role in his approach to the ice cream shop. While you and your kids spend twenty minutes trying to decide which of the 259 flavors you want, the Peaceful man always orders the *same* thing: vanilla. There's just something about the color white that seems to appeal to him. I guess it's an easygoing, noncontroversial color. No one's going to be offended, no one's feelings will get hurt if you order vanilla ice cream.

STEADY

When it comes to his career, the Peaceful man is best described as competent and steady. He probably won't start his own business, but he makes a wonderful business partner. He makes an excellent administrator because he is content to perform routine tasks, day in and day out. Most school administrators (and many elementary school teachers) are this temperament.[2]

He's probably not going to become the next president of General Motors. Instead, he will be among the often unsung heroes, the "Steady Eddies" who are the true backbone of every organization. He may not be loud like the Popular man, or detail-oriented like the Perfect man. He may not shake things up like the Powerful man. But no company in the world could survive without these folks who quietly get the job done behind the scenes. He doesn't ask for credit or glory. He's a team player, liked and admired by his coworkers.

SOLID FINISHER

Although the Peaceful man is not one for launching big projects, he's definitely the man to have on hand when it comes to *finishing* a project. His specialty is persistence. I remember when we first moved into our new home and I wanted to make a bold design statement. You know, by painting the walls with bold colors. One day, when Cameron was at work, I painted the dining room dark green. I mean a dark Army green. Imagine my husband's surprise when he got home and heard me humming "We're in the army now. We're in the army now!" Needless to say, he was not pleased.

You see, he wanted white walls. That's the way they had it in the model. That's the way they were when we moved in. And, as far as he was concerned, that's the way they should stay. No need to launch a big project to change the status quo. Since the Peaceful man is a peacemaker by nature, he decided not to make too big of an issue about the green in our dining room *provided* (and the key word here is provided) I agreed to let the rest of the walls in the house stay white. I went along with it at first, but one day I got to thinking: "White walls? How dull. What kind of a statement do white walls make?" Then a brilliant idea struck me. I knew that if I went out and bought the paint and got the project started, he couldn't stand seeing it left undone.

So, guess what I did? I went out and bought purple paint (oh, don't gasp . . . it's a light purple!) and casually rolled a bit of it on each wall. Just enough to get the project underway. Then, he couldn't stand the lack of harmony in the walls, so he slowly, painstakingly finished the job. Well, I'm ashamed to admit such a story. Shame on me for doing such a thing! It just goes to show that understanding the temperaments can be a dangerous thing at times. Let me encourage you to do as I say, not as I did: resist the temptation to use your newfound knowledge to manipulate your unsuspecting husband.

A MAN OF QUIET INTEGRITY

When Cameron was up for a promotion last year, his boss went to the vice president to seek approval. The VP was a young, hard-driving, successful executive, with whom my husband had very little contact. But guess what he had to say about Cameron? That in his entire career, only three people had profoundly influenced him. Cameron was one of them. Why? Because of his quiet integrity.

That's what the Peaceful man is all about.

Now, my husband hasn't made it to the top of the corporate ladder, despite all the years I tormented him and goaded him on. He's never raked in a six-figure salary, never won any awards. But I know one thing: he could go back to any company he has ever worked for and be warmly received. All of that is not to say the Peaceful man cannot have a successful career. Former presidents Gerald Ford and George Bush were both Peaceful men who achieved tremendous success. They climbed to positions of power, not by sheer force of their will or because of their charismatic personalities, but because of their character. What's more, the Peaceful type does not have any enemies; everyone likes him. While flashier men fizzle out and more brilliant men burn out, the Peaceful man steadily works his way to the top. He remains loyal to the company and will rarely quit a job, no matter how unpleasant the situation becomes. If your husband has been with the same company for many years, you can bet he has strong Peaceful tendencies.

One of my absolute favorite movies is *Chariots of Fire*. It recounts the true story of British Olympic gold medalist, Eric Liddle. The movie recounts Eric's steady progression to the Olympic Games. He's not flashy. He's not driven to beat the competition. He simply knows that God has given him an extraordinary gift and he wants to use it for God's glory. This is in sharp contrast to the other leading figure in the movie, a Powerful type, who prepares for the Games with a vengeance, bending the rules in a headlong rush to win at any cost. If you ever want a vivid portrayal of the contrast between God-confidence and self-confidence, the difference between one who is called and one who is driven, by all means, rent the movie. It's a fascinating character study.

Eric methodically prepared to compete in the 100-meter race. However, when he discovered that the race was to take place on the Sabbath, he refused to run. When the British Olympic Committee got word of this, they were furious with him. I mean, hey, they didn't know it was going to become an Academy Award-winning movie. All they saw was their great hope of glory, dropping out of the race. They called a high-powered meeting with the Prince of Wales himself in attendance and tried to intimidate Eric into backing down from his principles. He was polite but completely unmoved. In his quiet, steady way he maintained his integrity.

Eric entered the 400-meter race (scheduled to be run on a different day), a race he was completely unprepared and unqualified to win. To everyone's astonishment, he won it anyway. He was a man of quiet integrity. What a picture of the incredible potential of the Peaceful temperament.

CARES FOR THE SICK

My girlfriend Carol (a strong Powerful mom) had invited us for dinner one evening. We talked in the afternoon and all systems were go. I was dressed and ready when the phone rang. Carol needed to cancel dinner. "Amy was asleep all afternoon and I figured, 'Hey, this is great. I can get lots done.' It never even occurred to me that something might be wrong with her. The minute Chris walked in, he put his hand on her forehead. Sure enough, she had a fever. Within minutes, he was wiping her head with a moist cloth and pumping her with fluids and medicine."

Now, if it were up to Carol, we would have gone ahead with our plans for the evening. But her husband is a Peaceful man and there was no way he was going to neglect a sick child. I tried to talk her out of bringing the dinner and a battle of the Powerful moms was underway. She won. She came rushing over with hot lasagna, garlic rolls, and salad. We stood chatting for two hours (about how to get our kids under control, of course). Meanwhile, back at the ranch, Chris aka Florence Nightingale, spent the evening caring for the sick.

SUBTLE HUMOR

People often tell me I should do stand-up comedy because I'm always cracking jokes and laughing loudly. But the truth is, my husband is much funnier than I am. It's just that he cracks *quiet* jokes. The Peaceful man has a wonderful, dry sense of humor.

I'll never forget the time when a dear friend had just found out that her husband had been having an affair. In fact, that he had been conducting affairs with various women throughout their sixteen years of marriage. Her husband had moved out and she was trying to put the pieces of her life back together again. Although she was a Christian, she had not been actively involved in a church for more than three years. She was sitting at our kitchen table and I was trying to persuade her to meet with our pastor. (The Powerful type trying to "fix" her problems, don't ya know?)

Anyway, I was going on and on about how wonderful our pastor is. Finally, I concluded my lecture with something along the lines of, "He is the kindest man you'll ever meet. He is so caring and gentle and wonderful. I know you will absolutely love him." To confirm that the detailed course of action I had laid out was correct, I turned to Cameron and said, "Don't you think so, dear?"

He had been quiet throughout my entire sermonette but now he quietly added, "Well, I think Pastor Paul is a great guy, too. But I'm pretty sure he's already married."

We all sat there howling with laughter for the next ten minutes! It was exactly the comic relief we needed. My girlfriend commented, "This is the first time I've laughed in weeks." That's the Peaceful man for you. He doesn't say much, but when he does, it's often incredibly funny.

LIFELONG FRIENDS

When you combine his loyalty, his knack for diplomacy, his subtle wit, and his aversion to conflict, it's not hard to understand why the Peaceful man keeps his friends for a lifetime. He's not big on huge parties and doesn't maintain a social calendar featuring a cast of thousands, though. Instead, he'll devote himself to a small band of friends: his golfing buddies, his fishing buddies, or in my father's case, his beer buddies. My dad has had the same circle of friends since he was a teenager. Which is remarkable, especially considering that he is now seventy-two years old! I can remember the same group of men gathering virtually every weekend, to swap stories over beer and fat pretzels at the kitchen table, or to putter around the garage working on old cars.

PEACEFUL WEAKNESSES

SLOW-MOVING

The wife of a Peaceful man is the most likely to hear comments about how lucky she is to be married to such a great guy.

He's so sweet, so lovable, so patient. Who on earth wouldn't be thanking the heavens above for such a precious gem of a guy? His wife, that's who! Believe it or not, this easygoing man has some extremely annoying weaknesses. Chief among them is that he appears to have only three speeds—slow, unbelievably slow, and comatose. I hate to admit how many times I've yelled, "Oh for crying out loud, let's GO," as my husband puttered around the house. His coworkers don't see this side of the Peaceful man because typically, he works very hard on the job and tries to be friendly toward everyone. However, doing so completely drains him of energy. When he comes home, he has absolutely nothing left to give to his wife and children. He shifts into low gear and proceeds to drive his family NUTS.

Speaking of driving, the surest way to spot a Peaceful man is on the road. He even *drives* slow.

UNMOTIVATED

Some Peaceful dads are not only slow, they are downright lazy. Now, I know that doesn't sound very nice, but it's true! They just can't seem to muster enough motivation to get anything accomplished. You ask your husband to take out the trash and he says, "Sure, honey." He's truly willing to get the job done, however, he lacks the motivation to get up off the couch and carry the bag to the curb. He has grand intentions about organizing the garage, but he can't muster the energy. He's been planning to repaint the house for years, but he can't muster the energy. He'd like to plant a garden, but he's never been sufficiently inspired to till the soil. Now, perhaps if you start the project, he'll get motivated to finish it. But not always!

Although most of these men will work steadily at their job, if they get laid off, you could be in for a serious problem. Why? Because they lack the motivation required for a successful job hunt. Or perhaps they have a job, but the pay is not sufficient to meet your family's needs or the job itself is unsatisfactory. He'll stick with it forever because he's not willing to put in the effort to make a change. (Please allow me to give a disclaimer here that not all Peaceful dads are lazy. Both my husband and my father fit into this temperament, yet both are extremely hard-working men. They'd never forgive me if I didn't mention that! As you read through the strengths and weaknesses listed throughout this book, please keep in mind that no one fits entirely into any of these temperament types. We're all unique!)

INDECISIVE

Sometimes the Peaceful man appears unmotivated, when in fact, he's merely indecisive. He doesn't like his job, but he can't decide if he dislikes it enough to move on. Besides, what if his new job turns out to be even worse? Fear—specifically, fear of making a wrong decision—is frequently the motivating force behind his inaction. So he makes up his mind not to make up his mind.

TV ADDICT

Behold the quintessential couch potato. As one woman noted, "When my husband and I got married, he and the couch became one." When the Peaceful man gets home from work in the evening, he heads directly for the couch. Ideally, he'd like to have a tray permanently set up by "his" chair so that he can eat dinner while watching TV. When the children try to talk to him, he mutters "huh" or waves them aside. His idea of a romantic evening together is asking his wife to sit down and watch TV with him. Within minutes, he'll be sound asleep. It's not unusual for a man with this temperament to spend most of his non-working hours dozing in and out of consciousness, which makes him essentially an absentee father.

By the way, the ultimate gift you can give your husband is an easy chair. He'll love it! However, if you really love him, you may *not* want to buy him one, because he'll never be able to get back up again. And you don't want your husband stuck in an easy chair for the rest of his life, do you?

This will sound shocking to some, and I admit it's a radical step, but I actually hid the television from my husband. Yes, I admit it! Every night after dinner, he would sit on the couch, click on the tube, and promptly fall asleep. Well, the kids needed daddy time and I needed hubby time! I felt that the TV was actually a stumbling block preventing him from becoming the kind of man he wanted to become. (The Powerful wife always thinks she's "helping" when everyone else thinks she's being bossy and controlling.) At first, he was in shock, but now he freely admits that his life is much better without that old TV monopolizing his time. He finally planted that garden he's been planning and he's even talking about organizing some of his paperwork. Would you take alcohol away from your alcoholic husband? Well, I removed my husband's addiction. Yes, he went through a period of withdrawal . . . but he's much better now!

RAIN ON THE PARADE

The Peaceful man is not big on generating new and exciting things for the family to do, which wouldn't be that big of a problem if it weren't for this particular character trait. Not only does the Peaceful man rarely instigate any new activities, he'll rain on your parade when you try. "Sweetheart, let's go out to dinner, just the two of us." "I'm too tired," comes the reply. "Hey, honey, I've got a great idea! Let's have a family picnic this weekend!" A grunt in response. "Honey, what do you think?" A grunt in response. He may not come right out and tell you "Forget about it, babe. Not gonna happen." He's too polite for that. But nine times out of ten, when time for the picnic rolls around, you won't be able to roll him out of bed. He'll just dig in his heels and refuse to go. "I don't feel like it," is all the explanation you'll get.

One woman exclaimed, after years of searching for common interests with her husband, "How can you cultivate common interests with someone who isn't interested in anything?" It's very hard, indeed. And without common interests, your marriage may be about as warm and cozy as a rainy day.

WHAT YOUR PEACEFUL HUSBAND NEEDS MOST FROM YOU[3]

If you've married a Peaceful man, you're very blessed with someone who is almost always there to meet your needs. However, don't lose sight of the fact that he, too, has emotional needs. Consider the following.

PEACE

His primary motivation in life is to avoid conflict, to live in harmony with himself and those around him. When he comes home at the end of the day, the worst possible scenario is for him to walk into chaos—kids screaming, the kitchen torn apart, a wife who's ready to kill someone, *anyone*. If this is what your husband comes home to, don't be surprised when he immediately retreats to the couch and his beloved television set. Don't be surprised if he promptly falls asleep. That's his way of escaping the madness. I know how difficult it is when the entire world's gone mad and life is racing at breakneck speed, but do your best to make your home a refuge from the storm.

A couple ideas that have helped me promote peace: First, Crock-Pot cooking! Sounds crazy, I know. But the beauty of it is that you make the mess in the morning and have all day to clean up the kitchen. That way when your husband comes home, you're not running around with a frying pan in your hand and flour on your face. I've also invested in a variety of relaxing CDs, such as those that capture the sounds of nature—a waterfall, a gentle ocean, the sounds of chirping birds. Well, you know the ones I'm referring to! I also have a collection of classical music and instrumental hymns and praise music. (He doesn't care for the lively praise and worship music; not peaceful enough!) If I can get the baby to sleep before Daddy gets home, that's a real bonus that enables us to have dinner in peace. I might even light the candles on the kitchen table (if I can find the matches!).

One of the most significant things you can do to maintain the peace is to provide your husband with "early warnings." That's because he requires plenty of advance notice about any upcoming events. If there is one thing he simply cannot stand it's a sudden change of plans. He had his heart set on sitting and watching TV and suddenly, you spring a dinner party at the Joneses on him. Since he's generally slow to warm up to an idea, he needs to prepare himself ahead of time. If you want to get this normally mild-mannered man's blood boiling, just try sneaking something up on him without warning! LOOK OUT!

I'll never forget one Wednesday evening my sister called to invite us to a birthday party for my niece. I hung up the phone, turned to my husband, and told him about the invitation. He hit the roof! I couldn't understand why he was so furious, but that didn't stop me from joining the battle. We argued vehemently for nearly forty-five minutes, when finally in exasperation I exclaimed, "What exactly is it that you have to do this Saturday that's soooo important that you can't attend my niece's birthday party?" Suddenly, he was quiet. "You mean it's on Saturday?" "Yes," I replied. "Oh, I thought you meant it was tonight. Sure, no problem. Of course, we can go." With that, we both broke into hysterics and literally rolled on the floor with laughter. He had his early warning. Peace was restored to the Partow household!

RELAXATION

You may label your husband "lazy," but his emotional need for relaxation is as legitimate as any other emotional need and it goes deep within your husband. If you divorce him from his beloved TV (even if it means having his channel surfer surgically removed from his hand), it's up to you to replace it with something else. How about a relaxing evening with you? Why not play soft music? Perhaps a leisurely walk around the block? Be creative and ask God to help you develop some positive alternatives.

PRAISE

Now this is the key that really turned around my relationship with my husband. When I began expressing sincere praise and honest appreciation for his many fine qualities, suddenly I discovered that my husband had "full confidence in me" (Proverbs 31:11). He began to rest more securely in our relationship. You're probably thinking, "If I start being nice to him, he'll see right through that old trick. If I start praising him, he'll get suspicious and accuse me of being insincere." If he's half-Perfect, you may be right. He may react that way. Then you'll just have to work doubly hard to ensure that you are praising him, not just flattering him. There is a difference. Flattery is superficial. Praise takes the time to really *look* for the good and genuinely cherish it. Here's how the Bible puts it: (don't mind my slight modification) "Finally, wives of Peaceful men, whatever is true, whatever is noble, whatever is right, whatever is praiseworthy—think about such things" (Philippians 4:8).

SELF-WORTH

Your husband needs you to reassure him that he's a valuable human being even if he never *accomplishes* anything of great value, according to the world's standards. It's quite likely that your easygoing husband will never achieve the sort of success the world applauds, that's why he so much needs *you* to applaud him. That's why he needs you to build his self-worth with loving reassurance, instead of criticizing and belittling him. The first time I heard the song, "The Measure of a Man" performed by 4Him, I drove down the freeway weeping. It said everything I knew I needed to say to my husband (so I bought him the CD, of course). The song reminded me that my husband's physical appearance, the amount of money he makes, or the number of brilliant thoughts he may have does not really indicate what kind of man he is. One line in particular has meant much to my husband, as I've assured him that I firmly believe it: "What's in the heart defines the measure of a man."

I frequently remind my husband of his many wonderful qualities: that people love him, that he's honest, hardworking, and loyal. I point out how wonderfully he handles the baby and how, whenever our children are discouraged, they turn to him. Who needs flash when you can have substance?

Well, I must tell you the results of the above paragraph, which I wrote about a year ago! As I've been working on this book, God has really been dealing with me about my attitude toward my husband. I've realized that, on a very deep level, I have been disappointed that my husband wasn't making a bundle of money "like all the other men in the neighborhood." I've felt like I was failing as a mother and it was *all his fault* because he didn't earn enough money, so I had to work, which left me feeling depleted and grumpy. God has shown me two things: first, that I am completely responsible for my attitudes and actions; pointing the finger at my husband is a cop-out. Second, that my job is to love my husband *whether or not* he provides the level of financial security I was hoping for.

As I've worked to rebuild my husband's confidence, it's almost like a light has gone on within him. "Yeah, I *do* have some great qualities! I *am* hardworking, honest, and loyal. The fact that people like me *is* an important career skill. My ability to resolve conflict and bring peace *can* make a difference for my company's bottom line." As he's lived out that newfound confidence on the job, his supervisors have taken notice. Recently, he received a promotion along with a significant pay increase, *plus* opportunities for substantial bonuses and a possible trip to Bermuda for both of us!

I just want to encourage those of you who are married to a Peaceful husband to ask God to help you *really believe* in your husband. Superficial words of praise are not enough. But as you come to genuinely believe in him, he will come to believe in himself. I often tell people who want to start their own business: "Believe in you and others will, too." Help your husband to believe in himself and other people will believe in him, too!

LOVING MOTIVATION

It goes without saying that you shouldn't nag your husband. Well, at least I hope it does. Solomon said it was better to live on a rooftop than with a nagging woman, and he was right. If nagging and goading could get the job done, believe me, ladies, my husband would have climbed Mount Everest and been the president of an international corporation by now. However, your husband does require "loving motivation." Now, I'll admit it's a fine line and I haven't gotten it all figured out yet. I can give you an example from my own life that may shed some light on the difference.

My husband has an extraordinary talent for the guitar. However, he hadn't played in years. When we began attending our current church, the music program . . . well, it left a little to be desired, to put it mildly. By the pastor's own admission, it was a weak link in an otherwise growing, dynamic church. I just knew that if my husband broke out his guitar, he could make a huge difference in the quality of our worship experience. I suggested it. I suggested it some more. I mentioned it a few more times. YEARS passed, with my weekly nagging sessions going unheeded. Finally I shut up. About three years after we began attending, I took my husband by the hand and walked over to the music director and declared, "This man is the most incredible guitar player you'll ever hear. If you don't recruit him, you're crazy." Then I turned around and walked away. The music director handled it from there and my husband has been blessing the congregation with his talent ever since.

Loving motivation works! Try it with your honey and see.

Part 3

Understand Your
Marriage

11

How the Popular Wife Entertains (and Annoys) Hubby

POPULAR WIFE + POPULAR HUSBAND

When two people who love the limelight get together, intense rivalry can result. Since both want to be the center of attention all the time, petty jealousy might develop if one starts to outshine the other. On the bright side, neither of you is inclined to hold a grudge, but if this issue constantly surfaces, there will be ongoing turmoil. One possible solution, of course, is to actively divide the glow. For example, one might shine in the area of the home and relationships, while the other shines on the job. Provided both are content with this scenario—that is, they get enough attention, approval, and affection—there shouldn't be an inordinate amount of conflict in this marriage.

This is probably a very fun-loving couple, who genuinely enjoys their life together. They no doubt have many friends and love throwing parties. Their children look forward to coming home (even though it's a wreck) and their friends all wish their parents were just like the two of you. You two are great together when life is great, but when tough times inevitably come, you may lack the internal fortitude to see you through. In particular, be on guard against financial set-backs. Neither of you may handle money well, so credit cards might be like a deadly weapon in your marriage. When you're having fun, you spend money. When you have a fight, you spend money. When you're worn out from a tough day on the job, you go out to dinner and spend money. Hopefully, one partner will land a sales job and make enough money to cover your cozy lifestyle. If not, you can expect money problems to be a significant issue throughout your lifetime, particularly in the retirement years.

POPULAR WIFE + PERFECT HUSBAND

Here's an extremely common combination and one that's fraught with heartache, if not handled properly. Unfortunately, there are a great many things about the Popular wife that genuinely bother the Perfect husband. For example, the Popular wife is disorganized and inaccurate, two of the worst crimes imaginable to the Perfect type. He thinks his wife is just a show-off and soon grows impatient with her tendency to exaggerate and invent wild stories. It's equally hard on her because she's inclined to think, "How did I manage to marry the *one person* in the world who doesn't like me?"

The Perfect husband enjoys people who are serious, intellectual, and deep, which often leaves his wife wondering why *on earth* he married a Popular type like her. However, if she wants him to be happy, she should try to have a sensible conversation with him . . . at least once a week.

This couple frequently gets into conflict over money management. One wife reported taking radical steps to eliminate the battle over money:

> The first thing I did was get rid of all my credit cards. I mean, I just had to admit I couldn't handle the responsibility. The so-called convenience wasn't worth driving my husband nuts over. We used to share a checkbook, but it made him crazy. I'd write out checks or make withdrawals and not tell him about it. Then he'd go to balance the checkbook and find all these withdrawals that I was too embarrassed to tell him about. We fought about it all the time.

So then he got me my own checking account and gave me a set amount of money each month that I was in charge of. Well, I'd spend all the money in the beginning of the month, but then I was too embarrassed to ask him for more money, so I would bounce checks all over the place. Eventually, I just said to him, "I can't handle a checking account. I want a cash allowance." Now I have no access to credit cards or checking accounts. He gives me cash for groceries, gas, and household stuff. It sounds crazy, but it's made a big difference in our marriage. Now I don't give him all that grief. My spending is controlled because I only get a certain amount of cash to spend. I do my best not to ask him for more.

If my husband had come up with the idea, I probably would have been mad at him. But I'm the one who chose it. It was creating too much stress. I had to admit I have no self-control. I've tried many ways and none of them worked. For me, this is easier.

Well, I warned you that she took radical steps. Your situation may not be that severe. Nevertheless, if you and your Perfect husband engage in constant warfare over money, you might consider some radical steps of your own.

Another battleground for the Popular wife and the Perfect husband is the house. Specifically, his desire for the perfect home coupled with her inability to get it together leads to major frustration on both sides. Believe me, I sympathize with your side of this battle. Nevertheless, I would strongly encourage you to take some action here. If you can possibly afford it, you might consider hiring a housecleaner to come once a week or even once a month. It may be well worth the expense if it keeps the peace. I have often hired housecleaners when involved with a demanding project; you don't have to make a lifetime commitment! Even if they only come once or twice, it might be just enough to get you headed in the right direction.

If you've got more time than money, buy some books on organization and get excited about it. With the right attitude, it really can be fun. Yes, fun! Kathy Peel is one of my favorite writers on the subject of housewifery. Her book, *The Family Manager*

(Word, 1996), is a wonderful place to start. Follow it up with *Do Plastic Surgeons Take Visa?* (Word, 1992). Donna Otto, Emilie Barnes, and Sandra Felton have all written upbeat, encouraging books for fledgling housewives like you. If you ever have opportunity to attend one of their live seminars, by all means do so. You can ride on the adrenaline for weeks! I'll bet you have some Perfect wife friends who would be willing to help you organize your home. Ask for their help. Even if you don't feel like it, do it for your husband's peace of mind.

As you may recall, the Perfect temperament has a heartfelt need for space. When I was a little girl, I shared a bed with my sister, Helen. We drew an invisible line down the middle and if I dared to cross over, she'd whack me over the head. Naturally, I gave her the same treatment. The wife of the Perfect husband often feels like a little girl who just put her toe over the invisible line.

Before John and Debra moved into their dream home, John worked closely with the architect on the design for his ideal home office. It was going to be his hideout, his haven of rest. Debra reports how well it worked out.

> He was so excited to put his desk in there. But soon after he moved in, I took it over. My papers were all over it at all times. The kids' toys were thrown everywhere and the kids were in and out. And he was really uptight. He suggested I get my own desk and put it at the other end of the office. He still wasn't happy, because my desk was piled a foot high. It wasn't a big deal to me, but it really bothered him. Even when I clean it, it never looks as good as his. They are neat piles in my mind, but in his mind, they are still piles. When we began to talk openly about it, I also discovered he was really offended that I didn't keep the kids out of there, out of his space.

The Popular wife's Day of Fun can often turn into the Perfect husband's Night of Depression. Barbara recalls one such occasion.

> I've always got a house full of kids. Well, on this particular day, I had a bunch of the neighbors' kids running around the backyard all afternoon. It had been rain-

ing for days, so they were covered in mud. To top it all off, we'd just bought a puppy and he was traipsing mud all over the house.

I decided to bring the kids in the house, because they were destroying the backyard. They quickly got bored so we decided to make cookies. Needless to say, they got cookie dough and sprinkles all over the place. We were having a great time. I figured I had plenty of time to get the house in order before my husband came home. Then all of a sudden, my husband pulled into the driveway. I knew he was going to be upset so I met him at the door and said, "Will you please leave? You can't come in right now." He said he just needed to grab something from his office, but before he could make it into the den, the baby came running out of the back room with frosting all over his face. My husband took one look at the backyard and the kitchen and went into shock. In my mind, it was a really fun afternoon; in his mind, it was completely unacceptable. He was very depressed that night.

Barb also reports several occasions when her husband called home from work to ask, "How is the *house* doing?" "I couldn't believe it," she says. "He didn't ask how are *you* doing, he wanted to know if the house was okay. How are you performing? Are you keeping up? I was very hurt. He wasn't interested in me; he was interested in the house."

The Popular wife resents the Perfect husband's pessimism, while he thinks her optimism is foolish and shallow. The truth is, she *is* a poor judge of character and may run with the wrong crowd or misread the intentions of male friends. She may also send out the wrong message in the name of being friendly. When her perceptive husband tries to warn her, she attacks him verbally rather than heeding his wisdom.

These two can learn a lot from each other, forming two halves of a wonderful whole, if they can get past their differences. Since you're the one reading this book—you're the one with the tools in your hands—I encourage you to take the first step.

POPULAR WIFE + POWERFUL HUSBAND

These two actually make a fairly harmonious couple, provided she keeps the social wheels turning at a fast enough clip while he conquers the business world. Because they are both extroverts with an abundance of energy, they'll enjoying staying active together. Pity the poor little Peaceful child born to this pair!

Conflict can arise if the Powerful husband views his wife as capricious and accuses her of getting nothing accomplished. She may not be goal-oriented enough for his taste. He may also feel she spends too much time talking, especially talking on the phone all day long. He wants to see results, not relationships. To ease conflict, the Popular wife should emphasize the results she has achieved through forming key relationships in the church and community.

If the Powerful husband's secondary trait is Perfect, then they may have another set of problems. After functioning in his extroverted Powerful mode all day at the office, he'll want to shift into his introverted Perfect mode in the evening. If the Popular mom has been at home all day without adult conversation, she'll be desperate for someone to talk to. Even when he's in high gear, the Powerful husband keeps communication succinct. He doesn't have the time or patience for long, winding stories; he wants people to get to the point. His natural tendency to become impatient with his wife's stories will be greatly magnified if his secondary trait is the Perfect type who views his home as a haven of rest, silence, and solitude.

If that's the case, the Popular wife should actively cultivate friendships with women, so that she has her share of adult conversation before her husband returns from work in the evening. She might also plan to go out one evening every week, after getting the children off to bed. This will give her husband at least one quiet night in the midst of each hectic week.

POPULAR WIFE + PEACEFUL HUSBAND

The Popular wife is almost always talking, talking, talking, LOUDLY, LOUDLY, LOUDLY. In the beginning, her Peaceful husband thinks it's cute. After all, he married her so someone could make conversation, but this is ridiculous. Doesn't she ever come up for air? Her incessant urge to make noise annoys her more reserved partner to distraction. Understand: he *needs* an opportunity to sit and work quietly, whether it's working on a crossword puzzle or paying the family bills. If the Popular wife fails to give him some time and space, he'll end up exhausted.

She loves nonstop activities, but if she expects her Peaceful husband to keep pace with her, she's in for a big surprise. If she *demands* that he keep pace with her, he will become literally sick with exhaustion. Larry and Denise are a case in point. Thanks to Denise, they had something going every night of the week. All good things, of course. Monday night, missions society. Tuesday night, small group Bible study. Wednesday night, prayer meeting. Friday night, youth group fun night. (She volunteered them to lead the youth group.) Saturday, household chores and extracurricular activities with the youth group. Sunday, church in the morning *and* the evening—with dinner guests in between. When Larry would beg Denise to slow down, she accused him of being unspiritual. She just couldn't understand what was wrong with that man. Where was his zeal for the Lord?

However, when she measured her spirituality as *God* does, not in terms of outward activity but inward fruits of the Spirit, Denise had to admit that her husband was far ahead of her. She may have been the chairperson of everything from the casserole committee to the missions society, but Larry was the one quietly cultivating a heart of love, joy, peace, patience, kindness, and self-control.

Another reason the Peaceful husband may not want to follow along with his wife's whirlwind schedule is because, quite frankly, she embarrasses him. He wants to be quiet and not make a scene. She actively tries to draw a crowd. She constantly overpowers and overshadows her husband. Eventually, he may resent her for it. She might also push and prod him along, thinking he moves too slowly, which again can yield resentment. She tosses out words without thinking and he takes everything to heart, which is yet another breeding ground for resentment.

Warning to the Popular wife: Your husband is the most prone to bitterness and resentment. Too many Popular wives are adored by absolutely everyone . . . except their own husbands. I don't want that to happen to you! You have so many wonderful qualities to offer to any husband, regardless of his temperament. Prayfully consider the suggestions in this chapter and seek to adapt your personal style so you can live in harmony with your partner.

12

How the Perfect Wife Drives Her Man Crazy

PERFECT WIFE + POPULAR HUSBAND

In the individual chapters on the Perfect wife and the Popular husband, we warned that the Perfect wife tends to drive people away while the Popular husband, with his flexible conscience, tends to wander. Again, I am not saying *all couples* with this temperament combination will end up a divorce statistic. However, based on years of dealing with women in bruised or broken marriages, I've concluded that this couple is the most prone to infidelity. As the eternal optimist, the Popular husband becomes frustrated by his wife's pessimistic attitude. His free-spirited nature gets crushed under the weight of her constant demands for perfection.

I met Barb, a trim, attractive woman in her late forties, at a women's retreat in Kentucky. Her husband of twenty years had just left her and she was reeling in shock. Barb was the church secretary and she did a perfect job running everything behind-the-scenes. Their weekly church bulletin was a thing of beauty with never a mistake in it. She even sang perfectly in the choir. Her home was perfectly decorated. In fact, it was the envy of the neighborhood. Even though her husband didn't make much money, with her knack for bargain-hunting and dollar-stretching (not to mention her exquisite taste) she managed to transform it

171

into something off the pages of *House Beautiful* magazine. But she wasn't some shallow, superficial woman. Far from it. She was often sought out by women in the congregation who admired her grasp of the Scriptures and the depth of her spiritual insight.

Everything was perfect. So why did her husband leave her? He found a less-than-perfect woman who accepted less than perfection from him. Was he right to do so? Certainly not; there's absolutely no excuse for his infidelity. We're not letting him off the hook here. He made the wrong choice. He committed a serious sin, one of the Big Ten. If our goal in this book were to find fault, this would be a no-brainer. We'd label him a jerk and be done with it. But our goal is to equip you *to make the most of your marriage*. And if that's your objective, forget about who's right and who's wrong, and pray that God will soften your heart and make you a more accepting person.

There is hope! This couple can have the most wonderful, passionate marriage if they savor the differences. My friend Cheryl, a Perfect type married to a Popular husband for thirteen years, shared the following story:

> My husband loves to tell stories, a quality I found attractive and engaging when we first met. I'm shy and soft-spoken, so I admired his ability to spin a yarn and hold an audience. After we were married however, I came to realize how much of his story-telling was fictionalized, and I took it upon myself to correct his every embellishment. One day my dad took me aside and reminded me that it would be okay, in fact it might promote marital harmony, if I let Mike go on with his stories and not try to correct every detail. I agreed to try and was presented my first challenge at dinner that night.
>
> We were out with two other couples and we started talking about the food at the Minnesota State Fair. A favorite of everyone there was the deep fried cheese curds. Mike and I had talked about making them at home, but hadn't actually made them yet. But since that wouldn't be a very good story, he started telling everyone how we made them all the time.

"Oh, they're great," he said, "we just get out the deep fryer and cook 'em up."

With my dad's words ringing in my ears, I just nodded and smiled. I was becoming part of this conspiracy. I was letting my husband get away with this story. He couldn't believe it! He became even bolder. "In fact, we just made them last night. We took them with us to a potluck dinner and our deep fried cheese curds were the hit of the whole dinner!"

Wow, now everyone wanted to make deep fried cheese curds at home, too. "You just use a deep fryer?" they asked. "Where do you buy the cheese curds?"

Mike was in his element until this question: "How do you make the batter?"

"Ha!" I thought. I knew he didn't have a clue about cooking. "Let's see you get out of this one, Mr. Smarty Pants." I looked over at Mike with a grin. But he just turned to me and said, "How *do* you make that batter, Cheryl?"

Cheryl reports that she and her husband are blissfully happy in their marriage . . . most of the time and that understanding the temperaments has gone a long way toward promoting harmony. I should point out that we're not overlooking the fact that her husband clearly crossed the line past "embellishment" with this particular story. If your husband embellishes to the point of falsehood, pray for him and privately "speak the truth in love." Cheryl, however, was absolutely *right* to resist the temptation to correct her husband in public.

PERFECT WIFE + PERFECT HUSBAND

These two perfect people should be perfect together, shouldn't they? Any problems? Just one: Heaven help their children! In terms of their marriage relationship, they may spend so much time analyzing one another that they never take time to enjoy life. Since both are prone to depression, theirs can become a dark, brooding marriage. One partner is likely to be Perfect-Powerful while the other is Perfect-Peaceful. As has been mentioned, the Perfect-Powerful is perhaps the most difficult combination to live with. Not only do they want everything done perfectly, they want it done their way NOW. The Perfect-Powerful partner's high-energy demands for instant action and total obedience can crush the life out of the Perfect-Peaceful partner, who is a low-energy, pure introvert. When the Peaceful tendency toward resentment joins forces with the Perfect tendency to hold permanent grudges, you can imagine the strength of the bitter root that might take hold. This is the couple who can live together in absolute silence for fifty years.

The best insurance for these two deep individuals is to actively maintain the romantic side of their marriage; both are incurable romantics. And love covers over a multitude of sins.

PERFECT WIFE + POWERFUL HUSBAND

His battle cry is "My mind is made up; don't bore me with the facts." And of course, the Perfect wife is president of the International Bore People with the Facts Society. She is extremely detail-oriented and cautious and will no doubt try to slow down her fast-action partner. Naturally, he has no interest in slowing down. Anne and her husband, Jack, decided to buy a new house, so she spent weeks putting together a scrapbook of clippings of the ideal house: a page for each bedroom, two pages of kitchen features, and so forth. She then typed up a chart listing the exterior and interior features they were looking for along with a rating system ranking the importance of each feature. Then, as they looked at each house, she could complete the form, tally the results, and make a logical decision based on the facts.

House #1 had a brick exterior, worth 10 points on a scale of 1 to 10. Since exterior sturdiness and durability were of extreme importance, that particular category carried a weight of 5 (10 x 5 or 50 points). She then rated each of the 20 features on the list (living room, fireplace, carpet condition, and so forth) and gave the house a total rating of 650 points. She did that for the next three houses, with ratings of 725, 350, and 450.

"Not bad for the first day of looking," she thought to herself, knowing it would take many months to find their ideal home rated at 1,000 points. When they got back to the realtor's office after their tour of homes, her husband dropped a bombshell. To her utter astonishment, he suddenly turned to the realtor and said, "We'll take (house #3)." (Isn't it amazing that he didn't even consult with his wife before making this declaration? Lest you assume he's just an awful guy, he later told her that it never even occurred to him that she *wouldn't* want to live in such an idyllic spot!) Well, she looked at her chart and realized it had the lowest rating. Before she knew it, her husband was putting in a formal, written offer on the house. He liked the backyard with the stream running through it. He didn't care that the bedrooms were small, the carpet was shot, and the kitchen appliances were outdated. He had always dreamed of having a stream in his backyard.

Anne tried to reason with him by showing him the charts. She had the proof, but she could tell he wasn't listening to a word she said. While they were sitting at the realtor's desk, debating the merits of the house, another couple called to say they were ready to make an offer. The realtor turned to Anne and Jack. It was a moment of truth. Would they trust the Perfect wife's flawlessly conceived and executed chart or the Powerful husband's childhood dream?

What would you do?

They followed the dream! They knocked down walls to expand the bedrooms, replaced the carpets, and installed new appliances. The one thing they couldn't have done was run a small stream through the backyard. Wouldn't you know that running water, teeming with minnows and tadpoles—serving as a magnet for creation—has been a continual source of joy for their family for the past fifteen years?

There's a time for analysis and a time for action. A time for checklists and a time to follow your heart. If you've got a Powerful honey, learn to trust his instincts. No, he can't always tell you exactly why, can't always provide chart-and-graph proof to support his case, but he has an uncanny ability to be *right*.

On the downside, he has an uncanny ability to run roughshod over your feelings. He doesn't like in-depth conversation or details. He's a big-picture person who likes to cut right to the chase. Express your viewpoint clearly, as Anne did in the above illustration, and don't allow him to turn into a total bully.

PERFECT WIFE + PEACEFUL HUSBAND

She wants everything to be perfect, but perfect takes a lot of work. That's a problem right there, because the Peaceful husband isn't that big on work. He would rather kick back in his easy chair than spend his weekends perfecting the house and keeping up with her endless checklist and charts filled with work. When he does complete her latest project, it's never quite up to her standards. She'll make him do it over and over and over again until it's done *right*—anything less than sheer perfection is never right in her book. He views her as too critical and judgmental. Since he can never please her anyway, eventually he figures, "Why bother?"

After the Perfect and Popular couple combination, I believe this pair is the second most likely to end in divorce. In this case, the Perfect wife's demands for perfection leave the husband feeling inadequate and emotionally drained. When he finally musters the strength to leave—and it usually takes many, many years—those outside the marriage will think: Here was a man with the perfect wife: the perfect hairstyle, the perfect house, the perfect cook, the perfect everything. What more could he want? It's not that he wanted *more*, he wanted *less*: fewer demands for perfection and fewer feelings of never measuring up to her high standards. In many cases, he will find another woman who will accept him as he is, rather than constantly demanding perfection.

Here again, we're not saying the Perfect wife is an awful, no-good person, while her husband is the innocent bystander who had no choice but to run off. No doubt his sluggish, cavilier attitude has been tormenting her for years. And no doubt his indifference has left her feeling compelled to pick up the slack, carrying far more than her share of the load with the house and the children. As usual, there's enough blame to go around. But why settle for "blame" when you can have the joy of a happy marriage? See if using your newly found tools doesn't make a huge difference in your relationship. That will be far more productive and gratifying than sifting through the wreckage, looking for evidence to prove you were right and he was wrong.

13

How the Powerful Wife Lords It Over Her Husband

POWERFUL WIFE + POPULAR HUSBAND

The Popular husband doesn't think being married to a Powerful wife is very much fun. He wants to have a good time, but she's bossing him around and giving him work to do. She also makes decisions without consulting him, which may or may not bug him. If he realizes that abdicating decision-making authority makes his life more fun, he may try to coast through the marriage and let her handle everything. That will work short-term, but will gradually erode their relationship.

Jane decided she'd pulled the wagon long enough for her "party boy" husband, Eric. One of the few places he'd agreed to help in the home was in taking out the garbage. However, when the task actually needed doing, he was always too busy, or waiting for the next commercial, or had his hands full, or something. Jane became tired of nagging and took the garbage out herself. The same thing happened with bill-paying. Eric told her to throw the bills on his desk and he'd take care of them, but they were never paid until panic forced her to do it herself.

Finally, she decided to stop mothering her husband. The next time the garbage needed to go out, she asked only once. After that, she started filling paper sacks beside the overflowing garbage can. The rest of the family made a fuss, but it took her husband five days of walking past the pile of refuse to notice it.

"I asked you to take that out the other day," Jane replied calmly. "I knew you'd get to it whenever you were able." She quietly communicated confidence in her husband, but also a line she would not cross.

Later, Jane took a similar action about the payment of their bills. Instead of bailing Eric out, she honored his commitment that he'd pay them. He didn't, of course, but after bill collectors began hounding him, he realized his wife was no longer going to mother him.

He said later, "I knew that all my life I just tried to get by. I didn't think of myself as lazy, but I suppose I was. I know I wasn't God's prize husband. Jane deserved better. But that day it hit me: Things weren't going to get any better if I didn't change."

What Jane had been trying to accomplish for twelve years, the bill collectors and garbage odors took care of in three months![1]

Because the Powerful wife is so capable, it's tempting for her to do everything herself. However, in the long run, that's not a wise decision. She needs to get her husband's input and allow him to shoulder his share of the responsibilities. If she learns to consult with him, then uses her considerable energy and talent to implement their joint decisions on the homefront, they can make a good combination.

POWERFUL WIFE + PERFECT HUSBAND

The Powerful Wife runs through life at break-neck speed, leaping obstacles in a single bound and "conquering" all opposition with her quick wit and sharp tongue. She thrives on action and is energized by spending time with people (especially when she gets to boss everybody around!). Unfortunately, this runs counter to her Perfect Husband's desire to stop and smell the roses, to enjoy the finer things of life.

The Powerful Wife is a big picture person, who doesn't want to get bogged down with details like "how's this gonna work out?" She's running with the vision and doesn't want anyone to slow her down. Meanwhile, her husband lives for details and is determined to slow her down at any cost.

If you want harmony in your marriage, have enough humility to admit that although you have great instincts, you're not infallable. Demonstrate respect for your husband by sitting quietly, listening to his careful analysis of the situation. It may very well be that his keen mind has honed in on a vital detail missing from your grand plan. Be thankful that he's willing to invest time preparing checklists and charts, and have enough sense to put them to good use.

Also remember that there are very few projects on this earth that need to be tackled right now. More often than not, haste makes waste. Be thankful that your detail-oriented husband is forcing you to do something you wouldn't otherwise do: namely, take time to carefully think things through before springing into action.

The Powerful Wife also has a tendency to run roughshod over her husband's feelings. (Don't be fooled by all those marriage seminars that insist it's always the husband hurting the wife's feelings; in your marriage, it's far more likely that you'll be the one hurting his feelings.) Your husband needs someone to listen to his innermost thoughts. Your tendency will be to brush him aside, advising him to "buck up" and "take it like a man." Nothing could be more detrimental to your relationship. Practice genuine listening and actively resist the temptation to offer him solutions. He doesn't want solutions; he wants empathy and compassion.

POWERFUL WIFE + POWERFUL HUSBAND

Wow, what a marriage. They'll either conquer the world or kill each other! When both husband and wife are Powerful types, you can bank on major turf wars. They will continually clash over control, which both of them want and neither wants to concede. The key for this couple's survival is to closely define territorial lines of authority. The Powerful wife must recognize that her husband is the lord of her household, whether she likes it or not. But they'll be happier together if Tarzan realizes that Jane needs a portion of the jungle to rule, too. Maybe a home business of her own or the chairmanship of a charity, or perhaps a small country to run . . . Whatever it is, she needs a place where she can exercise her natural urge to take charge in a positive, productive way. A healthy dose of mutual respect will go a long way toward keeping this marriage strong.

Also focus on the incredible potential you have together. I've met Powerful couples in joint ministry who accomplished unparalleled feats for God. More precisely, they allowed God to work *through them* to accomplish much.

POWERFUL WIFE + PEACEFUL HUSBAND

When I was gathering stories for this book, I sent an email to several friends. Here's one response:

> I printed out your email and walked into the kitchen where my husband and I began to predict each other's temperaments. We discovered that I am a Powerful Choleric and he is a Peaceful Phlegmatic. I asked him what he thought you meant by "lord it over your husband," and he said it had to do with bossing him around all the time. I thought about that for about two seconds then exclaimed, "I do NOT boss you around! You just need a lot of reminding!" He just looked at me and smiled, then we both burst into laughter.

Yes, the Powerful wife feels she is "helping" her husband by providing him with twenty-four-hour-a-day, seven-day-a-week reminders. She's not. She's nagging him. And like the Perfect wife, she can drive her man away if she's not careful.

She steamrolls her agenda over her husband and the rest of the family. She's gonna do what she wants to do and if anyone has an alternative plan, she doesn't want to hear about it. If her Peaceful husband, in a sudden wave of resolve, puts his foot down and pursues *his* agenda for the family, she'll do everything in her power to make life miserable. And she's a pretty powerful lady!

The Powerful wife's tendency to act now and think later gets the family into one difficulty after another and her take charge attitude often causes a scene in public. I used to do this constantly—as in *daily*—and my husband would just die inside. Here's a word of encouragement for you Powerful wives: at this point, I only cause a scene every few weeks. So there is hope for you! Since the Peaceful husband wants to avoid conflict at all costs, he becomes extremely upset over these incidents. One of our former neighbors (a *Christian*) had gotten into so many fights with local store owners that her family was embarrassed to shop for everything from videos to groceries. On one occasion, she got so rowdy "standing up for what was right" she was literally banned from shopping at one establishment. Her low-key Peaceful husband suffered humiliation after humiliation. Eventually, resentment began creeping into the marriage. The Powerful wife could learn a thing or two from her Peaceful husband about how much further kindness gets you than anger.

The Powerful wife also spends money without consulting her husband, which makes him angry, frustrated, and resentful. One time, I called an organization to ask if they would be willing to donate books for a charitable cause. Let me emphasize that: a donation. Somehow, I ended up purchasing sixty-five dollars worth of cookbooks. After I hung up the phone, I sat in shock, realizing what I had done. I knew my husband, who works so hard at putting together and following the family budget, was going to be furious. Worse than that, I knew how much it hurt him when I completely disregarded his carefully written-out budget proposals.

What on earth to do? On this occasion, I actually handled it right. I immediately started praying, "Lord, I don't want to dishonor my husband like this. I know he will be hurt and upset. HELP!" A few hours later, the phone rang. The woman said my credit card number was written down incorrectly on the order form. I practically screamed, "GREAT! CANCEL THE ORDER!" Well, that's not quite the reaction she was expecting. I'll bet she was completely baffled when she hung up the phone. But that night, there was peace in the Partow household.

What if I had been my usual pigheaded self? What if I had said, "Oh, so what? Big deal? I did it and I can do whatever I want. He'll just have to change his budget and make it work." I am ashamed to admit how many times that has been my attitude and how many times I have discouraged my husband.

Florence Littauer describes a typical scenario in the Powerful-Peaceful marriage:

> The Phlegmatics don't like to be pushed, and yet when they are left on their own, they don't get around to doing what they promised to do. Dotty, a Choleric

friend of mind who is trying to keep from running everything in the home, gave her Phlegmatic husband, Lewis, a major decision to make. In discussing vacation plans, he chose a certain resort on the coast. Lewis was to make the reservations. Each time Dotty asked if he had made them yet, he told her he would do it when he was ready, and she should stop nagging him. On the day they were leaving, Dotty summoned up a smile of hope and asked sweetly, "I assume you did make the reservations." His low-key comment was, "They always have cancellations." She was furious and they drove in silence to San Diego.

When they asked the desk clerk for a reservation, he laughed at them. "You expect to walk into a beach resort in August and pick up a room? You must be kidding. There's not a space in town."

"That was insult enough," Dotty told me, "but then Lewis turned to me and said, 'You should have reminded me to call.' I lost my mind on that, burst into tears, and ran out to the car where I hit my fists on the fenders. I vowed I'd never count on him for anything again."

They finally found one room in an old motel next to an all-night diner. Lewis went promptly to sleep on the lumpy mattress, while Dotty lay awake livid all night.

In the morning Lewis said, "This may not be a luxury motel, but think of the money we saved."

Unfortunately, this scenario is typical of the merry-go-round the Choleric wife and Phlegmatic husband are on. He doesn't want to be pushed around and tells her so. She holds back, and then tries not to check on him. He neglects his responsibilities, and the ax falls. She gets upset and knows she can't trust him. She takes back control, and he tells everyone she picks on him. She comes across as the heavy and he looks like the typical henpecked husband. [2]

Here's a warning for the Powerful wives: your husband is the most prone to burnout. If you keep lording it over your husband, you will crush his spirit, and your marriage will become a sad, empty shell. Sure, you'll get your own way, but you certainly won't get the man you married. You'll spend your life with only a shadow of the man he once was . . . and could have become.

Does it have to happen? Is your marriage doomed from the start? I sure hope not, considering this is the marriage combination I'm living with. I'll tell you honestly, it's been tough. But I'm here to testify that no matter how hard I tried—and believe me, I tried hard—I never succeeded in changing my husband. None of the self-improvement programs I developed for *his* self did a drop of good. I tried it all: books, audiocassettes, videos, seminars, training programs, Bible studies, small groups, you name it. I pushed and prodded. The more I pushed, the more he resisted.

When I finally began to understand the temperaments, when I finally accepted him and began trying to meet *his* emotional needs rather than trying to get him to meet mine, I saw remarkable progress in our marriage. Remarkable changes. I trust and pray it will be the same for you. Two resources that have been particularly helpful to me are *The Excellent Wife* by Martha Peace and *The Power of a Praying Wife* by Stormie Omartian. There's so much you can learn from each other; don't settle for second best.

14

How the Peaceful Wife Smothers Her Honey

PEACEFUL WIFE + POPULAR HUSBAND

If I were picking a wife, I'd pick a Peaceful wife. The truth is, she is by far the easiest temperament to live with. However, she does have some faults, in particular her tendency to smother the ones she loves. Generally speaking, this is a very harmonious marriage, especially if the wife is content to play the background role while her husband uses his personality to win friends and influence people. If he lands in a "people" position, like sales, he'll be able to bring home the bacon, which she will quietly, slowly fry up in the pan. That slow business could be a problem for the fast-moving Popular husband, who may get annoyed that she can't keep pace. In particular, he wants their house to be the center of the action: Super Bowl parties, company picnics, and the like. He wants to drag home a dozen basketball buddies and have her spring into action with refreshments. Since she doesn't do well with surprises—and she definitely doesn't "do" springing motions—he may get frustrated with her lack of spontaneity and enthusiasm. One of my best friends is the Peaceful type, and she is so slow-moving, even my Peaceful husband says it gets on his nerves.

Since both the Popular husband and the Peaceful wife avoid work, their house will never be the neighborhood showcase. Then again, they probably won't care!

Warning to Peaceful wives: We've had a warning for each of the wives, so even though you're a sweet lady, we'll issue one. You create selfish, dependent husbands who become a burden to you in your old age. And when you are gone, they are incapable of caring for themselves and become a burden to their family. What's more, *they know* they are a burden, and feelings of uselessness depress and overwhelm them. Stand by your man, sure, but don't let him stand on you. Let him stand on his own two feet or he may forget how.

PEACEFUL WIFE + PERFECT HUSBAND

These two may conflict because the Perfect husband wants the perfect house and she just doesn't have the energy or initiative to create and maintain "house beautiful." As a rule, she avoids extra work whenever possible, whereas he thinks the extra mile is the starting point. If he wants to impress clients or cohorts with beautifully arranged dinner parties, he'd better be prepared to shell out money for a caterer. When his drive for perfection comes up against her brick wall of indifference, deafening silence can result.

This couple may also become completely isolated, because both are introverts and because both of them can wield the silent treatment like a deadly weapon. This couple can live together in virtual silence for fifty years. Their marriage is dead, but they won't do anything about it.

I recently stayed in the home of a Peaceful wife and Perfect husband. Within an hour of my arrival, I realized that this was *not* her idea. The husband, who was actually Perfect-Powerful, was the chairman of the elder board of the church at which I was conducting a weekend retreat. Without consulting his wife, he had volunteered her to play hostess for the weekend. I'm sure he assumed she would muster her energy and rise to the occasion. She didn't. He was a successful executive with a major corporation and had provided her with a huge mansion, which she had obviously neglected over the years. The guest room was run down. There was nothing in the guest bath: no soap, no shampoo, no towels, nothing. When I awoke in the morning, there was nothing to eat and the hostess slept right through the first session of the retreat. She showed up around lunch, still looking like she'd just awakened.

Prior to my departure, he pulled me aside for a private conversation. (His wife had gone directly back to bed after the last session of the retreat.) We talked for some time, and I was deeply moved by his love for God and his concern for spiritual things. With tears in his eyes, he asked what to do about his wife. "She just doesn't seem to care about spiritual things. I had really hoped this weekend would give her the jump-start she needs. I try not to say anything, but I worry about her. All she does is sit in front of the television all day. She never wants to get involved at the church, never wants to learn anything new. She's a Christian but she just doesn't seem to care."

I could sense his disappointment and encouraged him to pray for his wife. The truth is, unless she makes a decision to rouse herself from her slumber, the marriage will continue to be a deep disappointment to them both. But it doesn't have to be that way. My friend Terre and her husband have been happily married for years. She shares her secret:

> We're both rather subdued so there isn't a lot of open conflict in our marriage. There is *one* thing that really gets on my husband's nerves, though: little mistakes and accidents that just happen in the course of everyday life. The perfectionist in him just can't abide them because, as he says, these things wouldn't happen if people would just *think* about what they're doing. Corny as it sounds, he gets especially upset over spilled milk! If anybody spills their milk, Steve literally jumps out of his chair trying to catch the upset glass. Then he turns on the offender and exhorts them to "THINK! Just THINK about what your hands are doing!" I usually just sit there and say something consoling like, "Oops, there goes another one."
>
> One day, after yet another spill, Steve sat down and moaned, "How many times do I have to go through this?" To which I muttered, "Until you get it right, I guess." Suddenly his perfectionist personality had a new angle to work on. These days, when somebody spills

their milk he starts to jump, then forces himself to let it go. You can almost see the gears going around in his head thinking, "I must get this right!" After it finally registers with me that there is milk running all over the table and onto the floor, I'll get up and clean it. Order is restored. Peace reigns and life goes on. We're learning!

PEACEFUL WIFE + POWERFUL HUSBAND

This is the way all couples are supposed to be, right? The husband is clearly in charge as the head of the household. He goes off to corporate America and makes bundles of money. Or he launches his own wildly successful company and makes even more money. He thinks fast and looks sharp. She is content to stay in the background, quietly applauding his many achievements. She is perfectly content to submit to his every whim, because, frankly, it's a whole lot easier than thinking for herself. She goes along with whatever he plans, because it spares her from putting forth any effort.

Provided he's content to do all the work and she's content to hold on for the ride, this couple will enjoy their quintessential marriage. Problems can develop if he wakes up one morning and says, "Wait a minute. I do all the work, all the thinking, everything. This woman is nothing but dead weight. She contributes nothing, accomplishes nothing. I might just as well toss her overboard." And boom, she's gone without a second thought. On the other hand, she may get tired of him walking all over her and treating her like a piece of furniture. She may just rise up and demand a little R-E-S-P-E-C-T, which he is unlikely to give. He only respects accomplishments, and the Peaceful wife is not big on accomplishments. She may just walk out on him after twenty-five years of being pushed around, and if she does, she'll never look back.

To avoid either of those unfortunate scenarios, the Powerful husband needs to respect his wife for her people skills. It may be helpful for her to delicately point out that everyone likes her and virtually no one likes him! And she, in turn, should try to demonstrate a little initiative from time to time, just to show her husband that she's still alive and kicking.

PEACEFUL WIFE + PEACEFUL HUSBAND

Ah, picture Mr. and Mrs. Peaceful, sitting in their lazy old rocking chairs, watching life go by. The truth is, these two easy-going people will probably get along just beautifully: no confrontation, conflict, or crisis. So what's the problem? Well, there's not much excitement, either. They may just bore each other to death! They'll also have a tough time getting anything accomplished, so let's hope they inherit enough money to live on. If not, their financial woes will present an ongoing problem. They will have difficulty making decisions because neither one wants to impose his opinion on the other. But, hey, I know plenty of couples who wish they had such problems!

Possible areas of conflict may emerge because of their secondary temperaments. One partner will probably be Peaceful-Perfect while the other is Peaceful-Popular. In that scenario, the conflicts between the Perfect and Popular temperaments will emerge (see descriptions above), although their overriding desire for peace should enable them to keep their cool.

Part 4

Understand Your Children

15

The Temperaments
in Your Children

Hopefully, by now you've gained a solid grasp of what the temperaments look like in action among *grown-ups*. But let's face it, we moms spend most of our time with kids. Can understanding the temperaments prove helpful for us in our role as mothers? You better believe it! In the next four chapters, we're going to sneak a peek into cradles, wander around playgrounds, and listen in on teen phone calls—all with a view to providing you with a powerful parenting tool.

To get us started, take a moment to study the following charts.[1] The charts cover three phases: baby (from birth to two years), child (from two to twelve), and teen (from thirteen up).

The first chart, Understanding Your Baby, compares and contrasts the four temperaments from birth onward. If you are beyond the baby stage, you can glance through this section chuckling, exclaiming Aha!, and lamenting the fact that you didn't have this parenting tool available to you sooner. No doubt, if you reflect back far enough, you can recognize your children's temperaments from the cradle on up.

If you have a baby at home or on the way, you'll want to take a much closer look. The point here is not just to gain information about different types of babies, but rather to equip you to handle your child effectively. These charts demonstrate, in a very graphic way, why one-size-fits-all baby management strategies don't work. Some babies do great on a schedule; others don't. Some will sit quietly in a playpen for hours; others won't. So take heart, mom. If you've got a Powerful baby and a Popular toddler on your hands, don't compare yourself to a woman with two Peaceful children. But her turn will come around soon enough, don't worry! When your kids are running the entire high school, she'll be trying to get her teens unglued from the television set!

It should be fairly obvious that an outgoing, adventurous baby requires a very different home environment than a quiet, serious baby. Unfortunately, parents often try to squeeze babies into one particular mold, assuming they are—or at least *should be*—all the same. The truth is, temperament is inborn. Any mother with more than two children can testify to the validity of that statement!

Our job as mothers is not to change our babies—well, okay, we do have to change their diapers, but you know what I mean. Our job is to train them to become all God intended for them. To help them discover the unique path he has ordained for them, even before they were born. "Train a child in the way *he* should go, and when he is old he will not turn from it" (Proverbs 22:6, emphasis added). Certainly, understanding their temperaments is a terrific first step to guiding them in the right direction.

The subsequent charts follow the progression of these temperaments into the "Child Phase" from ages two to twelve and then into the "Teen Years." Here again, one glance reveals the futility of trying to conform our children into a predetermined mold. There are four distinct temperaments with an infinite variety of degrees and combinations possible. In the following four chapters, you'll find expanded information on identifying and meeting the needs of your children.

Understanding Your Baby

Popular Baby	Perfect Baby	Powerful Baby	Peaceful Baby
Bright and wide-eyed	Serious	Adventuresome	Easy-going
Curious	Quiet	Energetic	Undemanding
Gurgles and coos	Likes a schedule	Outgoing	Happy

Wants company	Looks sad	Precocious	Adjustable
Shows off	Cries easily	Born leader	Slow
Responsive	Clings	Strong-willed	Shy
Screams for attention		Demanding	Indifferent
Knows he is cute		Loud	
		Throws things	
		Not sleepy	

UNDERSTANDING YOUR CHILD

POPULAR CHILD	PERFECT CHILD	POWERFUL CHILD	PEACEFUL CHILD
Daring and eager	Thinks deeply	Daring and eager	Watches others
Innocent	Talented	Productive worker	Easily amused
Inventive	Musical	Sees the goal	Little trouble
Imaginative	Fantasizes	Moves quickly	Dependable
Cheerful	True friend	Self-sufficient	Lovable
Enthusiastic	Perfectionist	Competitive	Agreeable
Fun-loving	Intense	Assertive	Selfish
Chatters constantly	Dutiful	Trustworthy	Teasing
Bounces back	Responsible	Manipulative	Avoids work
Energized by people	Moody	Temper tantrums	Fearful
No follow through	Whines	Constantly going	Quietly stubborn
Disorganized	Self-conscious	Insistent	Lazy
Easily distracted	Too sensitive	Testing	Retreats to TV
Short interest span	Hears negatives	Arguing	
Emotional ups and downs	Avoids criticism	Stubborn	
Wants credit	Sees problems		
Tells fibs	Won't communicate		
Forgetful			

UNDERSTANDING YOUR TEEN

POPULAR TEEN	PERFECT TEEN	POWERFUL TEEN	PEACEFUL TEEN
Cheerleader	Good student	Aggressive	Pleasing personality
Charms others	Creative— likes research	Competent	Witty
Gets daring	Organized	Organizes well	Good listener
Joins clubs	Purposeful	Assumes leadership	Mediates problems
Popular	High standards	Problem solver	Hides emotions
Life of the party	Conscientious	Self-confident	Leads when pushed
Creative	On time	Stimulates others	Casual attitude
Wants to please	Neat and orderly	Excels in emergencies	Quietly stubborn
Apologetic	Sensitive to others	Great potential	Indecisive
Deceptive	Sweet spirit	Responsible	Unenthusiastic
Creative excuses	Thrifty	Too bossy	Too compromising
Easily led astray	Depressed	Controls parents	Unmotivated
Craves attention	Withdrawn	Knows everything	Sarcastic
Needs peer approval	Inferiority complex	Looks down on "dummies"	Uninvolved
Con artist	Inflexible	Unpopular	Procrastinates
Won't study	Suspicious of people	May become a loner	
Immature	Critical	Insulting	
Gossips	Negative attitude	Judgmental	
	Poor self-image	Unrepentant	
	Revengeful		
	Lives through friends		

16

Understand the Popular Child

THE POPULAR BABY

BRIGHT AND WIDE-EYED NEWBORN

For our first stop on the tour of cradles, let's take a peek in on the Popular baby. No need to tip-toe in, because she is wide awake — as always! If this baby's mom was banking on the little tyke sleeping eighteen hours a day, she's in for a big surprise. The Popular baby arrives on the scene with an innate eagerness to explore her world.

When you start swapping notes with the neighbor down the street who gave birth a few weeks before you, don't be surprised if you walk away feeling more than a little sorry for yourself. She reports that her baby started sleeping twelve hours a night from day one. During the day, he sits, quiet and contented, in his baby swing for hours on end.

Meanwhile, back at your house, your Popular baby never sleeps more than a couple hours at a time. I know, because I've got a Popular baby! When she turned six months old, I finally convinced my husband to let her cry it out at night. He, of course, thought that sounded like cruel and unusual punishment. To which I responded, "Is living with a seriously sleep-deprived wife any less cruel and unusual?" Well, I had him on that one!

He had to agree that my behavior has been more than a little unusual lately. So, we struck a deal. If Taraneh awoke between midnight and six A.M., I could ignore her pleas. I'm happy to report that she's learning to cry herself back to sleep.

Nevertheless, if you're hoping your baby will mysteriously turn into a sleeper, I've got a bit of bad news. It turns out that some children are non-sleepers *by temperament*. It's not that you're a bad mother who hasn't trained the baby properly. The Popular baby is just too excited about the world to waste time sleeping. She is exceptionally alert, bright-eyed, and aware of her surroundings.

CURIOUS

Speaking of surroundings, the minute the Popular baby goes mobile, LOOK OUT. These are the babies who wreak havoc in the nursery, rip apart the kitchen cabinets, and decorate the wallpaper with the contents from their diapers. If you've got a Popular baby, by all means, childproof your house! These babies are in nonstop motion, exploring everything in sight. They're fascinated by lights, Cheerios, silly faces, everything. To put it bluntly, your Popular baby's insatiable curiosity is bound to take you on the ride of your life!

WANTS COMPANY

Popular babies are eager to communicate from a very early age; they'll begin gurgling and cooing at just a few months old. This is a wonderful baby, *provided* someone will sit and keep him company during every waking hour, which wouldn't be such a problem if it weren't for characteristic number one (namely, he never sleeps). People will often ask you, "Is he a good baby?" Tough question! He's sweet, but sweet-around-the-clock is still exhausting! So the answer is "Yes, he's wonderful, but I'm awfully tired!" You may appreciate the fact that he enjoys your companionship, but at 3 A.M., you're probably not that great of a companion.

The Popular baby is not mean-spirited or ornery, he just wants company. No doubt you've heard someone described as a people-person. Well, you've got a people-baby, that's all.

SHOWS OFF

The Popular baby is a natural-born show-off. She has her little bag of tricks and the moment an audience assembles, she springs into action: squealing, laughing, flapping her arms in the air, in short—*performing*. We attended a company picnic when Taraneh was fourteen months old. She walked up and down the picnic aisles waving at everyone as if she were Miss America in all her splendor! Now, if you expect to put your little show-off in the playpen and let her entertain *herself* for an hour like "the book" says you should do, you'll be very disappointed. After all, there's no point in showing off when no one is watching. It's amazing how a little baby can figure that out after spending just a few months on the planet.

RESPONSIVE

Perhaps the most enjoyable temperament trait of the Popular baby is responsiveness. You smile, he smiles. You close your eyes, he closes his eyes. You make a funny sound, he laughs. This is very reassuring for the new mom who wants to compare her baby's progress to the charts in "the book" to make sure he can see, hear, taste, smell, and communicate according to schedule. Your Popular baby will never disappoint you on that score. He's totally attuned to his environment and responds eagerly to any stimulus.

SCREAMS FOR ATTENTION

Talkative, responsive, entertaining—wow, what a perfect baby! There is, of course, one small problem with the Popular baby. He *must* have an audience at all times. He's not one to sit idly by, watching the world passively and peacefully. He wants attention with a capital A, and he wants it around the clock. When he doesn't get it, he screams his little head off. To some extent, you can train your baby in the fine art of NOT being a spoiled brat. But the bottom line is, his temperament longs for attention and that will never fundamentally change (unless you crush his spirit, which is something you want to avoid at all costs). Again, the Popular baby isn't bad, just time-consuming.

KNOWS HE OR SHE IS CUTE

I hate to brag but I've established a tradition of telling my readers the whole truth about my life. So here goes: My baby, Taraneh, is the cutest, most adorable baby in all the world. Especially according to Taraneh. It's hard to explain how I know this, but I get a clear sense that she *knows she's cute!* During the baby and toddler phase, this is a somewhat endearing quality, but it needs to be handled properly. A teenager or adult who "knows she's cute" is not the least bit endearing. Haven't you met a few?

THE POPULAR CHILD

DARING AND EAGER

Picture the Popular child on a playground at about six years old. The first thing you notice is that he's in perpetual motion, like a tornado destroying everything in his wake. When this kid arrives on the playground, everyone knows it. Within minutes, he'll have introduced himself to the other kids, learned everyone's age, and established himself as the center of the day's action.

The second thing you'll notice is that he's *constantly pushing the limits*. He'll not only swing on the swings, he'll try to see if he can make the swing go up and over the bars. He won't be content to climb the monkey bars, he'll have to try it one-handed or upside down with one leg. This is amusing unless of course, you happen to be the ever-cautious Perfect type, in which case you can expect this eager little boy to subtract at least ten years from your life expectancy.

INVENTIVE AND IMAGINATIVE

The Popular child not only has imaginary friends, he invents entire imaginary worlds. Popular boys will build giant cities filled with exciting characters. Popular girls will carry on entire conversations between ten of their Barbie dolls, using a different voice for each. My daughter Leah, who has strong Popular characteristics, continues to amaze me with her skits and puppet shows. Everyone who meets her can plainly see she has a flair for the stage. If I had a dollar for everyone who told me she's going to be an actress, I could pay for acting school!

I recently overheard Leah explaining to an adult that she was a children's author, and proceeded to describe her latest writing project in great detail. The other day, she took out a piece of paper and wrote "LEAH'S BOOK" across the top of the page. With her vivid imagination (combined with her Powerful child determination), I have no doubt that book will become a reality.

CHEERFUL, ENTHUSIASTIC, AND FUN-LOVING

You can ask the Popular child, "Do you want to play wash the dishes with Mommy?" Provided you're convincing enough in your attempt to make it sound like fun, she'll shout "Hip, hip, hooray!" Before you know it, she'll be up to her eyebrows in dish soap and having a grand old time.

The Popular child's overriding motivation in life is to have fun. Rather than being frustrated by it, use that characteristic to your advantage. If mom is enthusiastic about cleaning and organizing, you can even overcome the Popular child's greatest weakness—namely, keeping his room in order. Make it seem fun and you can get him to do virtually anything. My friend Jill has invented several clean-up games including "Race to the Finish" where they try to see how quickly they can clean the room. Or they quickly divide the toys into two piles and see who can put their pile away faster. The other game is "Mr. Inspector," where mom puts on her inspector's hat and comes to make sure the room is neat and tidy. If it is, Mr. Inspector often has a reward hiding in his hat.

Of course, kids also need to understand that life isn't always fun. But more often, moms need to understand it *can* be fun. Look for balance.

The Popular child is eternally cheerful. He skips around singing Zip-a-dee-doo-da all the day long. The entire world can come crashing down around him, and he'd still smile and sing. What a joy to be around a child like that!

CHATTERS CONSTANTLY

Of course if you asked the Popular child's *mother* if raising him is pure joy, she'll probably admit that his constant exuberance occasionally gets on her nerves. The Popular child chatters constantly and we do mean *constantly*. This may not sound like a huge weakness, but many mothers of Popular children would give anything for even a moment of silence. Imagine the poor Perfect mom who longs for solitude with this little tyke underfoot singing Zip-a-dee-doo-dah twenty-four hours a day. Or imagine the Peaceful mom who gets so bone-tired and longs for an afternoon nap. Do you think this little chatterbox is gonna keep quiet while mommy gets some shut-eye? I don't think so! Just last night, my Peaceful husband (who lives with four Popular females) was complaining about our constant chattering at the dinner table: "I wanted to tell you about my day at work, but I can't get a word in edgewise!"

POOR FOLLOW-THROUGH

If you give an assignment to your Popular child, you can be sure of one thing: unless you personally follow up and make sure the job is done properly, it probably won't be. Even when he has the very best intentions, the Popular child is terrible at follow-through. Again, it's not that he is consciously trying to be disobedient, but rather than he is easily distracted. You send him to feed the dog and along the way, he bumps into his big brother and starts telling him about the day's events. Next thing you know, a neighborhood friend stops by looking for someone to play with. Guess what? Poor Fido is left starving.

One helpful tool we've found is the Choreganizer (1–800–225–5259). It's a set of six laminated chore charts and about fifty laminated chore cards. Each morning, I insert several chore cards in each of the children's charts. After they complete (that's the key: *after they complete*) each chore, they transfer the card to a little storage pocket at the bottom of their chart. At the end of the day, dad or mom checks the charts to ensure that all the work was finished. The children receive chore dollars for each completed item. We take away chore dollars for incomplete items. This system has worked wonders in a family filled with Popular types!

SHORT INTEREST SPAN

Since the Popular child is so much fun to be around, you can expect a never-ending stream of invitations to participate in this or that extracurricular activity. Jenny wants your daughter to join gymnastics and gets her all fired up about her Olympic potential. You shell out the $35 registration fee, spend $50 on leotards, and invest another couple hundred in lessons. Pretty soon, your future Mary Lou Retton is bored stiff.

Then along comes dancing lessons. She vows to dance her way through college and you're roped into another round of lessons.

Then it's soccer. Then it's Girl Scouts. Then, then, then.

If you're one of those parents who earnestly wants your child to excel in a particular area, the Popular child will probably frustrate you left and right. She just can't seem to stick with anything long enough to get past the basics. You can encourage more fortitude and stick-to-it-iveness and you should. However, it's quite likely that your Popular child will struggle against a short attention span throughout his or her life.

EMOTIONAL UPS AND DOWNS

Day One: Life is great! I'm the most popular kid in the history of the school.

Day Two: Life is horrible! I don't have a single friend in the entire world.

Sound familiar?

If so, you've definitely got a Popular child on your hands. You may wonder if seven-year-olds really *can* suffer from PMS. They can't, but they can sure take the family for a ride as they run the roller-coaster gamut of emotions each day. The Popular child's emotions remind me of a joke we used to crack about New Jersey's weather. "If you don't like it, wait a minute." Unlike the Perfect child who can get depressed for long periods of time, the Popular child quickly bounces back from life's disappointments and heartaches.

He may have struck out in the last inning with three men on base in the championship game and you think he's scarred for life. He's holed up in his bedroom, vowing never to show his face in public again. Then the phone rings. There's a party at Bobby's house. Before you can say, "It's only a game, son," he'll be out the door humming, "Take Me Out to the Ball Game," cracking jokes about the stupid game that was "no big deal" anyway. Up, down, up, down. And so it goes. Just wait till high school!

DISORGANIZED

When you combine the Popular child's drive to have fun with his short interest span and lack of follow-through, you've got a formula for disorganization. You've got the bedroom that legends are made of and where diseases are bred. Here again, the wise parent will accept the fact that this child is not naturally organized. He is never going to find delight in color-coding his books or organizing his toy shelf in size order, like the Perfect child. However, if you can train him into an organizational routine, you will save him untold hassle and heartache later in life. (See the information above on the Choreganizer.)

FIBS

Because the Popular child lives for the moment, they will say whatever seems expedient for the moment, even if it's not true. If they get caught, they'll usually try to charm their way out of it or declare, "I was just kidding!" Well, this tendency to tell little white lies or fibs is no joking matter. It's certainly not cute. Reign it in now, before it turns into wholesale lying in the teen years. The Bible says, "The LORD detests lying lips, but he delights in men who are truthful" (Proverbs 12:22). You might make a habit of calmly asking, "Is that *exactly* what happened?" or "Is there anything else I should know?" or "Is there anything else you'd like to tell me?" Then, obviously, if you catch the child red-handed, there need to be serious consequences.

FORGETFUL

One of the Popular child's favorite fibs—in fact, one of her favorite all-around excuses is "I forgot." We heard this so much from our daughters that we established "forgetting" as an act of disobedience in its own right. Our children need to respect us enough that they make it a point to remember. So, for example, if we give one of our girls a job to do and she claims she forgot, we simply remind her that remembering what mom and dad tell you to do is Job #1! It's not an excuse at all. Don't let your children become little con artists.

THE POPULAR TEEN

POPULAR

Now your little shining star really comes into his or her own. Your Popular daughter will be the Homecoming Queen and Miss Congeniality all rolled into one. Your Popular son will be the star of the school play. Phones ringing around the clock, gifts from various admirers arriving left and right, cars squealing up and down the street—such is life when you've got a Popular teenager in the house. Smart parents will open their home and make it the center of the action for the local teen crowd. That's what we've tried to do.

JOINS CLUBS

There's not a club in the high school that a Popular teen won't join. I must have belonged to about fifty of them, from the women's liberation club to the foreign language club, and every club in between. Now that I'm approaching my twentieth class reunion, it's time to come clean: One of my chief motivations in joining all these clubs was to have my picture splattered all over the yearbook. Don't laugh, it worked! Here's Donna in the chess club, looking intellectual. Here's Donna in the snowboarding club, looking athletic. Here's Donna . . . Well, you get the picture. (Pardon the pun!)

As mentioned under the Popular child, your teen will probably continue to have a short attention span, which will incline him to jump from activity to activity. To encourage more fortitude and the development of real skill in a few particular area, you might want to limit how many clubs he can join. The objective is not to spoil his fun, but to help him get the most benefit and enjoyment out of the clubs he does join.

CHARMING

As you surely know by now, the Popular type isn't exactly big on work. Unfortunately, school is just bursting with work. Not to fear, the Popular teen refines work avoidance to an art form. (Boy, have I seen this trait!) They'll lie awake at night, but not doing homework. Oh no! They lie awake dreaming up ways to *get out of* doing homework—or work of any kind. They are so charming, they get away with doing the absolute bare minimum required and still land on the Honor Roll. They won't make straight A's, but they usually pull out mostly A's and Bs, because the teachers like them too much to label them average. Unfortunately, there's a downside to all this charm, which we shall discuss in a moment.

WANTS TO PLEASE

Perhaps the most winsome quality of the Popular teen is their earnest desire to please their parents. They so much want you to be proud of them, mom! If you'll reward their efforts with the attention, approval, affection, and acceptance they yearn for, you may save them from untold heartache. However, if they realize you are impossible to please, they'll give up. Instead, they'll focus on pleasing their peers and the beginning of sorrows will be at hand.

DECEPTIVE

The Popular teen has some extremely dangerous weaknesses that you absolutely must face. In fact, they are often in the greatest danger of involvement with drugs, alcohol, and sexual promiscuity because of their strong need for peer approval. What makes them especially vulnerable is their ability to deceive mom and dad about what's really going on. They'll smile in your face and convince you that everything's okay. And they are so persuasive, you'll end up feeling guilty for ever doubting them. The truth is, they are master swindlers and con artists when they set their mind to it. They can use their incredible charm to completely dupe their parents.

When my husband and I were active in youth ministry, we saw this happen time and time again. We would have teens admit to us they were sexually active, involved with drinking alcohol, and experimenting with drugs. Meanwhile, their parents would be naively proclaiming, "Thank God, our children would *never* do anything like that." It was actually very sad. Don't be paranoid and don't subject your teen to a twenty-four-hour-a-day Spanish Inquisition, but be alert to their deceptive tendencies. Believe the evidence, no matter how creative and convincing they are at explaining it away.

Nikki used to come home from school every day with tales of her classmate John's outrageous behavior. He shaved his head and hung out with a crowd of skinheads (that is, violent white supremacists). He tormented the bus driver and the one black student on the bus. He openly smoked marijuana and bragged about dealing drugs. One of John's neighbors told me she frequently overheard him and his friends in his backyard, spewing profanities and trying to top each other with tales of their weekend escapades. One day, I asked John's mother how he was doing and she began to regale me with stories of what a great kid he was and how they'd never had a drop of trouble with him. I've often thought of telling her what I know, but since she's a Popular mom herself, I don't think she'd believe me anyway. (Remember, the Popular mother often denies the truth about her children.)

Don't be deceived, parents of the Popular teen. Open your eyes and admit the truth!

EASILY LED ASTRAY

Here's the root of the Popular teen's problem. Because he craves attention and thrives on peer approval, he is notoriously easy to lead astray. As a result, he'll do virtually anything to gain it. The main reason we decided to take our teenager, Nikki, out of public school was this temperament weakness. Although your teen will resist you, be absolutely vigilant in monitoring his friends. Much diplomacy is needed here. When Nikki moved in with us, we casually (okay, perhaps not so casually) mentioned the kids in the youth group who met with our approval. Needless to say, she avoided them like the plague. Teens don't want to feel like their friends are handpicked by mom and dad. In fact, they'll often deliberately pal around with a particular kid just because mom and dad disapprove.

We were absolutely appalled at the friends Nikki brought home from school during her first year with us. We tried to be polite, but you could take one look at the kids and see they were nothing but trouble. (Some books you *can* judge by the cover.) Then we started learning the facts: arrests for shoplifting, joy riding in stolen cars, running away from home, and sexual promiscuity. I remember saying to her on one occasion, "Can't you find even one friend who doesn't have a juvenile record?"

Our solution has been encouraging Nikki to invite her friends to our house. She can have anyone she wants as often as she wants. Last Friday, she had a slumber party with four girls. Tonight, we're having a surprise birthday slumber party. As we spend time with these girls, Nikki sees with her own eyes that they don't fit our lifestyle or standards. We don't have to say anything. The contrast is obvious. Besides, how much trouble can they get into with Cameron a/k/a Hector Protector hovering over them?

Gradually, Nikki has found a new circle of wonderful, godly teens. When she invites them to our home, there are no tales of juvenile mischief. What a relief! We are confident that these girls are leading each other in the right direction. So, if you have a teen being led astray by the wrong friends, persevere. Pray that God will bring new friends to build your teen up, not tear him or her down.

WON'T STUDY

The Popular teen will continually amaze her parents by her aversion to studying. This kid will do *anything* but schoolwork. My Popular teen is no exception. She'll bake me little treats, write me encouraging notes, offer to baby-sit, even clean her room—imagine that! *Anything* but her schoolwork. If I'm not careful, she'll graduate from homeschool a total ignoramus. This past summer, when our teenager was on a mission trip to Africa, my thirteen-year-old Popular niece came to stay with us to be homeschooled. Believe it or not, she used the exact same study-avoidance strategies! Right down to baking goodies and writing me letters! Amazing!

GOSSIPS

Gossip gets attention. And for the moment when you're "spilling the goods" it brings approval. Unfortunately, it also gets you in plenty of hot water. You can plead with your Popular teen not to do it and give her a lecture about its evils, but five minutes later, you'll overhear her on the phone, back in the gossip game. Of course, be careful not to use real-life examples when discussing the evils of gossip. About a year ago, I overheard Nikki and Friend #1 in the living room, gossiping about Friend #2. I launched into a lecture about the perils of gossip which led to a lecture on the perils of bad friends, which deteriorated into all three of us gossiping about Friend #2. Lo and behold, a few days later, the *mother* of Friend #2 called to give me a piece of her mind. It seems Friend #1 promptly reported every word we said to Friend #2's family and it all began with a lecture *against* gossip.

WHAT YOUR POPULAR CHILD NEEDS MOST FROM YOU

We've already discussed the emotional needs of the Popular temperament, but just to recap, they include attention, approval, affection, and acceptance. Your Popular children need lots of people around and they enjoy staying active. Remember, their overriding goal in life is to have FUN. They are lousy at detail work and just can't stand dull tasks or routines. All kids need to perform chores and household responsibilities, but if you can make them fun and switch them around a bunch, your Popular child will perform better. Try blasting some upbeat music and acting like lunatics while you clean—that's what we do!

The Popular mom should get along quite well with the Popular child, provided she remembers to share the spotlight and occasionally draws a line in the sand. They won't get much work done (which will drive the Perfect types around them crazy), but they should have a very harmonious mother-child relationship.

The Perfect mom needs to use great caution in raising a Popular child. Realize that your child will never be a perfectionist and will never perform up to your lofty ideals. Although the noise will drive you crazy, encourage your Popular child to bring their friends home, and don't make a fuss when they destroy your perfect house. If you constantly criticize your child or with-hold your approval until she "gets it right" you will drive her away from you. She will get her needs met by her peers, and you won't like the results. Be careful!

The Powerful mom will revel in the popularity and personal success of the Popular child. However, if you try to bring the Pop-ular child under your total control, he'll do whatever it takes to gain freedom. Be extra sensitive to your child's need for affec-tion. My husband constantly tells me I'm not affectionate enough with our three girls, who all have strong Popular traits. If I don't give them affection, they'll fall prey to the first fast-talking guy in a Camero who tells them they are pretty. I don't want that to happen to my girls, and you don't want it to happen to yours! The other danger is setting lofty goals that your Popular child doesn't have the inclination or drive to pursue. You thrive on accomplishments, but they thrive on relationships. Don't try to remake them to fit your image of success.

God help the Peaceful mom trying to keep pace with a Pop-ular child! Although it doesn't come naturally to you, try to drum up some enthusiasm for your child's antics. I know how much you love peace and relaxation, but you'll have to wait until your retirement years to get it. On the other hand, don't allow your Popular child to keep you forever on the run. Here's how Annie Chapman puts it in her book, *Smart Women Keep It Simple*:

> Children need to know they can't do it all. This, of course, flies in the face of everything America stands for, but I don't care. Kids live stressed, harried lives, hooked on the adrenaline of over-achievement because we don't believe they can make it to adulthood without Spanish classes and Art Appreciation and soccer and Library Story Hour and a track meet and kiddie computer class.
>
> We've got to help our kids slow down and learn to live. There are sandpiles to dig in, bicycles to ride, snow forts to construct, and (gasp!) maybe even books to read.
>
> Mothering without being smothered means we *limit what we're willing to do* for our children. It is not in a child's best interest to have a mature, capable adult at

his beck and call twenty-four hours a day, waiting to feed him his favorite foods, then clean up his messes, entertain him when he's bored, and pacify him when he's cranky. We're mothers, not handmaidens to royalty.[1]

Wonderfully said and great advice to all moms of Popular kids—and every other kind of kid!

BIBLE VERSES FOR THE POPULAR CHILD

Although you need to resist the temptation to preach to your Popular child, you can certainly encourage him or her to ponder Scripture passages that address areas of need, including the following:

A righteous man is cautious in friendship. (Proverbs 12:26)

Do not be misled: "Bad company corrupts good character." (1 Corinthians 15:33)

A gossip betrays a confidence, but a trustworthy man keeps a secret. (Proverbs 11:13)

A gossip betrays a confidence; so avoid a man who talks too much. (Proverbs 20:19)

Like a city whose walls are broken down is a man who lacks self-control. (Proverbs 25:28)

My dear brothers, take note of this: Everyone should be quick to listen, slow to speak and slow to become angry, for man's anger does not bring about the righteous life God desires." (James 1:19)

17

Understand the Perfect Child

SERIOUS AND QUIET

As I began exploring temperaments from birth, it was so interesting for me to talk with my mom about how different her babies were. Her first four children each fell into a different temperament category, in the following order: Powerful, Popular, Perfect, and Peaceful. (God knew she needed a break on number four!) She said one of her strongest impressions of her third baby, my Perfect sister Nancy, was how serious she seemed, even as a baby.

"She was a pleasant enough baby," she recalls, "but very shy and reserved. It still stands out in my mind all these years later, because she was so different from my first two babies." Because of the Perfect baby's serious nature, he or she sometimes appears somewhat sad, as if to say, "I was so happy in that perfect womb environment, why'd you have to drag me into this imperfect world?"

LIKES A SCHEDULE

The other remarkable thing about Nancy was her love of schedules. "She wanted to do everything at a certain time and in

210

a certain way, every day," my mother recalls. "And it wasn't a schedule I put her on, she put herself on it. She would eat at the same time almost down to the minute. She wanted to sleep exactly the same time every day to the point where I could set the clock by her. Whether we were out or at home, it almost never varied."

I almost have to chuckle when I hear moms triumphantly announcing that they "managed to get the baby on a schedule"—and I take one look at the baby and know exactly who got whom on a schedule!

CRIES EASILY

The Perfect baby cries at the drop of a hat. But it's not the angry, demanding cry of the Powerful baby. It's a plaintive, unhappy, disappointed-with-life cry. Perhaps the surest way to spot a Perfect baby is at the door to the church nursery. They do *not* want to let go of mom. No way! They cry and raise a ruckus. They're not about to entrust themselves to imperfect strangers.

THE PERFECT CHILD

OBEDIENT

If you are looking for an obedient child, look no further. Child discipline doesn't get any easier than this: just look at them disapprovingly and they fall in line. They thrive on the security and stability that comes from knowing and following the rules. In fact, the more rules, the better they like it. They'll even make up rules for doing everything a "certain way." This is a wonderful trait for both you and your child, but do guard against becoming too self-congratulatory—you might just get a Powerful child next time! Meanwhile, enjoy your perfectly obedient little one.

PERFECTIONIST

Perfect children carefully line up their toys in size order, hang their clothing according to type and color, and keep their bedrooms perpetually neat and tidy. If you put one of their belongings away in the wrong place, they'll notice immediately. They may even get upset about it. My friend Joan recently told me about several incidents with her Perfect son, who attends kindergarten in the afternoon. "One day he came home extremely upset. Someone from the morning class had left some papers in the desk they shared. Another time he was distraught because the teacher changed their seating arrangement. He couldn't believe it. He wanted his seat back. When she insisted he had to move, he actually counted how many additional steps he had to take to get to his new seat. He was very displeased, and he made sure the teacher knew it. He was respectful, but he made his point!"

THINKS DEEPLY AND ENJOYS READING

My friend Joy recalls how she and the doctors thought their was something seriously wrong with her daughter Molly's hearing.

She was two years old and hadn't spoken a word. One day, we were sitting in the car and she suddenly piped up with a complete sentence. I literally drove off the road! From that day forward, she communicated in complete sentences. It was almost as if she waited until she could get the grammar and sentence structure *perfect* before she spoke. By the time she was three, she began reading and could write about sixty words.

Another time in the car, when she was about four, she asked me what a particular word meant and I told her we'd look it up in the dictionary when we got home. She asked what a dictionary was, and I explained it was a book full of words that told what each one meant. She didn't say anything more about it. It was late at night by the time we got home and she was already asleep, but the next morning, the minute she woke up, she came running into the kitchen jumping for joy, "Where is that book you told me about?"

Another friend of mine, also a Powerful mom, home-schools her five-year-old daughter, Hannah. She reads on a fifth-grade level, does second-grade math, writes poetry, and—get this—wakes up at 5 A.M. to write and illustrate her own books. We went to the library with this family and the little girl picked out a biography on Louisa May Alcott. Now, my daughter loves the movie *Little Women* and I thought that was saying something. Hey, it sure beats watching cartoons, right? But this little girl had not only read *Little Women* in its entirety, she was so enthralled with the literary stylings of the author, she was studying her biography. Talk about a deep thinker.

TALENTED (OFTEN MUSICAL)

The Perfect child has extraordinary talent, often in the musical area. We recently attended a violin recital featuring a five-year-old who performed an entire Mozart concerto *from memory!* Now if one of my kids so much as sang "Jesus Loves Me" at age five, they would have been strutting around like a peacock for hours afterward. This unassuming little guy simply bowed and quietly took his seat. The Perfect child assumes everyone is that talented, and later in life they are disappointed to discover that's not the case.

TRUE FRIEND

The Perfect child will not be surrounded by a cast of thousands like the Popular child, but those friendships they do form will be deep and lasting. They aren't interested in large groups or clubs, they're interested in spending time with one or two very best friends. They may even develop an imaginary best friend, whom they'll play with for hours on end. Actually, if you surround them with too many children, they'll find it physically draining. One mom reports that she found her five-year-old son taking a nap in the middle of his own birthday party!

INTENSE

Like most moms, I often compare my children to the other little tykes in the neighborhood. Now that I understand the temperaments, I realize how fruitless this enterprise really is! Well, one of my friends who has a Perfect child was constantly telling me how her four-year-old daughter worked on the computer for hours each day. I didn't understand the temperaments at the time, so I thought, "Aha! If only we bought a new computer with a CD ROM and all the latest bells and whistles, Leah wouldn't need constant playmates and baby-sitters. I'll just put her on the computer and let her work by my side in my home office." What a joke! She played with the $3,000 contraption for two days and that was the end of it.

Only the Perfect child has the intensity required to stick with a task for hours on end. This intense approach often causes them to move rather slowly. While the other kids whiz down the toy aisle, the Perfect child stands and quietly ponders. They want to choose the perfect toy and that's going to require quite a bit of analysis.

DUTIFUL AND RESPONSIBLE

My niece Amy is another classic example of a Perfect child. I remember one time visiting her when she was just three years old. I sat down to color with her and show her how much fun life could be. (She seemed way too serious for a child. I knew that couldn't be *normal,* right?) It took me a few minutes to figure out what was going on, but as I would shove a crayon back in the 64-count box, she would take it out and put it back in the "right" place. When a crayon lost its edge, she'd sharpen it right away. And if the teensiest little bit of peel or crayon residue landed on the floor, she'd pick it up, place it in the little palm of her hand and walk over to the trash can to deposit it in the *right* place. I remember thinking, "This is her idea of fun? I'd hate to be here on the off days!"

But her behavior was not only normal, it was *typical* of the Perfect child. They are dutiful, responsible, and one-hundred-percent dedicated to the task of doing things right.

MOODY

Speaking of off days, the Perfect child has plenty of 'em. They want life to be perfect and it rarely is. As a result, they fall into deep melancholy moods that can last for days or even weeks. These children are particularly hard hit by divorce, death, or other life traumas, which they experience intensely. One of my daughter Leah's little friends, Bethany, is so moody that I've actually learned to take her emotional temperature before greeting her. If all seems well, I'll give Bethany a nice smile and a warm hello. If her little black cloud is overhead, I'll greet her nicely but I won't dare smile. I used to rush up to her and start gushing about this or that, but I gradually realized she didn't appreciate my Mrs. Cheerful routine. These kids are extremely offended by what they perceive as superficial attempts to cheer them up. Before I understood that, I thought Bethany was a bit odd. Actually, she's perfectly normal *for her temperament*.

WHINES

Another distinctive about Bethany—and the rest of the Perfect kids—is her tone of voice. She rarely talks. She whines. To her, the world is filled with disappointments and crises. When other kids see the ice cream man, she sees an accident waiting to happen, or she's reminded of her cousin's neighbor's niece who was run over by an ice cream truck. When other kids see her beautiful Barbie playhouse, she sees one of Barbie's shoes was put back in the wrong place. Next thing you know, it's "Mommy, Mommy, Rachel took the shoes out and she won't put them baaaaa-ack." The incessant whining can really wear a mom down. (Unless, of course, she's a Perfect mom, in which case she'll commiserate over the lost shoe and begin whining *herself*.)

HYPER-SENSITIVE TO CRITICISM

Now, if mommy says something about the incessant whining, the child will take it as criticism. So mom has to constantly walk a fine line: if she's too flattering, the child will take it as patronizing and insulting. If she's not flattering enough, the child will take it as a backhanded insult. It's tough to say the right thing. And saying the right thing is of paramount importance, because the Perfect child will actually shut down under criticism or even perceived criticism. She will withdraw and refuse to communicate. When that happens, trying to get her to talk will be like pulling teeth.

When disciplining this child, often no more than a disapproving glance is all that's needed.

THE PERFECT TEEN

GOOD STUDENT

If it's straight A's and scholarships you're after, the Perfect teen will probably deliver beyond your wildest dreams. A possible exception may occur if he's become so discouraged with less than perfection, that he won't even try. Typically, however, these are the teens who land straight A's, perfect attendance, perfect citizenship, and every other "perfect" achievement. I remember calling them goody-two-shoes and really being annoyed with their drive for the perfect test score. I recently saw a fifteen-year-old doctor interviewed on a TV talk show, and he fit the Perfect teen profile to the tee, right down to having a love for research. In fact, he was devoting his life to researching Parkinson's disease.

ORGANIZED AND PURPOSEFUL

Perfect teens are extremely well organized, including their bedroom closets and school lockers. For them, all of life must be neat and orderly or they get extremely upset. If they have siblings, the biggest complaint you'll hear from the Perfect teen is that "so-and-so went in my room." If her sister borrows a sock, the Perfect teen will be able to tell you which one is missing and where in the sock drawer it was removed from. I remember one of my best friends in high school—Beth—kept each item of makeup on a certain part of her vanity. I'm not talking "general area" here; she knew where they belonged within a microscopic fraction of an inch. I once put a bottle of nail polish in the wrong place and she was shocked at my carelessness. She explained, in great detail, about the importance of putting the lipstick in color order and the catastrophes that might befall should they be misplaced.

CONSCIENTIOUS AND ON TIME

Perfect teens are equally conscientious about their stewardship of time. Not only because they want to do everything just right, but also because they are thoughtful and sensitive to others. They wouldn't want to keep other people waiting or inconvenience them in any way. As a result, they usually have a very sweet spirit about that. Although they are not outgoing like the Popular or Powerful teen, once their peers get to know them, they are greatly admired for their depth of character. Needless to say, they are always a hit with the teachers.

THRIFTY

They are also a big hit with thrift-shop owners! I had never even *heard* of thrift shops until that fateful day when Beth let me in on her little secret. She always had the most funky, avante garde outfits—and I mean that as the highest possible compliment. One time, she showed up at a school dance in the most adorable vintage army jacket, and I was dying to know where she bought it. She told me I'd never believe it, but if I was up for an adventure, she'd show me. A week later, she introduced me to the mysterious world of consignment. It looked like a bunch of junk to me. I wanted to turn around and walk out. But Beth Ann started picking through the piles and sure enough, she came up with a fabulous sweater for about $3. I was hooked! To this day, I love consignment shops, although I'm not nearly as savvy as my Perfect friends. They always seem to come up with better "finds" than I do. My greatest victory was a brand-new, still-had-the-tags-on-it Neiman Marcus dress that retailed for $350—I paid $35. Thanks Beth!

DEPRESSED AND WITHDRAWN

Although Beth and I had many special times together, I also remember her dark moods. She would go through long periods of deep depression when she would withdrawal from friends and even from her family. She would hide under her blankets and refuse to go to school. Although she was one of the most talented musicians in the school band, she lacked self-confidence. In fact, she had a terrible inferiority complex. She was very beautiful, but she didn't think she was thin enough. So she began starving herself. It turned into anorexia and her weight dropped below ninety pounds. Eventually, her search for the perfect body landed her in the hospital, where she was fed through intravenous tubes. It was very tragic to watch.

Now, don't panic, moms! I'm not saying all Perfect teens are doomed to anorexia, but I do believe they are the most prone, because they are most likely to be searching for the perfect body. However, Popular teens may turn to anorexia for attention. Powerful teens may become anorexic if life is out of control; in the midst of chaos, they discover that their body is the one thing they can control. Again, don't panic, but do be on guard.

SUSPICIOUS OF PEOPLE

When I tried to tell Beth that she was thin enough, she didn't believe me. The Perfect teen is very suspicious of people and is always alert to secret agendas. When I tried to convince her to eat, she would accuse me of wanting her to gain weight. This is an extreme example, of course, but don't be surprised if your Perfect teens experience similar emotions. Generally speaking, they tend to have a negative attitude toward people and toward life. Even when they present a sweet spirit outwardly, they can inwardly have a very critical spirit.

REVENGEFUL

Just as the Perfect teen does a super job of keeping track of school assignments and other responsibilities, she does a super job keeping track of who wronged her. Every careless word uttered from a Popular teen is recorded in her mind and probably even in her diary. Then she begins plotting her revenge. She may never carry out the revenge, but she'll spend hours rehearsing the verbal lashing she'd like to give all those careless cads.

WHAT YOUR PERFECT CHILD NEEDS
MOST FROM YOU

The greatest emotional needs of your Perfect children are for silence, space, security, and stability. From a very young age, they thrive on routines and schedules. That's not hard to understand, when you consider their driving motivation is to have everything perfect. They'll do quite well if you give them a place to call their own. This is especially important if they have loud, messy brothers and sisters roaming the house. You've got to give them a way of escape. Frequently assure your Perfect children that you believe in them and think they are first-rate. Help them find at least one area where they can pursue excellence—whether it's music or academics or some other specialty. They'll be much happier with themselves when they can produce something of quality that brings them satisfaction.

The Popular mom needs to be especially cautious in raising a Perfect child. Your tendency to "cheer them up" will frustrate and anger them. They can't stand trivial fun and games. Nor do they like the noisy parties and chaotic houses you so delight in. Don't try to turn your Perfect daughter into a cheerleader, and accept the fact that your Perfect son will never be the life of the party. Although you love to talk, respect their need for silence and solitude.

The Perfect mom will be absolutely delighted with her Perfect daughter. And the delight should be mutual, provided mom doesn't push too hard for perfection. In most instances, these two form a deep, lifelong friendship that few other mothers and daughters share.

The Powerful mom also must use care, otherwise she can literally crush the spirit of her sensitive Perfect child. The Powerful attitude of "get the job done and move on" and "when it's good enough, it's good enough" stands in sharp contrast to your child's desire to make everything perfect. Don't push! Let your perfect child work at his own pace, even if you consider it too slow. Learn to value excellence and consciously work to develop emotional sensitivity, realizing you tend to hurt your child's feelings without intending to.

The good ol' Peaceful mom can do an excellent job parenting the Perfect child. However, don't be surprised when your Perfect child begins pointing out how YOU don't measure up to her standards! You may be pleased as punch with your Perfect child's performance, but she'll be critical of your less-than-perfect performance. Stand firm and demand the respect that is due you as the authority figure in your home. If you do, you'll gain this child's respect and devotion.

BIBLE VERSES FOR THE PERFECT CHILD

Although you'll be tempted to believe yyour Perfect child really is perfect, remember that the Bible says all have sinned and fall short ofthe glory of God. Perhaps more than any other temperament, your child is prone to the most serious (yet socially acceptable) sin: Pride. We may euphemize pride by labelling it "confidence," but God says he hates a proud spirit. Your child's pride may also manifest itself in a judgmental and unforgiving spirit. Some verses for you to emphasize include the following:

> For by the grace given me I say to every one of you: Do not think of yourself more highly than you ought, but rather think of yourself with sober judgment, in accordance with the measure of faith God has given you. Who are you to judge someone else's servant? To his own master he stands or falls. And he will stand, for the Lord is able to make him stand. (Romans 12:3;14:4)

> There is only one Lawgiver and Judge, the one who is able to save and destroy. But you—who are you to judge your neighbor? (James 4:12)

> Bear with each other and forgive whatever grievances you may have against one another. Forgive as the Lord forgave you. And over all these virtues put on love, which binds them all together in perfect unity. Let the peace of Christ rule in your hearts, since as members of one body you were called to peace. And be thankful. (Colossians 3:13–15)

> Do not be anxious about anything, but in everything, by prayer and petition, with thanksgiving, present your requests to God. And the peace of God, which transcends all understanding, will guard your hearts and your minds in Christ Jesus. Finally, brothers, whatever is true, whatever is noble, whatever is right, whatever is pure, whatever is lovely, whatever is admirable—if anything is excellent or praiseworthy—think about such things. (Philippians 4:6–8)

18

Understand the Powerful Child

THE POWERFUL BABY

BORN LEADER

I remember the excitement and high hopes I had when my daughter Leah was born. Like all new moms, I had visions of peacefully rocking my little cherub, while instrumental hymns and lullabies serenaded her to sleep. The Perfect baby, perchance? It didn't quite work out like that. The nurses at the hospital where Leah was born had a nickname for her. They called her the "leader of the pack." I was wondering what that meant and was secretly hoping that she was showing early signs of genius. Well, that wasn't it, exactly. One of the nurses took me aside and said, "You've got a real crier on your hands."

The Powerful baby doesn't cry for attention as the Popular baby does; nor does he cry from disappointment as the Perfect baby does. Instead, he cries to control everyone around him. It's his way of exerting his presence and establishing himself as the ruler from Day One. This isn't surprising, given that his driving motivation is to control as much of the world as he possibly can! It wasn't long before several of our relatives provided Leah with another nickname: The Dictator.

You'll notice in this first section on babyhood that we don't have much nice to say about the Powerful baby. Well, there's no denying it: this is by far the toughest baby to handle. But stay tuned, there's wonderful news as the baby becomes a little boy or girl, if child training is handled properly.[1]

STRONG-WILLED AND DEMANDING

Let's be honest: we're talking about the poster baby for the International Association of Strong-Willed Children here. The Powerful baby arrives in the world with his fists clenched and an attitude the size of a professional football player. If he doesn't get exactly what he wants the instant he wants it, the Powerful baby SCREAMS. Notice I didn't say *cries,* I said *SCREAMS* at the top of his lungs. If you've got a Powerful baby, you're in for the battle of a lifetime.

We've certainly found that to be the case with our two older girls, who are both half-Powerful. These girls work over-time, inventing new ways to exert every ounce of power they can muster to control their environment. And yes, Leah was like this from birth onward. To say that she was a demanding baby would be the understatement of the century. I had been working as a youth director throughout my pregnancy and all the teenage girls couldn't wait for the baby to arrive. They were all vying for the opportunity to be the official babysitter. Then Leah arrived. After a few minutes she had them all running for cover! My mom has eight kids and twenty-two grandkids, and even *she* was running for cover! No joke!

The Powerful child only understands one time frame. NOW. Feed me NOW. Pick me up NOW. I want my diaper changed NOW. But hang in there, mom, the Powerful baby soon becomes a Powerful teen, and I think you'll be extremely pleased with the wonderful person your child has the potential to become. Believe me, I know!

ENERGETIC AND ADVENTURESOME

The Powerful baby is a bundle of energy and she is con-stantly into everything with a vengeance. She is in a hurry to get things done and she rushes headlong past all the baby mile-stones. That's the neat part where you get to brag to all your friends. Powerful babies think cribs and highchairs were created to be climbed out of. That's the part where you're glad you have health insurance coverage. Like the time Leah found out what she could do with a hanger. She scratched her cornea.

According to "the book" babies should play quietly for at least forty-five minutes each day, content to examine the toys mom and dad provide. Ha! We attempted to put Leah into "playpen time"—what a JOKE! She couldn't stand being fenced in like that. She wanted to explore the whole house. She *demanded* to explore the whole house.

The Powerful baby can be downright aggressive. Take a walk by the church nursery sometime and, invariably, you'll see a Powerful baby crawling after the other babies and sending them running for cover. At the risk of sounding sexist, Powerful baby boys tend to be particularly aggressive and can pose a health hazard to other, more docile babies.

PRECOCIOUS

Here's another upside of Powerful babies: they are often very bright. They are not necessarily the smartest (that honor is usually reserved for the Perfect babies), but they are definitely the *first to get there!* My mom often tells stories about my oldest brother, Jimmy, who could crawl at three months, walk at nine months, and carry on complete conversations before his second birthday. At the age of two, he could go gather worms (from underneath logs) for fishing, stopping to chat with the neighbors along the way. My mother was the youngest in her family and had no idea what kids were *supposed* to be able to do. They didn't have "What To Expect the First Year" back then. After she brought a few more babies into the world, she realized just how precocious her oldest was. There's no quicker creature on knees than the Powerful baby. They're in a big hurry to conquer the world and heaven help anyone or anything standing in their way!

THROWS THINGS

The Powerful temperament begins its grab for power from the high chair. They can get great big adults to bend down just by throwing a toy. "Throw the toy, Mommy jumps. Throw the toy, Mommy jumps. Hey, this is fun. I like power!" Pretty soon, Mommy gets sick of jumping. But when Mommy doesn't jump NOW, the Powerful baby throws a fit in addition to throwing the toys. Moms, stand firm and show that Powerful baby who the *real* boss is. Teach it to them now before they turn into toddlers! (Trust me on this one, ladies!)

NOT SLEEPY

The Powerful baby has no time to sleep. He is out to conquer the entire world in a matter of months. And since he is precocious, he knows the only way to conquer the world is to stay awake. "The book" says babies should sleep anywhere from sixteen to twenty hours per day. Imagine my surprise when Leah was *awake* sixteen to twenty hours per day! Even now, Leah doesn't have the slightest interest in sleep. What's exciting is that she now has all those sleepless hours to "accomplish" things, like reading books on an eighth-grade level, even though she's only seven years old. This past week, she reread the entire Felicity series of six historical fiction novels over the course of two days. She did it while the rest of the kids her age were napping!

THE POWERFUL CHILD

A FORCE TO BE RECKONED WITH

Leah was an only child for five years, but one Powerful child is the equivalent of ten Peaceful kids. Then we added twelve-year-old Nikki to the family. In the early days, Nikki was quiet and sullen around the house, and I assumed she was Peaceful or Perfect. Boy, was I wrong! When we gave her the temperament test, I couldn't believe the results. She *also* has strong Powerful traits.

When my youngest daughter, Taraneh, was only five months old, an older woman in the church turned to me and said, "Wow, this baby really wants what she wants when she wants it!" And I thought, "Oh, Lord, please help me! Not another one!" I relayed her comments to my Peaceful husband, who responded calmly,

"God is determined to force you to deal with your weaknesses. That's why he keeps sending you kids who are *just like you.*"

If you want proof that Dr. Dobson's strong-willed child has come to life in my living room, read the following message, written by my daughter, Leah (who was six at the time). She wanted to invite a friend over and I had told her, "Sure, as soon as you finish cleaning your room." Here's what she thought of that:

As if the content of the message isn't evidence enough, look very carefully at the stick figure self-portrait. Did you notice that her hands are on her hips?! That sums up the Powerful child: determined, strong-willed, hands-on-hips. I love the way Florence Littauer puts it: The Powerful child "looks out of the cradle and wonders to herself, 'How long before I take over this entire house from mother?'" [2] That's too true to be funny!

DARING AND EAGER

I need to quickly add that Powerful children have some marvelous strengths. They are brave, daring, and eager. They are the kids on the front lines, making things happen: building forts, organizing neighborhood productions, running lemonade stands and various home enterprises. When I was a child, I was always up to something new. I remember one time when the carnival came to town and my mom said I could go if I came up with the money. So I held a huge fund-raiser and earned $25 in a single day, selling everything from comic books to Barbie dolls and lemonade. Once I set a goal, I stayed focused until I achieved it. I find my girls to be the same.

Recently, we were driving through the Indian reservation near our home. It was almost 120 degrees, yet many of these families are living in unair-conditioned trailers. Seven-year-old Leah was outraged. "That's not right, Mommy. When I grow up, I'm going to become the governor or the president and get this straightened out." I looked over at her and said, "Honey, I'm sure you will. I'm sure you will." Notice that she doesn't want to be a schoolteacher or ballet dancer, she wants to run the country!

Another of her proposed projects is to defeat Satan, and this kid means business. She actually has developed a battleplan which includes converting Stephen King to Christ (long story!) and eliminating Halloween. I thought you might enjoy her self-proclaimed "book" that follows on the next page.

PRODUCTIVE WORKER

Given the proper training and encouragement, the Powerful child is an extremely productive worker. Since I was the youngest of eight, I often managed to weasel my way out of doing any household chores. But when I did set to work, look out! I was the white tornado! In particular, if I had invited a friend over, I would set a goal to get the whole house cleaned. I would throw myself into a cleaning frenzy and work like a maniac for hours at top speed. That's another characteristic of the Powerful child: they move very quickly. Although I'm still not a big fan of housework for housework's sake, if someone's coming to visit, few people can out-clean me.

One day, I decided I couldn't stand my dirty wooden baseboards for another second. I filled a bucket with hot water and some Murphy's Oil Soap and asked my daughter, Leah, what she had planned for the day. Boy, was she excited. She rolled up her sleeves and the two of us set to work. Would you believe she scrubbed those baseboards on her hands and knees for six

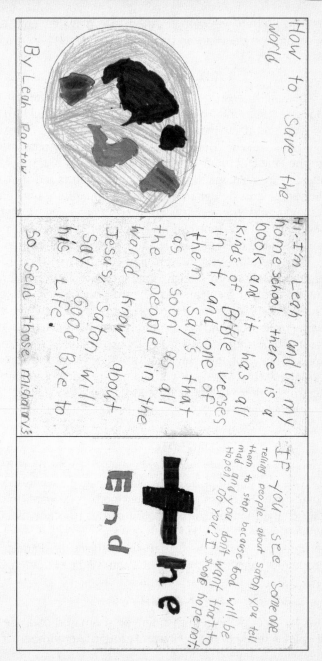

How to Save the world

By Leah Partow

Hi, I'm Leah and in my home school there is a book and it has all kinds of Bible verses in it, and one of them says that as soon as all the people in the world know about Jesus, Satan will say Good Bye to his Life. So send those missionarys

IF You see someone telling people about satan you tell them to stop because God will be mad and you don't want that to Hapen, Do you? I shood hope not

the End

hours? And when we were finished, she declared enthusiastically, "Mom, we ought to do this more often!"

SELF-SUFFICIENT

This child doesn't expect mom and dad to entertain him. He doesn't sit around waiting for mom and dad to tell him what to do next. Youth worker Jason Wrench recalls one of his family's famous stories: "Both of my parents and my older brother were [the Peaceful type]. When I was two years old, we went to a museum in Williamsburg, Virginia. They strapped me into a stroller and I quickly became restless. I apparently noticed that my six-year-old brother looked tired, because I unstrapped myself, climbed out, put *him* in the stroller, and tried to push!" These kids are extremely self-sufficient and self-motivated.

They are often very mature and capable and they excel in emergencies. My mother recalls that when my Powerful brother Jimmy was only three years old, she was working on her sewing machine and the needle ran through her fingernail and got stuck. He came over, broke the needle and helped her get her finger out of the machine. Only a Powerful child can pull off a feat like that!

As a result of their self-motivation, Powerful children are exceptionally trustworthy. If you tell them to do something, you can count on them to get the job done. You don't have to follow behind and double check.

COMPETITIVE

The Powerful child wants to win, to be the best. It's not enough for him to participate in the school play; he wants to be the star of the play. He doesn't want to play football; he wants to be the captain of the football team. When it comes to academics, he is never satisfied with an A. He has to have *the highest A in the class.* If he finds out one of his classmates (usually the Perfect type) scored a 99% when he scored a 98%, he will be extremely upset.

BOSSY

After a couple years practicing on mom and dad, the Powerful child is ready to boss *the world* around. Remember: control is their goal! They constantly tell the other kids what to do. When Leah has playmates over to play dolls, she tells them, sentence by sentence, exactly what they are supposed to say. When I suggest that she let her friends make up their own dialogue, she informs me that they don't know what to say. You see, the Powerful child doesn't think she is being bossy, she thinks she is helping the poor dummies out of a bind.

You need to work closely with your Powerful child in this area. Left unchecked, the other kids will soon get sick and tired of your kid bossing them around, and then you've got a new problem on your hand: no one wants to play with your unpopular child. We went through a period like that with Leah, during which she memorized the following slogan: "Everyone likes to boss, but no one likes to BE bossed." I carefully monitored her playtime and whenever I noticed her becoming bossy, I would just say, "Remember, Leah," and she would chime in "Everyone likes to boss, but no one likes to BE bossed." She's improved so much that her teacher reported she was one of the most popular kids in the first grade! (If you are a bit confused by the reference to a "teacher" other than mom, I've homeschooled her most of her life but she attended public school last year.)

We've also worked to find some positive outlets for Leah's innate urge to boss. For example, she loves the American Girls historical fiction novels and loves to reenact the stories. We discovered that the company actually published a theater kit, complete with four scripts and—this is the key—a director's handbook. We bought the package, and Leah is so excited to be directing this production about Felicity and the American Revolution! She has assigned everyone in the family roles to play and gives us instructions about where to stand and how to say the lines. She even sat and highlighted everyone's lines in their individual play books, to make sure no one lost their place in the dialogue. We feel this is a productive outlet for the "bossy" temperament.

BULLIES

An *unproductive outlet* for the bossy temperament is the tendency to bully. This is especially common among Powerful boys, who beat up on other kids in an effort to get things done "my way and my way NOW." If your son is a bully, deal with it. Don't listen to his constant excuses about how he was fighting the lions of injustice or defending the family honor. Even if he gets into a fistfight every week, he always seems to have a justifiable reason. Taken individually, the bully is quite convincing in defense of his actions. But when you string all the incidents together, you see a clear pattern that needs to be stopped.

TEMPER TANTRUMS

If you've ever seen a child throwing a *serious* temper tantrum, you've probably witnessed a Powerful child in action. They are the masters of the art. Again, they get a goal in mind (such as a piece of candy or a particular toy they want), and then they will do whatever it takes to achieve that goal. They learn at a very early age how to use public humiliation as a tool to manipulate their parents into giving them what they want. If you don't deal firmly with this, it will become a major battle.

This is one area where I must say we've won the victory. We decided early on that we would never give our children anything they pleaded for in any store. If it's not on the list, we're not buying it. If they see something they want, we tell them we'll consider adding it to the list for the next time we visit the store. But we certainly aren't going to buy it on the spot. As a result, our children rarely bother us in stores. If only we'd been that firm and consistent about nap times and bedtimes! If you've got a Powerful child, the only way to defuse temper tantrums is to make sure they never get rewarded. Never. Easier said than done.

INSISTENT

The reason it's so difficult to resist the Powerful child is because he is so insistent, so relentless in pursuit of his goals. If channeled properly, this can become a wonderful force for good, but it can also be dangerous. It can lead to a child who is constantly testing you, constantly pushing you to the limits to see what he can get away with. I can tell you from experience that parenting such a child becomes an exhausting ordeal.

Here's how H. Clay Trumbell puts it, referring to this tendency as "teasing":

> Many a child does not expect to get what he wants, if it is out of the ordinary line of his daily needs, unless he teases for it; therefore he counts teasing a part of his regular duty in life, as truly as "beating down" the city shopkeeper on his prices is supposed to be the duty of the shopper from the country. So, when the answer "No" comes back to him, in such a case, he meets it with the appeal, "Do let me. Oh, do!" and then he enters upon a nerve struggle for the mastery over his parents at this point, with the idea in his mind that it is a single question of who shall be most persistent in adhering to his side of the conflict. . . .
>
> Most parents give way, sooner or later, in some of these conflicts with their children. It may be that they are less determined than their children, and that they are simply tired out by the teasing. It may be that they are moved by their children's earnestness in the matter, and that they yield because of their tenderness toward the little pleaders. It may be that their first answer to the appeal is a thoughtless one, and that their fuller considering of the matter leads them to see it to be right to reverse their impulsive decision. Whatever be the parents' reason for their course in such a case, if they give a negative answer to their children's first request, and an affirmative one in response to more or less teasing on the children's part, they train their children . . . to believe that teasing is an important factor in a child's progress in life; and of course they are responsibile for their children's continuance in the habit of teasing. . . .
>
> No parent can have the truest respect of a child, while the child knows that he can tease that parent into compliance with the child's request, contrary to the parent's real or supposed conviction. For the child's sake, therefore, and also for the parent's, every child ought to be trained not to tease, and not to expect any possible advantage from teasing.[3]

The reality is, every time you let your Powerful child win one of these contests, he becomes more resistant, more argumentative, more determined to get his own way. If you really love your Powerful child and want him to achieve his full, God-given potential, help him to channel his insistent nature toward positive ends.

UNPOPULAR

If left undealt with, this insistent quality, this tendency to "tease" as Trumbell calls it, will cause your child to become very unpopular. No one wants to be friends with a child who absolutely insists on having everything go his way. No one wants to spend time with someone who wants everything his way, *right away*. And if it isn't so, he makes everyone around him miserable. As a result, he himself is often unhappy. In fact, of all the temperaments, the Powerful Type "is the least happy because it is most likely to call forth opposition to itself."[4]

THE POWERFUL TEEN

TREMENDOUS POTENTIAL

Although the Perfect teen usually has the most talent and the Popular teen has the most friends, the Powerful teen has the most potential. To borrow a phrase, they are the "most likely to succeed." The Powerful teen is a force to be reckoned with: capable, aggressive, goal-oriented. If they have a clear vision of their future—where they want to go and who they want to become—they will pursue it relentlessly. I remember a close friend of mine in high school, Robert, who was determined to go to the Naval Academy. The caption under his high school year book picture sums up his philosophy "Challenge yourself to the limit and to @#*# with everyone else." Well, we could do without the profanity, but it's certainly a classic Powerful teen slogan. They know what they want, and they won't let anyone or anything stand in their way.

YOUTH WITH A MISSION

The Powerful teen is a youth with a mission. Nikki recently entered the contest to become the 1998 *Brio* Girl (*Brio* is a magazine for teen girls published by Focus on the Family). Here's how she responded to the essay question "As a Christian teen, what is one thing you'd change about today's youth and why?"

> I'm on a mission to let teens know where their home really is. Teens are looking for security in all the wrong places: boyfriends, sex, alcohol, parents, friends, popularity, appearance, school performance. The list goes on. None of these things bring security. Believe me, I know! I grew up not knowing God's Word, surrounded by alcoholics, drug addicts, and criminals. I was neglected, and mentally and physically abused. I was left homeless at age twelve, when both of my parents went to jail. None of my relatives would take me in. I searched long and hard for a place to call home. I've lived in more than fifty places, including in cars. The search ended when I found my REAL HOME in Jesus Christ. Jesus said, "Abide in me." In the original language, abide means "settle down and make your home." I finally have a home that no one can take away from me. With the help of God and my new parents, I've finally "settled down and made my home" in Christ. I want to be the *Brio* Girl so I can share this message with as many teens as possible: you'll never find your home in anything or anyone but God.

Now if all that horrible stuff had happened to a Perfect teen, she would be too depressed to help anyone else. The Popular teen would be too busy looking for new friends to care about anyone else. The Peaceful teen would never take action because it would involve too much work. Only a Powerful teen can respond to that much adversity with a take-charge attitude and a determination to use her pain to make a difference in the world. We are so proud of Nikki, we could just burst. Out of nearly two thousand teens, she was selected as one of the top twenty finalists and was featured in the November 1997 issue of *Brio*.

Earlier this year, Nikki heard about Teen Missions International and applied to go on a short-term mission assignment to South Africa. She needed to raise five thousand dollars. At first, we hoped fifty people would just take out their checkbooks and hand over one hundred dollars. It wasn't that easy! When the money didn't just start flowing her way, Nikki decided to be a tentmaker and earn her way to Africa. She handmade thousands of cloth bookmarks, which she sold at my speeches for a minimum one-dollar donation. It was incredibly hard work, raising that much money in dollar-bill increments, but she was a teen on a mission. She did it!

ORGANIZES WELL

Although the Powerful teen is not hyper-organized like the Perfect teen, they are as organized as they need to be to achieve their goals. They are especially adept at efficiently organizing their study schedules so they invest just enough time to make the grades they need, while still pursuing other activities. Like running the entire high school, for example! During the teen years, the Powerful personality begins to assume leadership roles, providing their negative personality traits have been properly checked. Otherwise, they'll become so unpopular that even though they are the best person for the job, they will "call forth so much opposition to themselves" that they won't be selected as class president, or whatever.

Mom, you can play a vital role, here! Work with your Powerful teen. Lovingly remind him or her that "Everyone likes to boss, but no one likes to BE bossed!" At the end of this section are some Scripture passages on humility and servanthood that you should encourage your teen to study and memorize.

SELF-CONFIDENT

In the best-case scenario, the Powerful teen is a tremendous asset to his school or any organization he joins. He absolutely oozes self-confidence. While the rest of the kids stare in the mirror, agonizing over their blemishes, he travels to Washington, D.C., to meet the president. He has a natural flair for problem solving and excels in emergencies. He has a natural sense of what will work. If given a leadership role, he can do a super job of motivating and stimulating other teens to "believe and achieve." He is extremely responsible and will carry through on the commitments he makes. In short, this is a great kid! Aren't you glad you persevered through those tough baby years? Now you've got bragging rights to the max!

TOO BOSSY

The only thing standing in between the Powerful teen and his lofty goals is his bossy attitude. All of the Powerful teen's tremendous potential will achieve nothing if he constantly brings opposition to himself. As mentioned repeatedly, if you can help your teen deal with this weakness, you will have given him an incredible gift.

CONTROLS PARENTS

Another great gift you can give this teen is refusing to be controlled by him. Remember, his strongest drive is for power and control. If he can rule your house, he surely will. He'll use bullying tactics, manipulation, deception—whatever it takes to get mom and dad to fall in line with his demands. Be on guard or he'll become a very difficult adult to live with, controlling his wife and children, not to mention his coworkers and anyone else he thinks he can bully. Demand the respect due to you and, in the long run, he'll thank you for your loving firmness. Give him positive and appropriate outlets for his urge to control (put him in charge of the pets!). If you train him properly, rather than becoming a controlling bully, he'll become a self-controlled leader.

KNOW-IT-ALL

Perhaps the least endearing of the Powerful teens traits is her know-it-all attitude. All teens struggle with this to some extent, but the Powerful teen is a nightmare of knowledge! She constantly looks down on all the "dummies" in the world, and her parents top the list of stupid people. The Powerful teen hurls out insults at the speed of light. She's got a keen mind and a sharp tongue, which she uses as a weapon to decimate anyone who dares to oppose her on any point. To her, these verbal volleys are a big game. She loves debating for the sake of winning an argument. She prides herself on impressing people with her superior intellect, but in fact, all she is doing is offending and alienating people. Again, this is where mom comes in, training the teen and giving her a proper sense of her place in the universe.

UNPOPULAR

If not held in check, these negative characteristics can combine to make the Powerful teen extremely unpopular. All of his talents and leadership abilities will be passed over and the positions of influence will be awarded to less capable students. (Even if the other students are *more* capable, the Powerful teen will never admit it. He always thinks he's the smartest.) As a result of these disappointments, he may withdraw and become a loner. And that would be a terrible waste, because God created these talented teens specifically for leadership.

WHAT YOUR POWERFUL CHILD NEEDS MOST FROM YOU

The Powerful child's greatest emotional needs are appreciation for achievements and opportunities for leadership. Applaud his accomplishments and respect him as a capable person. The worst crime you could commit would be to "baby" him. Actually, a worse crime would be allowing his weaknesses to overtake and neutralize his many fine strengths. Encourage your Powerful child to participate in family decisions and to assume an appropriate leadership role in the home. One very practical thing you can do is give your child something to control: whether it's his own room, the garage, the backyard, or ideally, a pet to boss around. Whenever you give him an assignment, use the phrase "You're in charge of . . ." That'll light his fire! He also enjoys checking things off on a chore chart or checklist as each item is accomplished.

Accept that your Powerful child is never going to be interested in sleeping or napping. He wants to be active and will avoid boredom at all costs. Another thing he avoids is playing games he can't win, but if you teach him how to lose, you'll be doing him a great favor.

The Popular mom will have her hands full with the Powerful child, but she'll love bragging about his many accomplishments to all her friends. The greatest danger here is that the child will grab the reigns of power from mom. In the short run, abdication will seem like an easier path for her, but it will come home to roost soon enough. (The voice of experience speaks!)

The Perfect mom will frequently feel hurt by the harshness and insensitivity of her Powerful child. Don't take it personally, but do train him and help him to take that "edge" off of his personality.

The Powerful mom and the Powerful child will either kill each other or conquer the neighborhood together. Leah and I have nearly killed each other, now we're setting out to conquer the world. We've recently begun work on a children's book we are coauthoring, although she hasn't let me get a word in edgewise yet!

The Peaceful mom will have her hands full with the Powerful child, but you can give her the greatest gift she'll ever receive if you teach her the arts of *tact* and *diplomacy.* If she can combine your thoughtfulness and mediation skills with her natural leadership ability, she'll be a powerful force for good in this world.

BIBLE VERSES FOR THE POWERFUL CHILD

Here are some selected passages that may be of particular help, although you should encourage your child to seek out and memorize others.

> A wise son heeds his father's instruction, but a mocker does not listen to rebuke. (Proverbs 13:1)

> But the fruit of the Spirit is love, joy, peace, patience, kindness, goodness, faithfulness, gentleness and self-control. (Galatians 5:22–23)

> My dear brothers, take note of this: Everyone should be quick to listen, slow to speak and slow to become angry, for man's anger does not bring about the righteous life God desires. (James 1:19)

> A new command I give you: Love one another. As I have loved you, so you must love one another. By this all men

will know that you are my disciples, if you love one another. (John 13:34–35)

An angry man stirs up dissension, and a hot-tempered one commits many sins. (Proverbs 29:22)

A man's pride brings him low, but a man of lowly spirit gains honor. (Proverbs 29:23)

A fool gives full vent to his anger, but a wise man keeps himself under control. (Proverbs 29:11)

Young men, in the same way be submissive to those who are older. All of you, clothe yourselves with humility toward one another, because, "God opposes the proud but gives grace to the humble." Humble yourselves, therefore, under God's mighty hand, that he may lift you up in due time. (1 Peter 5:5–6)

19

Understand the Peaceful Child

THE PEACEFUL BABY

EASYGOING

Ah, to have a "low-need" baby. Can you imagine it? If you can, then perhaps you've brought a Peaceful baby into the world. She's what dreams are made of. My friend Susan has five kids and she reports that her Peaceful child, Jana, is by far the easiest to raise. "Even from birth, the difference was amazing. She would sleep contentedly for eighteen hours a day. The first night we brought her home from the hospital, she slept twelve hours through the night. She's been doing that ever since, plus she takes long naps during the day. No matter what we do or where we go, she's cool with it. My other babies were so demanding, but she doesn't demand a thing."

HAPPY

The Peaceful baby has a pleasant disposition and is quick to adjust to circumstances. Going to the grocery store? No problem. A different schedule every day of the week? No problem. Freezing cold out and you've got the baby dressed in a T-shirt? No problem. Messy diaper? No problem. Susan recalls one particular morning, when Jana was a few months old, she was lying in bed and her husband brought the baby in and put her beside Susan. The baby was smiling and just plain happy to be alive. She reached over to hug her and realized she was drenched all the way through to the bed. She opened up her diaper and discovered she also had a "mess." Yet she didn't complain. Jana would be content to sit in messy diapers all the day long; she rarely fusses unless she's overtired.

SLOW

The Peaceful baby doesn't race through the milestones. In fact, if you're looking for something to brag about, you'll probably have to brag about how well she sleeps, because that's going to be her greatest quantifiable accomplishment. They move slowly and they take their time to begin sitting up, crawling, walking, and so on. They'd rather be carried, anyway! It's less work!

One of the Peaceful children in our neighborhood will be in kindergarten this fall and yet he can barely speak. I was talking with his mother one day and she commented, "I know he could talk if he wanted to, but if he can get what he wants by pointing, he figures that's easier." There you have the quintessential Peaceful characteristic: always looking for the easy way out.

SHY

The Peaceful baby is also very shy. You take her to show her off at church and she hides her head under your arms. At first it's cute, but then you end up twisting and contorting her to try to prove she does, indeed, have two eyes and one nose. This reserved characteristic will last throughout the Peaceful person's life.

INDIFFERENT

Don't waste your money on lots of exciting toys, and don't load down the playpen with expensive playgyms filled with bells and whistles. Frankly, the Peaceful baby just isn't interested. He's perfectly content to just sit and watch the world go by. He's already figured out that it's less work to watch other people work than to actually work yourself.

THE PEACEFUL CHILD

EASILY AMUSED

It doesn't take much to amuse the Peaceful child. Joan recalls that her son Jason "would sit and play for hours on end, amusing himself with quiet games. Basically, he was content to raise himself. There was one small problem, though. I never found a punishment that fazed him. If I sent him to his room, he was perfectly content to sit and play quietly. Well, that was no punishment. So I took away the toys. So he sat and read quietly. Then I took away the books. He was in there quietly for almost an hour and I figured he'd fallen asleep. When I went to check on him, he was sitting in front of the mirror making faces at himself. What was I going to do? Take the mirror away? I had to laugh. He was just perfectly content no matter what."

Certified Personality Trainer Arlene Hall tells the story of her three-year-old nephew, Tim, who amused himself by squeezing an entire tube of toothpaste around the bathroom. When his five-year-old sister ran to report his misbehavior, he ran and hid under his bed. When his mother called out, "Come here," she heard a sweet little voice softly reply, "I'd rather not get involved, thank you." That's classic Peaceful child behavior: fleeing in the face of conflict, determined to stay as uninvolved as possible.

LITTLE TROUBLE

Joan reports that Jason was very little trouble. "One time we were going on vacation with a car full of children. The kids were all acting like lunatics, demanding this, that, or the other thing. Not Jason. He climbed into the backseat and never said a word for three solid hours. He was like that all the time. No matter where we took him, we'd put him on a chair and there he'd sit. He'd never get down or get into trouble. Wherever we put him, that's where he'd stay."

Whenever staying out of trouble constitutes less work than getting into it, you can count on the Peaceful child to peacefully cooperate.

As you can see, the Peaceful child is just plain lovable! He is so agreeable and easy to get along with. He rarely fights with his siblings and he would never dare to fight with mom or dad.

AVOIDS WORK

Now, if you're starting to think, "Hey, we oughta call this kid the Perfect child," I'd better set you straight. The Peaceful child does have some weaknesses. Chief among them is work avoidance. If she puts her clothes on inside out and backward, *even when she realizes it,* she won't go to the trouble of fixing it. Her favorite pastime is watching television because she doesn't even want to work at playing. In many cases, these kids won't shine academically. They tend to be average or below average in almost everything they undertake.

This can be extremely discouraging to parents, like the Powerful or Perfect type, who want "nothing but the best" for their kids. The Peaceful child doesn't want the best; he'd rather take a rest. One Powerful dad, who was determined that his son should follow in his footsteps as a basketball star, reports his disappointment: "Whenever the coach would put him in the game, he would stay down the end of the court, slouching and biting his fingernails, casually waiting for the game to come to him." If this dad understood the personalities, he wouldn't have been the least bit surprised. The Peaceful child will do whatever he can to avoid work. But he won't put his hands on his hips and shout, "No." Instead, these children are very sly and creative in their attempt to weasel out of work. In that sense, it's much harder to see that they are being rebellious. That quiet rebellion can foment and become a huge problem during the teen years.

On the bright side, their desire to avoid work can sometimes yield great innovation. Milly Potter, a speaker from Australia, told me about her son Nathanial who, like most Peaceful children, had *one thing* he cared about. (More about the "one thing" principle in a minute.) In his case, the one thing was fishing. Milly reports that whenever she wants to motivate him to complete his schoolwork or chores, she uses fishing as the incentive. The promises of grades or getting into a great college don't faze him; but he gets excited about fishing! At school, the kids were given an assignment to make something, anything, for a woodworking class. Nathaniel made a "trolley" with wheels so that he could push his fishing box rather than carry it! If necessity is the mother of invention, the desire to avoid work is often the father!

TEASING

The Peaceful child often gets a big kick out of "firing up the troops" in a negative sense. He is a master at playing the role of instigator. The Peaceful child quietly teases his siblings, pressing all the right (or wrong) buttons, then when they react like a band of lunatics, he sits quietly and smugly, rejoicing in his ability to get a rise out of others with so little effort. Unfortunately, his brothers and sisters often make it too easy for him by falling for his bait.

One of his favorite games is "The last word in." I can remember one of my Peaceful siblings frequently playing this game. We'd be debating about some childish controversy, and the Powerful and Popular children would be passionately arguing our side of the case. He'd sit in absolute silence, wait for a lull in the conflict, then quietly toss out some inflammatory remark. Off we'd go again. Just when the controversy seemed to abate, he'd toss out another remark. In exasperation, one of us would yell, "Okay, that's enough. Just end it." But he never would; he always had to have the last word in.

Often my mother would walk in, assuming that the kids making the most noise were the guilty parties. I'm sure there was enough guilt to go around, but I think the one who instigated the trouble deserves a harsher punishment. A good verse to remind this child of is Proverbs 6:19, which includes among the seven things God *hates,* "a man who stirs up dissension among brothers." That's pretty serious business. Be alert, mom. Just because your Peaceful child isn't making as much noise as his siblings doesn't necessarily mean he's not making trouble. Consider establishing consequences for the crime of "needling your brothers and sisters."

FEARFUL

Even though he might like to audition for the school play, he won't because he's afraid he won't get the part. He'd like to try out for baseball, but what if he doesn't make the team? He'd like to make friends with the new kids down the street, but what if they don't like him? The fear of rejection or failure can immobilize this child to the point that he drops out of life before his life has even begun.

Don't be like the father of one of my childhood friends who decided to teach his son to swim by throwing him into the river. That just intensified his fear of water. Don't toss your child into overwhelming situations, but don't let him constantly languish on the sidelines, either. Look for balance. Whenever possible, walk with him through the scary places: offer to coach him in dramatics and to be there supporting him at the audition. Or recruit dad to help refine his batting skills *before* the big day. Offer to meet the new mom and have her bring the kids over to your house. You may be thinking, "But shouldn't I make this kid stand on his own two feet?" Yes, you should, but in these early years, stand close by. Help him to overcome his fears; don't intensify them with an insensitive approach. Remember that overcoming fears is hard work, and work is something this child would rather avoid. Therefore, you'll have to provide loving motivation to help him discern why waging war with the "stuff that goes bump in the night" is worth his while. And even if he doesn't win the part, make the team, or befriend the new kids on the block, reassure him that you think he's terrific anyway. Consciously build his self-worth and he'll grow into a wonderful, capable adult.

THE PEACEFUL TEEN

PLEASING PERSONALITY

Although the Peaceful teen is not very outgoing, he will gradually build quite a following of devoted friends. He has a very pleasing personality and because he never loses any friends, he'll often end high school with more friends than the so-called Popular kid who has alienated his band of followers with his selfish and immature antics. Incidentally, don't be surprised if your Peaceful teen keeps for life the friends he makes during these years.

I often talk with women who are concerned about their Peaceful son's career prospects. In many cases, they worry needlessly. Although the climb may be a bit slower, the Peaceful temperament can go far on the strength of his pleasing personality.

There's just something about this guy that makes others *want to help him*. It's almost as if they look at him and say, "What a nice guy, but he might not make it if I don't help out. I'd better roll up my sleeves and pitch in."

One of my fellow speakers, Kathleen, reports that her son, Craig, virtually coasted all the way to the U.S. Naval Academy.

> He's incredibly smart, so "acing" his tests was never a problem. But homework? That was another story! Fortunately for him, everybody liked him so much that his friends did his homework for him. He didn't want to go to the trouble of reading, so he studied Cliff notes and listened to the books on tape. He didn't make the decision to apply to the Academy until late in his senior year. He should have begun the process in his junior year. He found another kid at school who was also applying and she told him exactly what to do, step-by-step, so he didn't have to do any research on his own. He kept procrastinating, so finally I did all the paperwork for him. We were concerned about how well he'd survive the hazing during his year as a Pleb, but we shouldn't have worried. They could yell at him all they wanted; nothing fazes him. He couldn't care less.

How's he doing at the Academy? Fabulously. Everybody likes him so much—and admires his calm demeanor—that he was selected commander of his unit. Kathleen recently asked what made him choose the Naval Academy. His response? "I'm guaranteed a job for life. I'll never have to look for work." Only the Peaceful teen will attend one of the most prestigious institutions in the world *to avoid work!*

WITTY

The Peaceful teen is the master of one-liners. Although he's not one to draw attention to himself, people will learn to listen carefully when he does talk, because even though he doesn't talk much, when he does, it's usually something very funny. His subtle wit will gradually become appreciated by his peers.

GOOD LISTENER

He's a great listener and enjoys playing the role of mediator. When Kristi is mad at Misti because Becki said she said that she said (well, you get the picture), the Peaceful teen will step in and make the peace between warring factions. Even if she is angry or hurt by what's been said, she'll be able to hide her own emotions and focus on bringing about resolution. She doesn't jump into leadership and is never splashy, but when pushed into a leadership role, she'll draw on her skills of diplomacy to do an exceptional job.

Joy Brown, a pastor's wife from South Carolina, recently shared this story about her daughter, Molly, who was seventeen at the time:

> One of my friends mentioned in passing that she had seen Molly at the local hospital, visiting with people in the ICU (Intensive Care Unit). I couldn't think of anyone we knew who was hospitalized, so I was really surprised. When she got home from school, I asked about it. She responded in her usual casual way: "Oh, yeah, Mom. A lot of times I stop by the hospital on my way home from school. Of course, they don't let me in to see the patients, but I just sit in the ICU waiting area, listening to the families, letting them talk about what they're going through. They like to tell stories about the person who may be dying in the other room. Then I'll offer to pray with them." I asked her how long she'd been doing this and she said, "I don't know. I guess a couple years." She was that way about everything. She never served to get the glory; she has a real servant's heart.

CASUAL ATTITUDE

A big part of the Peaceful teen's charm is his cavalier attitude, which is considered very cool at this age. That's why "what-EVER" is the most popular saying among teens right now. They all say it, but only the Peaceful teens can say it and mean it. They really do feel like "whatever" happens is okay by them.

In most cases, this is the perfect attitude to have toward teenage trivia. Their clothes are fashionably rumpled and they live by the motto: "Why stand when you can sit; why sit when you can lie down?"

As Young Life leader Sherri Shaffer points out:

When all the kids are yelling back and forth insisting we go to this place or another, the [Peaceful teens] won't say where they want to eat or what they want to do. Most leaders try to force them to state an opinion, not realizing that they honestly don't care. It's not so much that they are shy or "just trying to be polite," they are content to do what the others want and appreciate not having to make a decision.

They also take sincere delight in observing the fun of others. Sherri continues:

When we take kids to summer camp, there will always be kids who don't say much, who do more observing than participating. Here again, leaders often make the mistake of trying to pressure them to get involved. Most people think that because [the Peaceful teen] doesn't join in all the activities, they must not be having fun. Actually, they enjoy observing from the sidelines. They enjoy the conversation and jokes even when they don't say much themselves. Sure enough, at the end of every camp, the teens who all the adults were concerned weren't participating enough, will come up and say, "This was the funnest week of my life!"

TOO COMPROMISING

This is where the "whatever" attitude becomes a real problem for the Peaceful teen. He can land himself in huge trouble out of sheer laziness or an unwillingness to take a stand. One of the most famous stories in our family involves my Peaceful brother John. He was suspended for smoking marijuana at school, but he swore to my mom that he had not been smoking it. She, being a

Powerful mom, marched directly to the school to find out what was going on and to do battle with the lions of injustice. The vice principal looked at John and said, "But I personally saw you with the joint in your hand." To which he casually responded, "Yeah, but I wasn't smoking it. I was just passing it."

Classic Peaceful teen line there, folks! Too often, their motto is "peace at any price"—even if it means compromising their core values.

UNENTHUSIASTIC / UNINVOLVED

Another big frustration with these teens is that they are just so unenthusiastic about everything. Mom tries to get them interested in this club or that club, and they just can't be bothered. It's possible for them to avoid participating in a single extracurricular activity during their entire high school career. They just lack the motivation to go compete with all those Powerful, Popular, and Perfect teens; it's easier to sit home watching TV. Your Peaceful teen will stay home from school activities for no other reason than she doesn't want to go alone, but she is not motivated enough to pick up the phone and make plans with a friend.

QUIETLY STUBBORN

Now, moms, listen up. If you get on a rampage about how important it is for your teen to "be true to your school" and get involved and "make a difference" and all that stuff, it will absolutely backfire. The Peaceful teen is quietly stubborn and he will take a secret delight in seeing you get all worked up about the fact that he's not going to the homecoming dance. Don't play the game.

On the other hand, he could be staying home because he's indecisive and can't decide whom to invite. Or because he procrastinated so long, he couldn't get a ticket. Wisdom will be needed to know how to help your teen without getting overly involved in living his life.

SARCASTIC

We mentioned one of his strengths is the Peaceful teen's wit. Pushed to an extreme, however, he can become extremely sarcastic. These teens also tend to think they are better than everyone else: not shallow like the Popular teen, not a "Goody Two-shoes" like the Perfect teen, not an obnoxious jerk like the Powerful teen. They can have great fun sitting on the sidelines poking fun at those who have the courage to step into the arena. And that's no way to travel through life.

WHAT YOUR PEACEFUL CHILD NEEDS MOST FROM YOU

Part of me was feeling very uncomfortable with the fact that I didn't have long, elaborate passages to write about the Peaceful child as I have about the other temperaments. I couldn't come up with cute or exciting stories. "What's wrong with you, Donna?" I kept wondering. "You know these temperaments inside out and backward." Then it hit me. There's no need for elaborate passages when you are dealing with such easygoing children! No need for stern warnings about crushing their spirit, dire predictions of teenage rebellion, or suggestions for overcoming their glaring weaknesses. For the most part, these kids have sturdy emotions, rarely rebel, and frankly, have no glaring weaknesses. They are just happy to be on the planet, hanging out, not doin' much. And it's hard to come up with exciting stories about kids who avoid excitement.

Realize that your child does not do well with conflict and confrontation, so try to deal with him in a calm, rational manner. If mom and dad are in constant conflict with one another, don't be surprised if your child runs to hide. He may "hide" in front of the television set, at his friend's house or, in the teen years, by using drugs or alcohol, or running away. But if there's conflict, he is guaranteed to flee.

Spell out exactly what his responsibilities are at home and at school, but don't expect him to take initiative or perform extra work. It ain't gonna happen. Accept that he moves at a slower pace than most kids; that doesn't make him bad, just slower.

Help him find an area in which he can really shine. One of the interesting characteristics about the Peaceful temperament is that, invariably, they have *one thing* they can truly excel at. They have a single-mindedness of focus, which when channeled properly, can have marvelous results. It may be in art, music, computers, sports, or whatever. So often, I meet with women who are deeply concerned about their Peaceful child's future, particularly if the child is a boy. "He doesn't seem to care about anything! How will he ever find a job to provide for a wife and family." I tell them to stop worrying and start searching for that *one thing!*

One mom shared with me about her son who had flunked out in seventh grade. He'd been labeled everything from lazy to learning disabled. She decided to homeschool him, which she did for the next two years. He didn't have much interest in anything *except* computers. That was the one thing he could get totally enthused about; the rest of his schoolwork was constant hassle. One day, she said in passing, "You know, you oughta just take the GED and be done with high school." "Can I really do that?" he said, leaping for joy at the thought of all the mundane homework he could avoid! Sure enough, he took the GED without having finished ninth grade. He scored in the top ten percent (smart kid, just couldn't be bothered) and immediately enrolled in the local college majoring in computers. He's a top student who volunteers his time helping people twice his age. His classmates love him because he's so patient, and they can't help catching his love for computers.

The best example of this single-mindedness of purpose in adulthood is former President George Bush. Although he was the easygoing Peaceful type, his single-minded devotion to foreign policy led him all the way to the White House. On the downside, it was a key factor in his failure to be reelected. He just couldn't muster any enthusiasm for domestic affairs or other issues brought up by his opponent during the campaign.

Well, Popular mom, you may or may not get much bragging rights. But can you accept your Peaceful child as the special gift he is? Let him slow you down and give you a perspective on what really matters. Don't push him to be outgoing; he's not. Don't push him to be jolly; he's not. Acceptance is the key to your relationship.

Your Peaceful child has some very significant emotional needs which can only be fulfilled by mom and dad. Most of all, he needs you to accept him for the easy-going person God made him to be. Don't push him; don't expect him to be a go-getter or the homecoming king. Give him the peace and relaxation he longs for. Praise him for his inner character and help him derive self-worth apart from "being the best." Try to provide loving motivation, but resist the temptation to nag and goad him on. Many parents report great results once they've identified the *one thing* their Peaceful teen cares about—and there's always one thing, but you may have to look very hard to find it. If he avoids chores or homework but loves hanging out with the guys, then tell him he must finish all his work before leaving the house.

Perfect mom, here again, you're not going to get perfection. Far from it. In fact, the Peaceful child often seems to intentionally aim for mediocrity. Accept it as a temperament difference, and not as proof that you've failed as a mother. Focus on your child's inner character, rather than hoping for perfect performances.

The Powerful mom needs to resist pushing her slow, Peaceful child. He may never change the world in the way you think he should, but remember: most of the world's greatest leaders have been diplomatic Peacemakers, not the Powerful warmakers.

The Peaceful mom should just enjoy her little kindred spirit.

BIBLE VERSES FOR THE PEACEFUL CHILD

Motivating this dear child to memorize Scripture may be a challenge, but try to make it easier by setting the verses to song or working on them together as a family.

> For this very reason, *make every effort* [emphasis added] to add to your faith goodness; and to goodness, knowledge; and to knowledge, self-control; and to self-control, perseverance; and to perseverance, godliness; and to godliness, brotherly kindness; and to brotherly kindness, love. For if you possess these qualities in increasing measure, they will keep you from being ineffective and unproductive in your knowledge of our Lord Jesus Christ. (2 Peter 1:5–8)

> Whatever you do, work at it with all your heart, as working for the Lord, not for men, since you know that you

will receive an inheritance from the Lord as a reward. It is the Lord Christ you are serving. (Colossians 3:23–24)

For God did not give us a spirit of timidity, but a spirit of power, of love and of self-discipline. (2 Timothy 1:7)

Lazy hands make a man poor, but diligent hands bring wealth. (Proverbs 10:4)

He who gathers crops in summer is a wise son, but he who sleeps during harvest is a disgraceful son. (Proverbs 10:5)

Diligent hands will rule, but laziness ends in slave labor. (Proverbs 12:24)

The Parable of the Talents (Matthew 25:14–30)

A Final Word

You did it! You made it all the way through this crash course on understanding the temperaments. By now, you should have been transformed into the perfect wife, perfect mother, and perfect friend. What's that? You're not perfect yet?

Well, I'm not a perfect wife-mother-friend, either . . . and I teach this stuff!

Reading this material won't make you perfect, but studying it and applying what you learn will certainly make your life easier, while making you a little easier to live with. I would strongly urge you to go back and reread the portions of the book you highlighted. Cut out the "Tool Kit" cards and carry them with you wherever you go. When you've got a few extra minutes (waiting in line or sitting at the doctor's office, for example), pull out the cards and prayerfully consider how you can implement these truths into your life.

At a minimum, I trust you've gained a greater understanding of why you act the way you do and how others perceive you. I hope you've begun building on your strengths and that you pray daily for power to overcome your weaknesses. I also trust that you have gained an increased appreciation for your husband and that you have developed some strategies to better meet his emotional needs.

This may sound strange, but authors learn just as much as they impart while writing a book like this. For me, researching the effects of temperament on children has freed me to accept that God has deliberately given me three challenging Powerful kids. (At first, I was mad at him for pulling such a dirty trick, but I think I'm over it now!) I used to look at women with Peaceful and Perfect kids and think that they were better moms, better

Christians, because their kids could sit down and shut up in public. I've realized that it's not that I'm a lousy mom, it's that God wants to transform my character. By sending three kids who share my Powerful temperament, he is forcing me to come to grips with my own weaknesses. It's painful, but at least I don't have the added burden of thinking I'm a failure as a mother. I hope you've found a measure of freedom, as well.

Thanks for reading along with me. If this book has made a difference in your life or you have a hilarious story you've just got to share, I'd love to hear from you.

Remember: God loves you and made you just the way you are!

BLESSINGS,
DONNA PARTOW

Zondervan Publishing House
5300 Patterson SE
Grand Rapids, MI 49530
email: DonnaParto@aol.com

Appendix:

Personality Test Word Definitions

STRENGTHS

1. Adventurous—willing take on new and daring enterprises with a determination to master them

   Adaptable—easily fits and is comfortable in any situation

   Animated—full of life; lively use of hand and arm gestures and facial expression

   Analytical—likes to examine the parts for their logical and proper relationships

2. Persistent—sees one project through to its completion before starting another

   Playful—full of fun and good humor

   Persuasive—convinces through logic and fact rather than charm or power

   Peaceful—seems undisturbed and tranquil; retreats from any form of strife

3. Submissive—easily accepts another's point of view or desire with little need to assert his own opinion

   Self-sacrificing—willingly gives up personal being for the sake of or to meet the needs of others

   Sociable—sees being with others as an opportunity to be cute and entertaining rather than as a challenge or business opportunity

   Strong-willed—determined to have his own way

4. Considerate—having regard for the needs and feelings of others

   Controlled—rarely displays emotions

Competitive—turns every situation, happening, or game into a contest and always plays to win

Convincing—wins through the sheer charm of his personality

5. Refreshing—renews and stimulates; makes others feel good

Respectful—treats others with deference, honor, and esteem

Reserved—self-restraint in expression of emotion or enthusiasm

Resourceful—able to act quickly and effectively in virtually all situations

6. Satisfied—accepting of any circumstance or situation

Sensitive—cares intensely about people and situations

Self-reliant—full dependence on personal cabilities, judgment, and resources

Spirited—full of life and excitement

7. Planner—prefers to work out a detailed arrangement for the accomplishment of project or goal, and prefers involvement with the planning stages and the finished project rather than the carrying out of the task

Patient—unmoved by delay; remains calm and tolerant

Positive—knows it will turn out right if he's in charge

Promoter—urges or compels others to go along, join, or invest on the basis of his personal charm

8. Sure—confident; rarely hesitates or waivers

Spontaneous—prefers all of life to be impulsive, unpremeditated, and unrestricted by plans

Scheduled—makes and lives according to a daily plan; dislikes his plan to be interrupted

Shy—quiet; doesn't easily initiate conversation

9. Orderly—methodical and systematic

Obliging—accommodating; quick to do a task another's way

Outspoken—speaks frankly and without reserve

Optimistic—sunny disposition; convinces himself and others that everything will turn out all right

10. Friendly—a responder rather than an initiator, seldom starts a conversation

Faithful—consistently reliable, steadfast, loyal, and devoted sometimes beyond reason

Funny—sparkling sense of humor that can turn virtually any story into a hilarious event

Forceful—a commanding personality whom others would hesitate to take a stand against

11. Daring—willing to take risks; fearless; bold
    Delightful—a person who is upbeat and fun to be with
    Diplomatic—tactful, sensitive, and patient
    Detailed—does everything in proper order with a clear memory of all the things that happened
12. Cheerful—consistently in good spirits; promotes happiness in others
    Consistent—stays emotionally on an even keel, responding as one might expect
    Cultured—interested in both intellectual and artistic pursuits, such as theater, symphony, ballet
    Confident—self-assured and certain of personal ability and success
13. Idealistic—visualizes things in their perfect form; has a need to measure up to that standard himself
    Independent—self-sufficient, self-supporting, self-confident; seems to have little need of help
    Inoffensive—seldom unpleasant or objectionable in behavior or speech
    Inspiring—encourages others to work, to join, or to be involved and makes the whole project fun
14. Demonstrative—openly expresses emotion, especially affection, and doesn't hesitate to touch others while speaking to them
    Decisive—quick, conclusive, judgment-making ability
    Dry humor—exhibits "dry wit," usually humorous one-liners that can be sarcastic in nature
    Deep—intense and often introspective with a distaste for surface conversation and pursuits
15. Mediator—consistently reconciles differences in order to avoid conflict
    Musical—participates in or has a deep appreciation for music; is committed to music as an art form rather than simply the fun of performance
    Mover—driven by a need to be productive; is a leader whom others follow; finds it difficult to sit still
    Mixes easily—loves a party and can't wait to meet everyone in the room; never meets a stranger
16. Thoughtful—considerate; remembers special occasions; quick to make a kind gesture

Tenacious—holds on firmly, stubbornly; won't let go until the goal is accomplished

Talker—constantly speaking; often telling funny stories and entertaining everyone around; feeling the need to fill the silence in order to make others comfortable

Tolerant—easily accepts the thoughts and ways of others without the need to disagree with or change them

17. Listener—willing to hear what others have to say

Loyal—faithful to a person, ideal, or job, sometimes beyond reason

Leader—a natural-born director; driven to be in charge; often finds it difficult to believe that anyone else can do the job as well

Lively—full of life; vigorous; energetic

18. Contented—easily satisfied with what he has; rarely envious

Chief—commands leadership and expects people to follow

Chartmaker—organizes life, tasks, and problem solving by making lists, forms, or graphs

Cute—precious, adorable, center of attention

19. Perfectionist—places high standards on himself and often on others, desiring that everything be in proper order at all times

Pleasant—easygoing, easy to be around, easy to talk with

Productive—must constantly be working or achieving, often finds it very difficult to rest

Popular—life of the party and therefore much desired as a party guest

20. Bouncy—a bubbly, lively personality; full of energy

Bold—fearless; daring; forward; unafraid of risk

Behaved—consistently desires to conduct himself within the realm of what he feels is proper

Balanced—stable, middle-of-the-road personality, not subject to sharp highs or lows

WEAKNESSES

21. Brassy—showy; flashy; comes on strong; too loud

Bossy—commanding; domineering; sometimes overbearing in adult relationships

Bashful—self-conscious; shrinks from getting attention

Blank—a person who shows little facial expression or emotion

22. Undisciplined—lack of order permeates most every area of his life

Unsympathetic—finds it difficult to relate to the problems or hurts of others

Unenthusiastic—tends to not get excited, often feeling it won't work anyway

Unforgiving—difficulty releasing or forgetting a hurt or injustice done, apt to hold on to a grudge

23. Reluctant—reserved; uncommunicative; especially when the situation is complex

Resentful—often holds ill feelings as a result of real or imagined offenses

Resistent—strives against or hesitates to accept any other way but his own

Repetitious—retells stories and incidents to entertain you, not realizing he has already told the story several times; constantly needs something to say

24. Fussy—calling for great attention to trivial or petty details

Fearful—often experiences feelings of deep concern, apprehension, or anxiousness

Forgetful—lack of memory usually tied to a lack of discipline and not bothering to mentally record things that aren't fun

Frank—straightforward; outspoken; doesn't mind telling you exactly what he thinks

25. Impatient—finds it difficult to endure irritation or wait for others

Insecure—apprehensive or lacking confidence

Indecisive—finds it difficult to make any decision at all (not the personality that labors long over each decision in order to make the perfect one)

Interrupts—a person who is more of a talker than a listener, who starts speaking without even realizing someone else is already speaking

26. Unpopular—intensity and demand for perfection can push others away

Uninvolved—has no desire to listen or become interested in clubs, groups, activities, or other people's lives

Unpredictable—may be ecstatic one moment and down the next, or willing to help but then disappears, or promises to come but forgets to show up

Unaffectionate—finds it difficult to verbally or physically demonstrate tenderness openly

27. Headstrong—insists on having his own way

Haphazard—no consistent way of doing things

Hard to please—a person whose standards are set so high that it is difficult to ever satisfy them

Hesitant—slow to get moving and hard to get involved

28. Plain—a middle-of-the-road personality without highs or lows and showing little, if any, emotion

Pessimistic—while hoping for the best, this person generally sees the downside of a situation first

Proud—one with great self-esteem who sees himself as always right and the best person for the job

Permissive—allows others (including children) to do as they please in order to keep from being disliked

29. Angered easily—a childish flash-in-the-pan temper that expresses itself in tantrum style that is over and forgotten almost instantly

Aimless—not a goal-setter with little desire to be one

Argumentative—incites arguments usually because he is certain he is right no matter what the situation may be

Aliented—easily feels estranged from others often because of insecurity or fear that others don't really enjoy his company.

30. Naive—simple and child-like perspective, lacking sophistication or comprehension of what the deeper levels of life are really about

Negative attitude—seldom positive and often able to see only the down or dark side of each situation

Nervy—full of confidence, fortitude, and sheer guts, often in a negative sense

Nonchalant—easygoing, unconcerned, indifferent

31. Worrier—consistently feels uncertain, troubled, or anxious

Withdrawn—a person who pulls back to himself and needs a great deal of alone or isolation time

Workaholic—an aggressive goal-setter who must be constantly productive and feels very guilty when resting; not driven by a need for perfection or completion but by a need for accomplishment and reward

Wants credit—thrives on the credit or approval of others. As an entertainer, this person feeds on the applause, laughter, and/or acceptance of an audience.

32. Too sensitive—overly introspective and easily offended when misunderstood

Tactless—sometimes expresses himself in a somewhat offensive and inconsiderate way

Timid—shrinks from difficult situations

Talkative—an entertaining, compulsive talker who finds it difficult to listen

33. Doubtful—characterized by uncertainty and lack of confidence that it will ever work out

Disorganized—lack of ability to ever get life in order

Domineering—compulsively takes control of situations and/or people, usually telling others what to do

Depressed—a person who feels down much of the time

34. Inconsistent—erratic, contradictory, with actions and emotions not based on logic

Introvert—a person whose thoughts and interest are directed inward, lives within himself

Intolerant—appears unable to withstand or accept another's attitudes, point of view, or way of doing things

Indifferent—a person to whom most things don't matter one way or the other

35. Messy—a state of disorder and disorganization

Moody—doesn't get very high emotionally, but easily slips into low lows, often when feeling unappreciated

Mumbles—will talk quietly under the breath when pushed, doesn't bother to speak clearly

Manipulative—influences or manages shrewdly or deviously for his own advantage; will get his way somehow

36. Slow—doesn't often act or think quickly, too much of a bother

Stubborn—determined to exert his own will; not easily persuaded; obstinate

Show-off—needs to be the center of attention; wants to be watched

Skeptical—disbelieving; questions the motive behind the words

37. Loner—requires a lot of private time; tends to avoid other people

    Lord over others—doesn't hesitate to let others know he is right or in control

    Lazy—evaluates work or activity in terms of how much energy it will take

    Loud—laugh or voice can be heard above others in the room

38. Sluggish—slow to get started, needs push to be motivated

    Suspicious—tends to suspect or distrust others or ideas

    Short-tempered—has a demanding, impatience-based anger and a short fuse. Anger is expressed when others are not moving fast enough or have not completed what they have been asked to do.

    Scatterbrained—lacks the power of concentration or attention; flighty

39. Revengeful—holds a grudge and punishes the offender, often by subtly withholding friendship or affection

    Restless—likes constant new activity because it isn't fun to do the same things all the time

    Reluctant—resistant or unwilling to get involved

    Rash—acts hastily without thinking things through, generally because of impatience

40. Compromising—will often relax his position, even when right, to avoid conflict

    Critical—constantly evaluating and making judgments, frequently thinking or expressing negative reactions

    Crafty—shrewd; can always find a way to get to the desired end

    Changeable—has a childish, short attention span; needs a lot of change and variety to keep from getting bored

Recommended Reading

Barnes, Emilie. *More Hours in My Day.* Eugene, Ore: Harvest House, 1994.

Felton, Sandra. *The Messies Manual.* Grand Rapids: Revell, 1983

Freeman, Becky. *Worms in My Tea and Other Mixed Blessings.* Baptist Sunday School Board, 1994.

LaHaye, Tim. *The Spirit-Controlled Temperament.* Wheaton, Ill.: Tyndale, 1993.

_____. *Transformed Temperaments.* Wheaton, Ill.: Tyndale, 1993.

Littauer, Florence. *Personality Plus.* Grand Rapids: Revell, 1992.

_____. *Personality Tree.* Nashville: Word, 1989.

_____. *Freeing Your Mind from the Memories That Bind.* Nashville: Nelson, 1989.

_____, and Marita Littauer. *Personality Puzzle.* Grand Rapids: Revell, 1992.

_____. *Raising Christians, Not Just Children.* Nashville: Word, 1988.

Omartian, Stormie. *The Power of a Praying Wife.* Eugene, Ore.: Harvest House, 1997.

Ortlund, Anne. *Disciplines of the Beautiful Woman.* Nashville: Word, 1984.

_____. *Disciplines of the Heart.* Nashville: Word, 1987 (out of print).

_____. *Disciplines of the Home.* Nashville: Word, 1993.

Partow, Donna. *Becoming a Vessel God Can Use.* Minneapolis: Bethany, 1996.

_____. *Families That Play Together, Stay Together.* Minneapolis: Bethany, 1996.

_____. *Homemade Business.* Colorado Springs: Focus on the Family, 1992.

_____. *How to Work with the One You Love.* Minneapolis: Bethany, 1995.

_____. *No More Lone Ranger Moms.* Minneapolis: Bethany, 1995.

Peace, Martha. *The Excellent Wife.* Bemidji, Minn.: Focus, 1997.

Roseveare, Helen. *Give Me This Mountain.* (out of print).

Notes

CHAPTER 1: TEMPERAMENT 101

1. Created by Fred Littauer. Personality Profile from *Personality Plus* by Florence Littauer, copyright 1992 by Florence Littauer, used by permission of Florence Littauer and Fleming H. Revell Company. NOT TO BE REPRODUCED. Copies may be ordered from: CLASS, P.O. Box 66810, Albuquerque, NM 89193, $1.00 each, 6 for $5.00, 12 for $10.00, 50 for $30.00, 100 for $50.00. Shipping for quantities: 6 add $1.00, 12 add $2.00, 50 add $3.50, 100 add $5.00. NM residents please add local sales tax. Credit card orders may be placed by phone, 800–433–6633.

CHAPTER 4: INTRODUCING THE POWERFUL WOMAN

1. Oswald Chambers, *My Utmost for His Highest* (Uhrichsville, Ohio: Barbour, 1991), 218.

2. Ruth Tucker, *From Jerusalem to Irian Jaya* (Grand Rapids: Zondervan, 1983), 257.

3. *From Jerusalem to Irian Jaya*, 259.

4. *Personality Plus*, 124.

5. *Personality Plus*, 126.

6. Andrew Murray, *Humility* (Springdale, Penn.: Whitaker House, 1982), 43–44.

CHAPTER 5: INTRODUCING THE PEACEFUL WOMAN

1. *Personality Plus*, 130.

CHAPTER 7: HE'S THE POPULAR MAN

1. Florence Littauer and Marita Littauer, *Personality Puzzle* (Grand Rapids: Revell, 1992), 201.

CHAPTER 8: HE'S THE PERFECT MAN

1. Tim LaHaye, *Transformed Temperaments* (Wheaton, IL: Tyndale, 1993), 163.

2. *Personality Puzzle,* 202.

CHAPTER 9: HE'S THE POWERFUL MAN

1. *Personality Puzzle,* 203.

2. *Personality Puzzle,* 203.

CHAPTER 10: HE'S THE PEACEFUL MAN

1. *Transformed Temperaments,* 191.

2. *Understanding the Male Temperament,* 87.

3. *Personality Puzzle,* 204.

CHAPTER 13: HOW THE POWERFUL WIFE LORDS IT OVER HER HUSBAND

1. Annie Chapman, *Smart Women Keep It Simple* (Minneapolis: Bethany House, 1992), 30–31.

2. *Personality Plus,* 159–160.

CHAPTER 15: THE TEMPERAMENTS IN YOUR CHILDREN

1. Florence Littauer and Marita Littauer, *Raising Christians, Not Just Children* (Dallas: Word, 1988), 78–81.

CHAPTER 16: UNDERSTAND THE POPULAR CHILD

1. *Smart Women Keep It Simple,* 52.

CHAPTER 18: UNDERSTAND THE POWERFUL CHILD

1. We strongly recommend H. Clay Trumbell's *Hints on Child Training* (Eugene, Ore.: Great Expectations Book Co., originally published in 1890).

2. Florence Littauer, *Personality Plus* audiocassette series (Albuquerque, N.M.: CLASS, Inc.).

3. *Hints on Child Training,* 58–59.

4. *Transformed Temperament,* 5.

Your Tool Kit

The following cards are your personal tool kit to take with you wherever you go! Cut them out and tuck them in the front of your Bible or in your purse, right away! The information on them will help you recognize "who you're dealing with" as you interact with family, friends, and strangers. More importantly, the cards will remind you of practical ways to make the most of your relationships.

PRIMARY MOTIVATIONS OF EACH TEMPERAMENT

Popular: to have fun and be loved. When dealing with this type, ask yourself, "How can I make this more fun?"

Perfect: to bring perfection to an imperfect world. Ask yourself, "How can I do this in an orderly fashion?"

Powerful: to control as much of their world as possible. Ask yourself, "How can I give this person a sense of ownership in this situation?"

Peaceful: to take life easy and live in peace. Ask yourself, "How can I promote harmony in this situation?"

POPULAR WOMAN

STRENGTHS TO BUILD ON	WEAKNESSES TO PRAYERFULLY OVERCOME
• Popular	• Permissive
• Talkative	• Forgetful
• Life of the party	• Unreliable
• Motivator	• Fussy
• Creative	• Messy housekeeper
• Accepting	• Overwhelming
• Optimistic	• Seems phony
• Refreshing	

PERFECT WOMAN

STRENGTHS TO BUILD ON	WEAKNESSES TO PRAYERFULLY OVERCOME
• Meticulous housekeeper	• Perfectionistic
• Organized	• Unpopular
• Perfectly groomed	• Rigid
• Wonderful hostess	• Prone to the blues
• Detail-oriented	• Unforgiving
• Thoughtful	• Cheapskate
• Frugal	
• Careful decision-maker	
• Gifted	
• Sophisticated	

POWERFUL WOMAN

STRENGTHS TO BUILD ON	WEAKNESSES TO PRAYERFULLY OVERCOME
• Take-charge woman	• Unpopular
• Courageous	• Mean
• Determined	• Self-centered
• Crusader	• Uses people
• Productive	• Impulsive
• Open and honest	• Bossy
• Effective disciplinarian	• Usually right, but often rejected

POPULAR TYPE VERSES TO LIVE BY

When words are many, sin is not absent, but he who holds his tongue is wise. (Proverbs 10:19)

My dear brothers, take note of this: Everyone should be quick to listen, slow to speak and slow to become angry, for man's anger does not bring about the righteous life God desires. (James 1:19)

PERFECT TYPE VERSES TO LIVE BY

Cast all your anxiety on him because he cares for you. (1 Peter 5:7)

An anxious heart weighs a man down, but a kind word cheers him up. (Proverbs 12:25)

POWERFUL TYPE VERSES TO LIVE BY

Be completely humble and gentle; be patient, bearing with one another in love. (Ephesians 4:2)

Each of you should look not only to your own interests, but also to the interests of others. (Philippians 2:4)

PEACEFUL WOMAN

STRENGTHS TO BUILD ON	WEAKNESSES TO PRAYERFULLY OVERCOME
• Comforting	• Unenthusiastic
• Thoughtful	• Uninvolved
• Attentive	• Fearful
• Loyal	• Sluggish
• Peacemaker	• Compromising
• Dependable	• Enabler/codependent
• Protective	
• Takes time for the children	
• Patient	
• Faithful	
• Devoted care-giver	

WHAT YOUR POPULAR HUSBAND NEEDS MOST FROM YOU	WHAT YOUR PERFECT HUSBAND NEEDS MOST FROM YOU
• Attention	• Stability
• Affection	• Space
• Approval	• Silence
• Acceptance	• Sensitivity

HOW TO RECOGNIZE THE POPULAR . . .

BABY	CHILD (AGES 2–12)
• Bright and wide-eyed	• Daring and eager
• Curious	• Inventive and Imaginative
• Gurgles and coos	• Cheerful
• Wants company	• Enthusiastic
• Shows off	• Chatters constantly
• Responsive	• Energized by people
• Screams for attention	• Disorganized
• Knows he is cute	• Easily distracted
	• Tells fibs

WHAT YOUR POWERFUL HUSBAND NEEDS MOST FROM YOU

- A sense of obedience
- Appreciation for accomplishments

WHAT YOUR PEACEFUL HUSBAND NEEDS MOST FROM YOU

- Peace
- Relaxation
- Praise
- Self-worth
- Loving Motivation

TEEN

- Cheerleader
- Charms others
- Daring
- Joins clubs
- Popular
- Life of the party
- Creative
- Wants to please
- Emotional ups and downs

- Apologetic
- Deceptive
- Easily led astray
- Craves attention
- Vulnerable to peer pressure
- Con artist
- Won't study
- Immature
- Gossips